The Great Days of the
EXPRESS TRAINS

60025
FLYING
SCOTSMAN
GRANTHAM

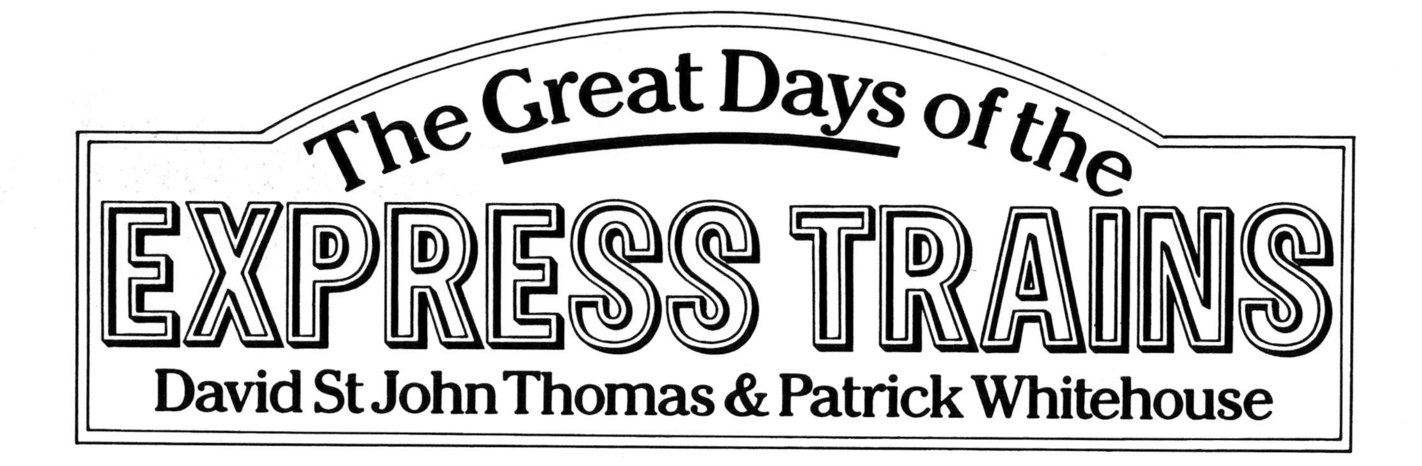

DAVID & CHARLES
Newton Abbot London

Half title page: Through glorious Gloucestershire. The familiar sound of a hard working GWR engine echoes across the Golden Valley as a Cheltenham to Paddington express climbs the final 1 in 60 gradient to Sapperton tunnel. The Castle is unknown and the train mostly MK1 coaches in red and cream; the dining car in Great Western so the date is likely to be mid 1950s.

Frontispiece: Storming out of the Cross. Sir Nigel Gresley's A4 Pacific No 60025 Falcon *in BR dark green takes the Flying Scotsman up Holloway Bank and out of Gas Works Tunnel in the early 1950s. The engine's home shed, Grantham, is marked both by the name painted on the buffer beam, LNER fashion, and by the new LMS-type shed plate, 35B, adopted by British Railways.*

The down Thames Clyde express crosses the river Eden north of Carlisle headed by rebuilt Royal Scot No 46109 Royal Engineer *in the mid 1950s.*

British Library Cataloguing in Publication Data

Thomas, David St John
Great Days of the Express Trains.
1. Great Britain. Railway passenger transport services, history
I. Title II. Whitehouse, Patrick, *1922–*
385.220941

ISBN 0-7153-9414-2

Book designed by Michael Head

Typeset by Typesetters (Birmingham) Ltd, Smethwick, West Midlands
and printed in Great Britain
by Butler & Tanner Ltd, Frome and London
for David & Charles plc
Brunel House Newton Abbot Devon

CONTENTS

The Up Mail (i). Colwyn Bay to the east of the station and on the resumption of double track sometime around 1930 probably the last year prior to the introduction of the Royal Scots on the North Wales trains. The train is the up Irish Mail consisting of fifteen vehicles including a then new steel-sided leading van. The time is around 2pm and if one was lucky a lunch period could encompass seeing both the up and down trains. The engines are still one hundred per cent LNWR – an Experiment 4-6-0 No 5546 Middlesex *(withdrawn 12/33) double heading a red-painted Claughton class four-cylinder 4-6-0 No 5903* Duke of Sutherland *(withdrawn 5/33). Note the very LNWR signalbox and tall signals with the up main starter carrying two arms, the taller of which could be easily seen from the western approach to the station. Just over the roofs of the fifth and sixth coaches are the panels of the glass station windscreen (typical of many LNWR stations) and a stopping train waiting in the up slow platform.*

1
INTRODUCTION

IT shows how popular our subject is that nearly every reader will have his own distinctive memory of a journey by a great express. Many of our lives were changed by a trip to another part of the country that only the railway made possible – for interview, national service, romance or perhaps something to do with the sporting or artistic worlds. Then there were holidays, the journey often being the best part.

The platform is deep with passengers, parents (who have insisted on bringing a ridiculous amount of luggage along) agitated, father ever moving a few paces further from the bridge by which we crossed, when at last (preceded by bells from the signalbox) hundreds of tons of metal and wood come hurtling in. It is not just memory; many express trains did genuinely enter stations at higher speeds than today's diesels and electrics. All eyes, of course, on the locomotive, and equal enjoyment whether it be the very latest type, an ancient rarity only kept to work on peak days, or a machine more normally used on freight duties which will give the crew a real challenge at express speeds.

Each compartment still has its own entrance on the non-corridor side, so dozens of doors open, and for a few minutes pandemonium reigns. But, yes, the seats dad reserved carry their magic pieces of paper, the luggage is stowed on the rack, and as if by miracle the train has not merely digested that vast crowd but there are three spare seats in our compartment. We spread out, relishing the knowledge that we shall not be stopping (at least not to pick up passengers) for a hundred or more miles. Even before we have started, we have checked which of the four places shown in the carriage photographs mum and dad have been to and trace our route on the map. Only the mirror has no attraction to the young.

If we have been on other long journeys, we know how each has a totally different flavour. Do the railways (sometimes individual parts of the same system) reflect the countryside they serve, or is the very country coloured by which line happens to run through it? The LNER is always dirty, unwelcoming, yet curiously efficient. The LMS often seems a confusing, over-powering line, but how their expresses get going once they are on their way, and how comfortable the carriages are. As for the Southern, there is always an antiseptic scent in its much less posh carriages, progress seems uneven as the engine (smaller of course) struggles uphill and dashes down. Even if dad does splurge and take us to the diner (beg pardon, Pullman), afternoon tea will be a mean thing, though you can always put a few of those wrapped-up sugar lumps in your pocket. The Great Western, now there is a railway that knows how

Oriental Wisdom
Just after nationalisation quite a number of foreign railwaymen came to Britain to gain experience. In one district commercial office a Chinese was studying the organisation of special services at summer weekends. One of the clerks had explained how relief trains were organised. This seemed to puzzle the Chinese. 'Please, why you run relief train before ordinary train instead of after?' said he. This puzzled the Englishman who had never really thought about it. With a flash of inspiration he said, 'If we ran it after, everybody would pack into the ordinary train'. 'Please, no need for relief train then,' said the Chinese.

Wind-blown trail
The Great Central overbridge at Nottingham Midland always provided interesting traffic. The Marylebone, Sheffield, and Manchester expresses slammed across on their tight Leicester–Nottingham schedules, usually GC Atlantic, 'Director' or GN Atlantic hauled. One train in particular always seemed to invoke the signalman at Weekday Cross box. This train was booked into Victoria 9.8pm but always had to slow up for the 'on' distant signal at Arkwright Street station. Sometimes I would hear the piercing windblown wail of a GN whistle proclaiming its urgent cry to the night as if defying the home peg to be 'on'. Rumbling nearer, the short low note of a GC type whistle, which meant that the train was double-headed, probably a Director, proclaimed Weekday Cross 'off' and a clear run into Victoria. I heard the distinctive 'phut' as snifting valves banged on to their seats, the renewed exhaust beats in irregular time as the drivers opened up, growing fainter until the night quietened once more. – Philip Spencer.

to serve tea and generally make you feel special, except that the carriage seats are nothing like as spacious as the LMS's. But everything is well-ordered, even Paddington quite understandable, while Birmingham Snow Hill is heaven compared to the LMS hell at New Street. And the engines, just like all those displayed in the model shops.

Nobody ever doubted that express trains had great character. Until even twenty-five years ago they generally provided the quickest means of making a long journey (and on some routes this is still true). We remember them partly because we used them on great personal occasions, though in truth they were equally fascinating even if you had just invested in a platform ticket to watch them come and go at your local station, or saw them thunder past from some country vantage point. The joy was equal whether you had just spotted the first of a locomotive class new to you, added another famous name, or completed the whole class. Many of the trains seemed of infinite length, and in truth many were much longer than today's, especially out of Paddington, Euston and Kings Cross. Each had its individuality, the roof lines for example rarely uniform, though it was naturally the destination boards

Fast from Dover

Whilst working at Bricklayer's Arms I used to see a lot of driver Sam Gingell who worked into the shed from time to time and whose runs were always notable. Two trips with him will always stay with me especially as they were with classes of engine which some might consider to be poles apart. The first was with a Standard class 5 4-6-0 No 73089 with speed reaching the mid nineties over Darneth viaduct on the dash to Farningham Road but the second was even more memorable. Sam Gingell and his mate Jim Williams formed as fine a set of enginemen as you could find on any railway, and when their turn came to take the 2.2pm from Dover Priory, which right up to the end of steam traction on this route was regularly hauled on Saturdays by an inside cylinder 4-4-0 a small band of reverent enthusiasts would be there. They were never disappointed.

The particular trip which I made with Sam Gingell was with No 31145, a rebuilt South Eastern & Chatham D class 4-4-0 with long travel valves and eight full bogies. Gingell gave us speeds in the forties on the 1 in 100 Sole Street bank and a maximum of eighty-six through Farningham Road, a real thrill with an engine by then over thirty years old and, of course, incorporating parts of old No 145 built by Dubs in 1903. – Norman Harvey

Up Mail (ii). Almost a decade later the up Irish Mail passes Conway (Conwy) Castle with a Royal Scot, No 6120 Royal Inniskilling Fusilier *on the head end. LNWR signals are still to the fore but the train is composed mostly of modern LMS steel-panelled stock. No 6120 has white-painted smokebox door hinges, a decoration (sometimes allied to white smokebox rims) applied at the home shed and winked at by higher authority.*

Highland intruder. In 1934 the eight 4-6-0s of the former Highland Railway Clan class were transferred to the Callander & Oban line to replace ageing and feeble CR 4-6-0s. Here, LMS No 14768 Clan Mackenzie *is approaching Strathyre with the 08.00 Glasgow Buchanan Street to Oban probably in the summer of 1937.*

that most demanded attention. Some people who would never get to the places listed on them still enjoyed a vicarious thrill at seeing them being linked up. Schoolboys who had not yet been beyond their own county would announce that because of delays caused by a flood or derailment they had tonight come home by the Taffy instead of the Hampton (Swansea instead of Wolverhampton), and even farm workers would note that the Perth was down today.

And therein lay much of the fun. The timetable was made up of dozens of individual trains taking time-honoured routes at time-honoured hours. In large parts of the country, no two expresses were anything like the same. Even the Londons had vastly different first stopping points, many of them 150 or more miles from the capital and down a branch line. They also carried through coaches for different ranges of main- and branch-line destinations. Then there were the cross-countries. Every major city was served by a range of them making through journeys possible to an incredible number of places. The Londons (or sections of Londons), cross-countries, semi-fasts and locals somehow knit into a vast, comprehensive national, regional and local service, most of whose details remained constant for decades . . . so that even those not especially interested in railways knew the best trains and times.

But each new timetable did, of course, bring change, and the pages were read avidly by railwaymen and enthusiasts alike. Collections of them, once the expression of the hopes and fears of the commercial and operating people, the plans for business folk and entertainers doing their rounds, line many book shelves as a record of how different, how colourful it was in the great days . . . with innumerable fascinating details like trains stopping only to pick up, and then perhaps only by request, running further non-stop at summer weekends, shedding slip

Christmas Bonus

With a big up-market clientele to serve, the GWR maintained a large fleet of first-class carriages, including well into the post-1945 era many non-corridor ones. At busy times, such as Christmas, it gave third-class travellers the bonus of going first . . . such as on the third part of the 11.55am from Paddington non-stop Newport (133½ toiletless miles), the train consisting of ten non-corridor firsts and two vans.

coaches, exchanging restaurant cars half way down single-track branches, achieving a mile-a-minute average for over a hundred miles.

So what were the great days? They began rather earlier than in the case of the country railway (the subject of our companion book). For while the railway best served its commercial interests – and never forget that primarily it was always a business – by providing minimal services out in the sticks, clearly long-distance traffic was always encouraged by speed and comfort. The Great Western discovered this early on, when the broad-gauge *Flying Dutchman* was by far the world's fastest train, 4½ hours to Exeter of course via Bristol as early as 1845. Sooner or later, nearly all express routes met competition, and this was undoubtedly the great stimulant, culminating in the famous Races of the 1880s and 1890s to the North out of Euston and Kings Cross. That was when the signalman at Kinnaber Junction, where the two lines for Aberdeen converged, determined which train would get through first. But progress was ever fickle, not least of all in Brunel's kingdom where after a preliminary 'great day' things really only woke up after the abolition of the broad gauge. The Salisbury accident, when a LSWR ocean special from Plymouth fell off the track at too high speed, was just one that discouraged recklessness, while the engineers were ever complaining of the cost of high speed, especially in track maintenance. Thus even the Races to the North (incidentally for grouse shooting ahead of the glorious twelfth of August) culminated in a treaty between East and West coast main lines not to beat each other . . . a treaty, as noted in later pages, that survived into the grouping era and resulted in the *Flying Scotsman* actually having to travel more slowly when it became non-stop to Edinburgh.

Though there always have been (and still are) great days, expresses making splendid runs through gorgeous scenery in sparkling sunshine, attentive waiters serving fine fare in the restaurant car, the era on which we concentrate is roughly 1920 to 1960, interrupted of course by the war. The variety of great expresses, most of them again one-offs of considerable individuality, was then at its peak. On most routes trains were longer and heavier, ran longer non-stop distances, and went through to a greater variety of destinations than is the case today. Though not all pre-war services were restored in the slow rebuilding after 1945, the great weeding out of destinations served by through trains or carriages from stations like Liverpool Street and Kings Cross is relatively recent. On some lines, such as those out of Waterloo with Bulleid's new Pacific locomotives, services ran better after than before the war. The main point however has to be that in the 1950s, and even into the early 1960s, you had to pinch yourself to recall that both Britain and the world had been through great upheavals since many trains were running exactly as they had in the 1930s, nationalisation not withstanding, in some cases hauled by the same locomotives and with coaches in the same livery. The continuity was especially obvious on the Western. The GW had, of course, been the only one of the Big Four of the grouping era (that is from 1923, when dozens of smaller railways lost their independence, until nationalisation on 1 January 1948) to retain

Scottish Connections

Some of the most complex through coach workings on the LMS involved the Anglo-Scottish services. Most in the 1920s and 1930s included through portions from Euston to both Glasgow and Edinburgh, some had coaches for Perth and Aberdeen as well. But from Preston northwards there were often added portions from Liverpool and Manchester to Glasgow and Edinburgh. The *Mid-Day Scot*, for example, after 1937 when the streamlined *Coronation Scot* had taken on the Euston–Glasgow early afternoon service, was basically a Euston–Edinburgh service as it left London but included a couple of coaches to Glasgow for passengers from intermediate stations. At Crewe a GW brake composite from Plymouth to Glasgow was attached, at Wigan through coaches from Manchester to Glasgow and Edinburgh were attached – in the middle of the train so that the respective Glasgow and Edinburgh coaches were together – and finally at Lancaster a through portion from Liverpool to Glasgow was added.

At Carlisle the train split for Edinburgh and Glasgow, the restaurant car being in the Edinburgh part, so that with an arrival time at Carlisle of around 7.45pm Glasgow passengers had to make sure that they had finished their dinner and were back in their proper part of the train. Southbound the through portions were different with the Glasgow portion being coupled at Law Junction just 18 miles after the start to the through Aberdeen–Euston coaches including restaurant car. A little further south at Symington the Edinburgh–Euston coaches, also with restaurant car, were attached and during the peak holiday season through coaches from Stranraer to Euston were tacked on at Carlisle so that the *Mid-Day Scot* became a hefty load.

its own identity. This went on into the early days of nationalisation so that some expresses hardly changed their appearance in half a century.

While the latest locomotive types and accelerated schedules of course had great publicity value – giving newspapers the excuse yet again to print ever-popular photographs of the expresses speeding past their most characteristic pieces of scenery – familiarity and individuality were two qualities also highly prized. Many trains became cherished institutions, pieces of the well-ordered establishment. In every part of the country there was always *the* train to London, the best in every way at gentlemanly hours. One such is portrayed in the chapter 'Day Trip to London'. Much of that portrait would be equally accurate about a score or more best-of-the-day trains to the capital; much, indeed, would apply equally to the best-of-the-day train from Scottish centres to Edinburgh and Glasgow, from all over Ireland to Dublin, and even from part of the North and North Wales to Manchester.

Our subject is highly complex and it would be all too easy to produce long catalogues of trains and their developments, of how the routes were built and improved, to tell once more the whole spectrum of railway history, technical and otherwise. Especially since we have completed our '150' series on each of the four great railways, their origins and major events, what instead we have tried to do is portray an age, to select trains

Great Western streamliner. During the 'streamliner mania' of the mid to late 1930s the Great Western felt that it might, perhaps, be slipping on some of its publicity. Two engines took on a semi-streamlined appearance with a bullnose to the smokebox, rear chimney and safety valve cowlings, lengthy overall wheel splasher and a wedge-shaped leading edge to their cabs. They did not become pretty. The locomotives involved were No 5005 Manorbier Castle *and No 6014* King Henry VII *seen here on the Cornish Riviera Express in the summer of 1936.*

Nº 4467

and incidents that make a wider point – to bring alive the days when you looked forward to a long train journey as one of life's real pleasures. The reliability of the great locomotives, the smartness of the station work, the general dedication of all involved, just what was it that enabled our railways to offer such service and personality?

One factor is undoubtedly the class system! It was the lot of the many to serve the few. Those memories of porters lined up along the platform as a great express arrived at the terminal are correct. Everywhere station work was smart because there were many hands to share it, and well-directed hands. In much of the country, though certainly not in the Home Counties after 1939, for every locomotive cleaner's vacancy there were dozens of applicants, and well might railway families take pride in the fact that the third generation of young men had been taken on by the railway company, as reliable a ticket to security as any. In recent years the word 'canvass' hardly seems appropriate when the chief steward remarks casually, after describing buffet fare, that lunch is being served in the restaurant car. But canvass they used to, gently opening each compartment door with gracious smile, offering the menu and mentioning that some dish looked particularly appetising today. If anyone had wavered, he would be given a second visit with an almost imploring gesture.

Competition between the companies (three or four, even five routes out of London to some cities, a full service of restaurant-car trains by three to, say, Manchester) is just one reason why everyone tried so hard. A seemingly inherent inability to prevent overprovision also resulted in inadequate business to go round. Optimism was eternal in railway management. Even though they might set out to cut back coal usage, periodically paring branch and stopping-train services, the urge to add was irresistible. You only need to see the scale on which stations were built in city, town and country to realise the truth of that. What was over the top today would surely be justified tomorrow. And the truth of the matter is that, for those who could afford to do so, travelling by express train was a joy because mere handfuls of passengers were usually being carried, station and other facilities greatly under utilised. Right up to 1939, not to have a whole compartment to yourself was considered real hardship on many trains. One remembers always having a compartment to oneself on those monster trains out of Paddington (at least mid week) well into the 1950s. When you went to buy your ticket, newspaper, porter, you expected instant attention. You were someone special.

You were especially special during the great depression, when even on the light-weight trains out of St Pancras you might have a whole coach, not just a compartment to yourself, and your patronage of the restaurant car would bring joy to the whole crew. After the overcrowding of the war years (caused as much by running fewer trains as by the numbers travelling) it was perhaps surprising that the old values returned even to the extent they did. Labour shortages took their toll; in the days of undoubted race distinction, at the end only Paddington could hold out against employing coloured porters. But, yes, there was

Through the cuttings to Edge Hill. A Liverpool to London express (probably the 11.15 Lime St–Euston) approaches Edge Hill No 1 signalbox (removed c1938) which straddles the up slow line. The engine is Patriot class No 5511 Isle of Man *and an Edge Hill (8A) engine. A train is signalled on the down slow and it is hoped that the new vicar of Edge Hill had someone watching his back – probably the signalman leaning over his balcony.*

Off the Face of the Earth

Though most passengers kept on checking, reading the destination board as well as the departure sign on the platform, asking the guard and other passengers (and then maybe getting confirmation from the driver) that this was the right train, many still somehow got on the wrong one. And in the days of much longer non-stop runs, scarcer return services, and before most private homes were on the telephone, that resulted in long disappearance off the face of the earth. But they were also the days before motorway pile-ups, abductions and most violent crime, so there was more puzzlement than anxiety. The attitude was rather that nobody could tell what would happen to you if you caught a train.

Teatime from Kings Cross. The 4.00pm Coronation and the 4.00pm Leeds express abreast at Gas Works Tunnel during the summer of 1938. The engines are newly built A4 Pacific No 4467 Wild Swan *(2/38) and one of Gresley's earlier A3 Pacifics No 4480* Enterprise. *The gradient here is 1 in 107, a notorious exit from Kings Cross, and No 4480's driver is making full use of his sanding gear.*

Bulleid power. The roar of steam from safety valves fills the night air as Merchant Navy Pacific No 35010 Blue Star *gets the all clear at Salisbury with an evening Waterloo–Exeter and Ilfracombe express (probably the 15.00 ex-Waterloo) in November 1960.*

a great period for the top expresses after as well as before the war, and on many routes when passenger numbers increased there was ample scope to provide extra services.

As is told in the piece on summer weekends, holidays with pay brought an enormous injection of new business. But the 1950s were the days that seaside landladies had it all their own way. You could start your holiday any day provided it was Saturday. Even in the thirties the summer Saturday schedules had blossomed on holiday routes, but now coping with the weekly changeover strained resources to the maximum. But still the class system, two worlds. Most who had to go on Saturdays found trains crowded, often scheduled more slowly, certainly more likely to be late. Mid week, when on some lines extra trains were now being run simply to keep the locomotives and rolling stock needed for the weekends busy, the old values persisted.

Hundreds of thousands who went by summer Saturday trains, excursion trains, commuter trains, never experienced the railway's best, and because it was not under pressure that best was extraordinarily good. Mention has already been made of regional variations. They were substantial, lines to the west and north of London always being far better served than those to the south and east, systems south of the Thames traditionally having the slowest and least comfortable trains . . . a tradition by no means yet dead. But even on the Southern care was taken to provide one or two showpiece trains above the rest.

They were the days that the metalwork on the locomotives of the best trains shone, when the names of the trains were almost household words,

End of the line. Beginning of the journey. Penzance station early in BR days, probably around 1951, with No 5964 Wolseley Hall *of Laira shed (83D) waiting to depart with the up Cornish Riviera. The engine is in the mixed traffic livery of LNWR lined out black with a red backing to the nameplate; something ditched as quickly as they dared by the Western Region. The train is ex-GWR (mostly Hawksworth) stock painted in British Railways' 'blood and custard'.*

35010

Unusual engine. Britannia Pacific No 70023 Venus *leaves Bath Spa with the down Bristolian in 1953. The whole is representative of the modern scene in early BR days – the new Standard locomotive and up to date BR Mk 1 stock. This was only a short lived period and it was not long before the Castles were back on the head of the weekday train, normally seven coaches. On Fridays, when it tended to be strengthened a King would often be substituted. By 1959 a 100 minute schedule was to hand requiring a start to stop average of 71mph. In May of that year No 7018* Drysllwyn Castle *made the trip in 93min 50sec.*

when the beaming guard wore a carnation in his lapel and you thought it perfectly safe to ask him to keep an eye on an unaccompanied nine- or ten-year-old on a journey half way across Britain – and to pass on the responsibility if he was being relieved en route. They were the days that railwaymen played trains and took pride in it. Given that you can still have a most enjoyable journey by train, how is it that we have lost so much?

For a start, the stability in the fifties was illusory. The big mistake was building a thousand steam engines after nationalisation. Scarcer labour, poorer coal: the diesels and electrics were overdue, but getting rid of steam so rapidly caused great upheavals. And while the passenger side had been going on much as before, freight was withering . . . so alongside the motive-power revolution was the other of cutting out branch lines and stopping train services along many sections of main ones. So far from being respected, tradition was now ridiculed, steam described as psychologically disturbing to the staff, historic pictures torn from office walls. Engine sheds and other depots closed, men were moved around, many made redundant. Who could retain pride in all that? In fairness, some did, but purely for their own job satisfaction, no longer feeling their contribution was really appreciated.

More people bought their own cars, but more also had occasion to go to London or some other part of the country. The passenger as well as the freight railway became a specialised instead of common carrier. The proportion of the working population who *sometimes* travel by train is now greater than ever, but many only do so for a day trip to London or other large city. Business pressures are greater and different. In the great days of express trains, there were few quality arrivals at large termini before ten, eleven o'clock perhaps seeing the peak, while the day's very first arrivals from some cities 200–250 miles away were not until noon or after. The proportion of the country from which you could spend eight or more hours in London by day-time train was extremely small. Now people get up earlier, work harder and longer. The first trains from cities like Plymouth arrive nearly four hours earlier than in the 1950s, even the early 1960s! Commuters pour in not from the traditional radius but from places along main lines a hundred or more miles away.

The railways were always primarily a business, but never has the need to rake in the money been greater. Since road provides competition everywhere, the railway needs to answer with speed and frequency more than its traditional character and comfort. Frequency means not only more trains but stopping more of them more often. That has been a great spoiler of the top expresses. A non-stop journey of 150 miles is quite different in character from that calling at Peterborough, Watford or Reading. But even with more stops, journey times are much shorter; add the changes in eating habits and you destroy the need for most restaurant cars, and most individual touches have gone. So even the *Flying Scotsman* is totally standard. In the colourful days we are writing about, people would walk miles to see one of the recognisably great expresses go past – and experience a genuine twinge of excitement.

The expresses were among the neatest, prettiest things you saw anywhere in the country. That they were headed by the most powerful locomotives of the line, driven by top link men, advertised the towns and cities they served, started their journeys at time-honoured hours but steadily finished them sooner, that they paved the way for better signalling and safety standards and were taking important folk on vital journeys . . . all that added to the romance.

So once more, though alas, only in imagination, buy your ticket and come along. It will cost you, for travel by ordinary as opposed to workers' or excursion train was never cheap; and going back in time you will be disappointed by the general dullness of the station, for following in the Victorian tradition of browns and creams (since they were far cheaper than brighter colours) there is no effort to emphasise points of architectural interest, though plenty of advertisements to divert you. Spotting the ads (a colleague collected 193 different signs in five hours including the famous Liptons Tea – largest sale in the world, The smoker's match Swan Vestas, Pears soap – for matchless complexions, When ordering Bass insist on seeing the label, Wright's Coal Tar Soap) was one way to keep the children happy. Note how even if we go back this far there are already many people interested in railways: the magazines are prominently displayed at the bookstall and there is a

Crossing the Fireman's Arm

Single lines were not just for country locals. Prestige named expresses such as the *Royal Highlander* north of Perth, the *Pines Express* through the Mendips, the *Cambrian Coast Express* west of Offa's Dyke, were routed by them.

For the most part such routes were controlled by single-line tokens (also known as tablets) which lent themselves to mechanical exchange. Engraved brass discs about three inches in diameter, they were placed in a heavy leather pouch in the lineside apparatus, from which they were snatched by the jaws of corresponding equipment on the side of the cab or tender. Three forms of this equipment were used, invented by Whitaker, Bryson or Manson, and they permitted exchange of tokens at up to 60mph. Mind you, it was no fun for the fireman, wresting the pouch from the jaws with one hand while hanging on grimly with the other to the bucking locomotive. And if the catcher did not take the pouch cleanly it would launch it into a high-speed trajectory which, by Sod's law, always ended up in either a thick patch of nettles and brambles or in a muddy ditch. That meant a crash stop, a lengthy walk back and a search for the errant token.

Manual exchange, practised at 30mph as for example on the West Highland was equally exciting. The signalman faced the train with the new token held up in one hand the other arm extended below it to take the surrendered token; the fireman leaning from the cab adopted a converse position. Bingo, each was left with the correct token – but only as a result of much practice. That raconteur of things Glasgow & South Western, David L. Smith, tells of the time in the mid-1920s when Mossgiel Tunnel on the G&SW seven miles south of Kilmarnock

continued overleaf

continued
was being relined, necessitating single-line working.

'Now you don't get much tablet working round Glasgow and some of the young Corkerhill boys probably thought tablets were things that you took for indigestion. Jimmy Sewell had a green hand firing to him . . . Jimmy picked up Garrochburn tablet himself and gave it to his fireman with these explicit instructions: "Look out on your side at the other end of the tunnel. A man'll come out with a thing for catchin' it. Hang the tablet on it." The fireman, if unskilled, was a most willing, conscientious boy. It *was* a pity that just as they reached the south end an engineer should have set up his theodolite against the four-foot.'

Diesels, track circuiting, single manning and Radio Electronic Token Block have taken all the tingling anticipation out of single-line working. Drivers mostly *stop* to pick up the token, or if they catch it at low speed, *throw the surrendered one on the ground* for the signalman to pick up!

group of engine spotters at the platform's end. A branch train comes in. Mainly men alight, all in hats and caps according to rank, but a porter is immediately handy to help two haughty ladies (each with hat box though no doubt the bulk of headgear has been sent Passenger Luggage in Advance) transfer to our train. We are reassured we are at the right platform by an arm (a finger pointing to the edge) listing calling places. Each train has its arm, numbered in daily sequence. We hear the signalman receive two bells, train entering section, from the previous box, and immediately he closes the level crossing gates, pulls off the signals and sounds the platform bell, three rings for an up train. The stationmaster and other porters hurry out, the porters positioning some carts opposite where the guard's van will stop.

A distant whiff of smoke, the sound of steam, and in comes the train, the usual assortment of coaches representing successive developments and builds. You of course know which will give the best ride, have the most comfortable upholstery. The whole platform bobs about with activity and, yes, let us have a cup of tea from the trolley. (The same attendant pushes it the length of every train morning and afternoon; one cold morning when we complained the tea was cold he assured us that the water had been boiled for the previous train.) But the activity is a bit illusory, for over half the people we took to be passengers are actually seeing others off or greeting friends, and some of the railwaymen don't really have much to do, though those who do are putting their all into it. The stationmaster supervises the addition of another coach. Even medium-sized stations have their pilot engine, junctions two or more, ever topping and tailing trains. Restaurant cars and through portions come on and off, as do horseboxes, vans and the rest of the valuable 'coaching' traffic – not that the latter is carried by the great named trains.

Right Away. One more train is off, each departure quite an event yet very routine, a load that might be making or losing a lot of money for the company, an engine that is a joy to drive or really out of sorts, passengers repeating the familiar and traversing pastures new with what range of benevolent or malicious thoughts we can only guess.

Passing Through

Today's *Flying Scotsman* is an HST, its only visible acknowledgement to longstanding fame the destination labels stuck on the glass windows of the doors. It moves from and to London, Edinburgh and Aberdeen just like any of its express push-pull sisters and to a casual observer is just another BR train.

The great expresses in steam or early diesel days could scarcely have been more different. They had charisma in red- or green-painted locomotives which hissed and roared round or even growled. Most had shining brass name-plates whose nomenclature clearly indicated their class and therefore their power status. In later days they carried headboards (as did some LNER services) with the train's name emblazoned on them. Who could fail to identify the *Flying Scotsman* then?

It was not only the locomotive but also the train which made itself known as it passed along its tracks, coaches carried roof destination boards (later fixed above the windows on their sides) so it was easy enough to spot the *Bristolian*, the *Atlantic Coast Express* or the *Red Dragon*, or dozens of lesser, unnamed trains declaring their routes: Liverpool–Bristol–Torquay–Kingswear, Paddington–West Wales, or on summer Saturdays even Wolverhampton–Birmingham–Ilfracombe. Great for passengers and great publicity value, and when the *Torbay Express* (eight coaches in summer, seven in winter) only went from Paddington to Kingswear one day and back the next, no great complications for the staff. But steadily the commercial men required better stock usage, the *Bristolian* set no longer just being that.

Water splash. The result of the fireman not withdrawing the scoop from the trough in time. The leading coaches of this down train on Bushey troughs receive an involuntary wash from the overspill. The offending loco is Patriot class 4-6-0 No 5518 named Bradshaw *in 1939. The LNW main line had the most generous provision of water troughs being spaced at intervals of approximately thirty-five miles, enabling smaller tenders of either 3,500 or 4,000 gallons capacity to be used without problems. Bushey was only 15 miles out of Euston.*

Changing destination boards (or even just turning them round to display blank) was not easy even on the platform side, positively dangerous on the other – quite out of the question with the arrival of the overhead catenary. So died one of the more appealing facets of the great express trains. Who could not be excited by the geography displayed along our great main lines.

And when these colourful trains ran through the countryside, there were other rituals to observe. The steam engine required constant cossetting, human hands were needed to couple it to the train at the terminus station – the gentle bump would alert passengers to the fact that their journey was almost ready to begin. The guard and driver would converse checking the number of coaches and the train's weight and bustling station staff see that the myriad of compartment doors were shut. And then there was water, the life blood of any locomotive whatever its shape, size or colour; even the earlier diesels needed water for train-heating purposes. Most express engines tenders carried 3,500, 4,000 or even 5,000 gallons of water but with a consumption of 35–40 gallons a mile (and many were not that good), tender replenishment was a constant need. Often (and invariably on the Southern) this would be done at station stops, though even here it required skill to top up a tender in three minutes – always hoping the engine had stopped within the limited 'reach' of the column. But on the great non-stop runs of yesteryear (on almost all routes longer than today) the fireman had to rely on the water troughs.

'Taking water' was one of those skills which has gone, though leaving memories of its folklore as well as technical details. Approaching the troughs would be a large lineside sign, with a zigzag line on it. The fireman would quickly drop the scoop and watch the water indicator on the tender rise with each thousand gallons taken. At the right moment he would tug on the handle to lift out the scoop. A second's delay and water would shoot into the air from the tender top and drench the front coach; lift too soon and you might be short and have the disgrace of having to stop at a tower. Some troughs were notorious for overflowing and travelling ticket collectors or guards would go along to the first

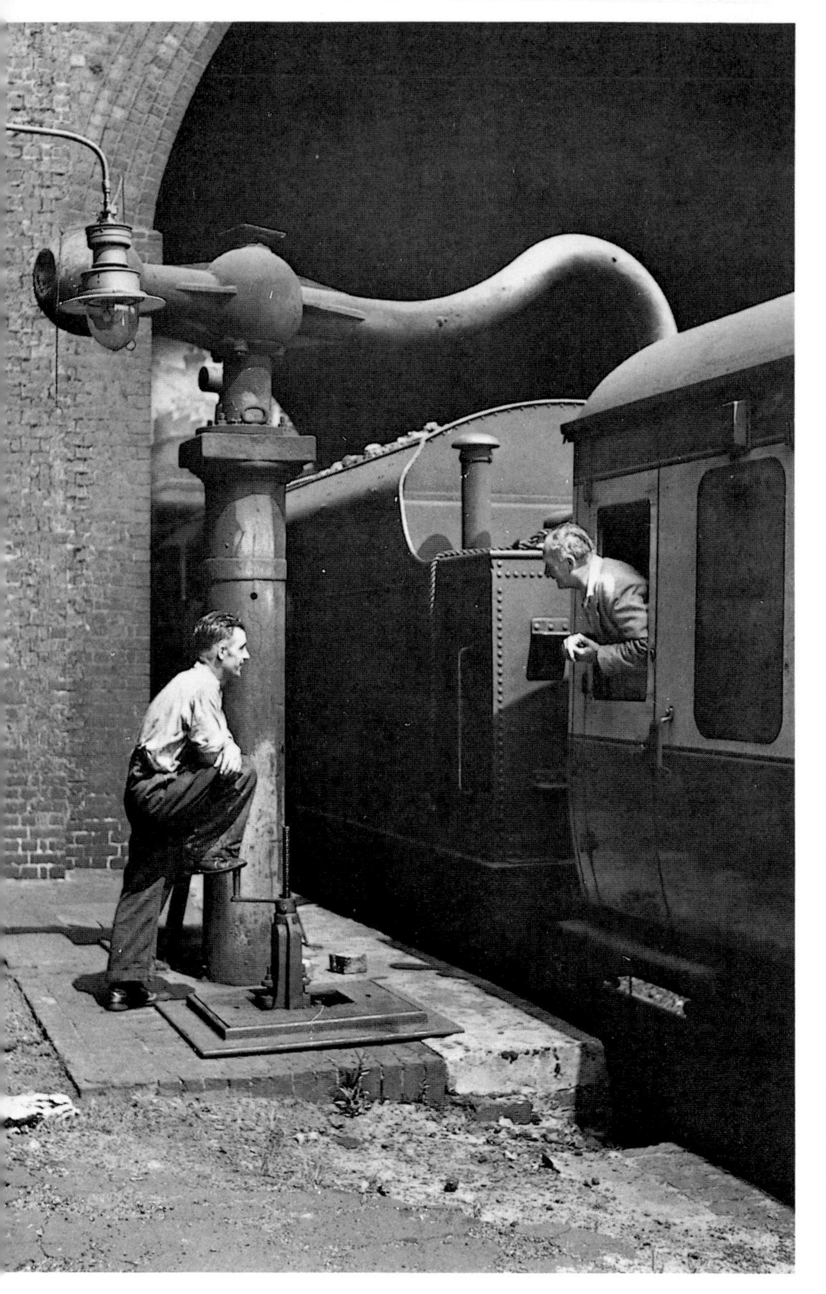

Taking advantage of a situation. Birmingham New Street station was very badly served with water columns. There were none on the Midland side platforms and only two on the LNW side. At holiday times when trains tended to queue up as far west as Bromsgrove or beyond drivers of up Midland trains frequently used an enforced signal stop at Five Ways to take water from the column there.

vehicle and close the windows as the train approached them. There were times when difficult passengers did not like the 'interference' and learned the hard way.

One reason for the great interest which non railwaymen took in railways was that, in steam days, they looked so difficult to run. Stations where regular engines or crew changes took place were hives of industry. The busy engine sheds beyond the platform ramps were usually covered in a cloud of smoke. Waiting for a train was never boring: there would be Pacifics or V2s or Castles or Halls moving on and off north or southbound trains, the whole area controlled by manual signalboxes with their bells ringing and their levers thumping. At Bristol as at Sheffield or Carlisle there were company or regional boundaries where old rivalries and loyalties remained. It was not only the engines which changed.

Then, during station stops at major centres the passenger's reverie would be interrupted by a dull clunk . . . clunk . . . clunk . . . clunk which grew louder and then, like an itinerant ghost, receded. He or she might get a bird's eye view of a cloth cap moving along the train on the side away from the platform. Here was the wheel tapper or carriage and wagon examiner at work, long-handled hammer in right hand and acetylene lamp in left. As he struck each wheel in turn, his trained ear was alert for any variation in the sound which might indicate a loose or fractured tyre; in a twist of the wrist he would apply the backs of his fingers to the axlebox to check that it was running cool. His lamp would pick out the brake-blocks, and between coaches the couplings and hoses, to see that all was well. But in the 1960s with the changeover to solid rolled wheels and roller-bearing axleboxes, epitomised by the B4 and B5 bogies, and a constant search for economies, one more skill was removed from the list.

Those were also the days of lodging turns where locomotive crews were expected to be away from home overnight as a matter of course; enginemen's hostels, like the one approaching Euston seen from the left hand side of the up train at Camden, were common at many terminal points and at busy changeover spots as Carlisle. The non-stop *Royal Scot* was never this with loco crews changing over outside Carlisle's Kingmoor or Upperby depots though the LNER did better with Gresley's corridor tenders allowing the exchange to take place en route.

Expresses which ran over single lines of course exchanged tablets or tokens – sometimes (as for example on the Somerset & Dorset) by automatic apparatus (that attached to the tender making contact with its opposite number set by the signalman on the lineside). Where automatic exchanges were not provided but the timetable demanded keeping on the move, there was great skill in making manual changes with the signalman. Carelessness could lead to a badly bruised arm. Then came the vital but absolute necessity to check that the section they were entering was that marked on the staff or tablet; carelessness here led to several terrible disasters.

Automatic exchange of mail at speed is yet another railway feature (described in the chapter on night trains) that has disappeared with standardisation.

To work on the railways in that not so distant past meant being part of a huge jigsaw puzzle, each piece interlocked and in many cases when the staff were known to each other if not personally then by sight. The locomotive crews in the top links knew their guards who knew the travelling ticket collectors, the signalmen at the sometimes hundreds of boxes en route, knew the men in the boxes either side of them and often their colleagues in the control office, they also knew the gangers and the telegraph linemen. The station staff also got to know those who stopped as they passed through on a regular basis and it all added up to a pride in the job.

Automatic tablet exchange. Two photographs relating to the automatic tablet exchange apparatus as used on the Somerset and Dorset section. These show (i) the tablet in its pouch as set up by the signalman and (ii) the lineside and locomotive tender apparatus as the exchange is made.

> **The Stationmaster's Day**
> He had come up through the ranks and what appealed most was the regular hours. Office hours, indeed largely office work . . . too much paper, nothing to help him except the mini-typewriter with a double shift key: press once for capitals, twice for figures and punctuation marks. He had to turn out half a dozen letters a day to titled people who expected a personal enquiry service by mail, tradesmen who were ever complaining, the superintendent of the Sunday school whose annual outing must not be allowed to go by road.
>
> The internal paper, instructions, cajolings from HQ, daily, weekly and monthly accounts, that took the real effort . . . a lonely job except you couldn't get on with it for all the callers. Tradespeople and even railway enthusiasts dropped in much as church leaders would on their minister. Everyone told him of their idea as to how the service should be improved but never listened to his. Then staff come to request holidays and make silly suggestions.
>
> Certain trains of course had to be supervised, definitely the important ups including any titled ones. Once or twice a day, when busy trains might clash, he would have to check how they were getting on in the booking office, even lend a hand. He checked there, the parcels office, the goods office, and signed the register daily at the several signalboxes under his control.
>
> The signalmen would phone him on the internal line if 'anything was up', and there would be calls from district office about specials and divided trains.
>
> Do his own paperwork he might have to, but at least someone lit his fire, tended to it when he was out (including a generous lunch hour when he mixed –
>
> *continued opposite*

2
BY TRAIN AND PLATFORM

IN the hours of darkness the traveller has dozed fitfully in his bunk listening occasionally to the sounds of a hard-working Duchess Pacific which was taken over from Camden men by a team from Crewe. He has crossed from Clydesdale and through the Forth/Clyde valley, clambered over the ridge between Strath Allan and Strathearn and stopped again at Perth. By now the motive power is a pair of Black Fives, and the first dawn light is breaking as he peers dreamily out of his sleeping-car window. Ben Vrackie stands out as a silhouette as the train emerges from the Pass of Killiecrankie and runs into Blair Atholl, where they stop for water, each engine in its turn. Adjacent, the small loco shed houses the bankers for the toil up Glen Garry to the summit of Druimuachdar. As daylight comes, the mountains which guard the pass are flushed with light; an awakening to remember.

At Aviemore it is time for breakfast, and, as the heavy express which has left London at 7.20pm the previous evening tackles its second long climb since leaving Perth, this time to Slochd Mhuic, the view from the dining car is of morning mists on the Cairngorms slowly dissolving to reveal distant peaks and heather-purpled moorlands tranquil under the early morning sun. It all conforms to the messages shouted out by the posters: 'See Scotland By Rail, take in the romance of the Highlands.'

It is now 1951. Little has changed over the last decade and more, though the old Highland line has again been tested with the exceptional demands of war traffic to Invergordon and Scapa Flow. This has seen to it that the motive power is standard and modern, so the sound of a Big Ben double heading a Highland Castle is something deep into the past, and the only surviving native 4-6-0 is *Clan Mackinnon* kept almost as an elderly pet at Inverness. The train arrives here at 9.7am, carefully backing over the triangle into the north-facing platform to make an across-platform connection with the stopper to Wick and Thurso. The traveller has arrived at the northernmost point for any express train in the United Kingdom.

Scotland has always proved fascinating with its combination of heavy trains and steep gradients and the powerful locomotives to ensure speedy competition between west coast and east. The dramatic passage of the border hills by the Dales of Annan, Nith, Esk and Teviot as well as by Grantshouse and Gala Water ensured a romanticism which only disappeared after the demise of steam.

For some, the magic may have died at the 1923 grouping. Before grouping the traveller could step on to the platform at Carlisle's Citadel and see the massive blue shape of a Caledonian engine – maybe even the

legendary *Cardean* – backing down to lift the heavy load of West Coast Joint Stock over the grades of Beattock. But for the next generation it was the Stanier hooter (which replaced the organ-like note of a Caley whistle) that spelt Scotland.

Modernisation in the shape of electrification first came to the West Coast main line. In the east, where the early alliances had flung great bridges over the Firths of Forth and Tay, the old order died harder. True, the Deltics had already begun to make their growling speedy way north from King's Cross by 1961, and towards the end of the following year the first five of Gresley's famous A4 Pacifics went for scrap. But there was to be a reprieve with a small number of engines moving up to Scotland. Years back, in the heyday of steam, few would have even entertained the thought that the final work of the great Pacifics of the streamline era would be over the former Caledonian main line between Glasgow (Buchanan Street) and Aberdeen. This Indian Summer for the A4s began late in 1963 and by 1964 the engines appeared quite at home on the smartly timed three-hour expresses. For years they provided sparkling performances over the racing ground between Stanley Junction and Forfar. It was on the instructions of James Ness, then general manager of the Scottish Region, that a test run had taken place between

Steam at the top. A double-headed London–Perth–Inverness express at Druimuachdar summit in the mid 1950s. The motive power is the standard product for the line at the time – double-headed Stanier Black Fives – their tenure ran for just on a generation.

continued
uneasily – with some of the town's high ups in the pub or restaurant of the moment), and one of the porters always made a point of finding today's *Times* in an empty compartment. Coffee came from the booking office twice daily. The bottle of sherry in the drawer lasted months and was for the occasional VIP including a reporter or of course tradesmen.

A4 Swan Song. Displaced by diesels from the East Coast main line, a small clutch of A4s took over the fastest Glasgow–Aberdeen trains in the summer of 1962 and ran them until withdrawal in 1966. Here one lifts the six-coach 07.10 ex-Aberdeen out of Stonehaven and up the 1 in 92 towards Carmont. It will call at Forfar, Perth and Stirling and be into Glasgow Buchanan St at 10.10.

the two cities on 22 February 1962; it was also very much due to Ness that the four Scottish preserved locomotives were returned to service in their old colours at around the same period.

But let us go back to the early post-war years, the last great days of steam on the East Coast main line, when the A4s were at their peak. The non-stop *Flying Scotsman* was reintroduced in 1948, only to be faced in August of that year by the severing of the route through flood damage between Grantshouse and Reston. The non-stop was diverted for three months via St Boswells and Kelso to Tweedmouth. Even with additional mileage the Haymarket drivers generally managed to reach Lucker troughs from Edinburgh without having to stop for water. In 1949 there was a speed trial when No 60017 *Silver Fox* reached 102mph on the descent from Stoke: the problem was that although the engine stood up well, the hard-pressed track did not. Arrears of maintenance in the war were compounded by poor working conditions and almost full employment, especially in the London area. To restore pride in the job, motive power superintendent L. P. Parker gathered most of the Eastern's A4s at Kings Cross Top Shed where matters were so arranged that many engines worked out and home with the same crews. Once more regular engines were allocated to top link men; *Silver Link* to E. Hailstone, *Mallard* to J. Burgess and E. Smith. Hailstone in particular was dedicated to his 'No 14'. It is said that he had special pins made for the middle big-end oil feed to give it a little more than the standard, and his front buffers were highly polished. 1952 saw a further step forward: the new *Capitals Limited* (in 1953 the *Elizabethan*) began its non-stop journey to Edinburgh at 9.30, ahead of the *Flying Scotsman*. Right

Coming for the Troops

On 17 February 1950 the SR had an unprecedented visitor in the form of LM Patriot 4-6-0 No 45516. It travelled down to Southampton Docks to pick up a troop train of its regimental namesake the *Beds & Herts Regiment* destined for Bury St Edmunds. The Patriot worked the train throughout to Suffolk. Today BR would charge a four-figure sum if a special engine were requested.

through its service to the end of steam over the East Coast route, engine crews took pride in running this prestige train to time.

Around the same period one can conjure up a journey south from Yorkshire's industrial heartland of Sheffield over the old Midland main line behind a *Jubilee* in good condition. The main part of the train has come down from Bradford and Leeds, so the knowledgeable traveller bides his time and finds a seat in one of the two restaurant cars, or the additional third coach attached at Sheffield. He settles down wondering how the performance will be with 'ten on'.

For the first forty miles or so speed is nothing to remember because of colliery subsidences. Once through Bradway tunnel the train gets moving and downhill acceleration takes it by Dronfield at a speed that no car could emulate on the winding alleyway that forms the main street. They drift down the sweeping bends over Unstone viaduct and towards Chesterfield at around seventy, and as Tapton Junction comes and goes the traveller wonders if the driver has forgotten to put his hand on the brake. By now Chesterfield's crooked church spire is in sight, speed begins to drop and they stop – gently! A mile or two south the distant main road shows short strings of cars pottering impatiently behind lumbering lorries awaiting chances to push perilously past.

The Erewash Valley is not a speedway but here and there away from

Kings Cross. The up Elizabethan running into Kings Cross in the fifties, hauled by A4 60009 Union of South Africa, *one of the class which has been preserved. The Capitals Limited non-stop between London and Edinburgh was renamed The Elizabethan in Queen Elizabeth II's Coronation year. To the right can be seen one of the Class N1 0-6-2 suburban tank engines. To the left, behind the train spotter, is the large electro-mechanical power box, which has now been superseded by the NX box on the up side at the exit from Gas Works Tunnel. This box covers as far as Sandy and, when it was built the track layout at Kings Cross was modified, eliminating the very difficult approach curve which The Elizabethan is negotiating, restricted to 8mph.*

the pits and their attendant subsidence, the fields and trees are lush and the driver can let go. Soon the long steel Great Northern viaduct near Ilkeston comes into view with a substantial passenger train advancing from the town; the fear is that it will pass overhead at the moment that will give the minimum view of its engine, but as always it is a compromise and it is identified fleetingly as a Gresley K2 2-6-0 with a Westinghouse pump.

Toton is always worth a peep and here are Garratts, Stanier 2-8-0s and even a Tilbury 4-4-2 tank looking reasonably clean which is a surprise as the class seemed to be dying in this area where it has been unloved since its arrival from its more successful days in the south east. Trent comes quickly, a tangle of junctions and some ferocious curves, with a 2-8-0 beginning to get a swing on a long coal train on the up goods line. The Soar Valley soon merges into the Quorn country and is a picture of pastoral peace: the Jubilee stalks through adequately at little less than 60.

Leicester produces a Claud Hamilton on the shed and – for contrast – a double-chimney class 4 2-6-0. They get away well until Knighton North box checks them, then the style of running livens. The Millhouses man opens up for the rise to Kibworth and hurtles down the far side. When the rail rhythm first sounds reckless it must be near East Langton: more curves as the train takes the right hand bend over the LNWR Peterborough line before Market Harborough and the engine can just be seen out of the window. The smoking chimney shows that the driver has shut off before the station which they race through at 66mph where

Station for Nowhere. Trent, between Derby and Nottingham, was purely a junction station, with single island platform, in the middle of fields and with only a footpath for access. Class 5 4-6-0 No 44918 (16A) approaches from Nottingham with an express for St Pancras. The Erewash Valley line comes in behind the first coach. Midland signals survive, but most have been converted to upper quadrant. The whole area is now greatly simplified and controlled from a new power signalbox opened in 1969.

Platform end at Temple Meads. Standing on the up platform looking west on 6 August 1956 one sees Bristol Bath Road shed containing a number of engine classes that would not have varied much over a generation. Left to right beyond the smokebox door of No 4903 Astley Hall *at the head of the 1.18pm Paddington–Weston-super-Mare express are a Castle, a Star, a 45XX 2-6-2T, a Hall, a Castle and a 43XX class Mogul. The leading coach on the express is an ex-GWR brake third.*

the limit is normally 50mph. So they get a wonderful run at the bank up to Desborough.

The driver lets *Bellerophon* run hard down the other side and soon there is a distant view of Kettering ironworks and the train flies down past Glendon like an LNER streamliner. They are soon into the eighties sweeping through Kettering at 84mph, Burton Latimer at 81mph, Finedon 80mph then somewhat excessively the driver eases to 54mph at Wellingborough. It is lunchtime now as the Jubilee pounds up to Sharnbrook summit and enthusiasm develops as they touch 84mph again on the way down to Oakley and continue smartly through Bedford and up the bank past Harlington. All in vain, for they are almost stopped by signals at Leagrave which makes them late arriving at Luton.

It takes thirty-three minutes for the remaining thirty miles to London with another severe signal check at St Albans, quenching anything more exuberant than 76 through Hendon. So they are five down at St Pancras but the Sheffield men have made a lively job of it. The traveller pauses as he passes the engine, unable to leave without a word with the crew. The fireman is ready to uncouple and is in a cheerful mood. 'Not a bad trip,' he says, 'and the coal was pretty fair.' By now both the crew and No 45694 have had enough and it is off to Kentish Town for the engine to be serviced and the men to sleep, ready for their return working at 8.50.

Newton Abbot 1937. A view taken from the western end of the down island platform of the rebuilt station showing the loco shed yard during late August in that year. Visible engines include an open cab 0-6-0 pannier tank (almost certainly rebuilt from a saddle tank) a 43XX 2-6-0 and three Castles. To the left of the Mogul is an old non-corridor clerestory coach used as an office. It is a busy afternoon and most of the Bulldog class 4-4-0s acting as pilots are out on the road. In addition to catering for the Torquay/Kingswear branch and the pilots/bankers, Newton Abbot shed also houses engines for the West to North route to Shrewsbury.

Hard into the attack. Stoneycombe quarry sidings on the climb up to Dainton summit on 23 March 1950. It is a North to West express with Star class No 4056 Princess Margaret *of Laira shed as the train engine and No 7812* Erlestoke Manor *from Newton Abbot as pilot. The Star has been repainted in BR green but the Manor and the train are in post-war GWR livery.*

Over on the Western, it is a Saturday in September, ideal for a day return from Bristol to Newton Abbot with sauntering at Taunton and Exeter en route. At Bristol Bath Road, clearly seen from the platform, not only are there Castles coming on and off for the north to west trains, the *Cornishman* to Wolverhampton via Cheltenham and Stratford, and various Londons, but not one of the last few Stars today. Now on to the 6.50 Leicester–Paignton: 10.50 off Temple Meads, arriving Taunton at 11.50, headed by No 7011 *Banbury Castle* and packed to the doors. The travelling ticket collector queries the cheap ticket availability: 'You're not travelling on the Midland now you know!' Taunton shed is close to the end of the down platform and sports No 6029 *King Edward VIII*, a Laira engine. Better not enquire why she's here as she may well have failed. There are some Moguls with their steps cut down to 8ft 4in for working over the Southern from Barnstaple Junction to Ilfracombe and a collection of those lovely little 45XX tanks for the Minehead branch. The *Cornish Riviera* comes through three minutes down at 13.02 and after that it is on to Exeter by the 9.20 Swansea–Kingswear, due out at 13.02 but running thirteen minutes late. Timekeeping is not helped by signal checks on the 1 in 80 climb to Whiteball; they will be having a problem getting bankers and pilots across the busy main lines for their return journeys. Exeter St David's is full of Southern engines going the wrong way after making their (still in BR days) mandatory stop. Exeter shed, by the up platform, is almost empty. But Southern's West Country and Battle of Britain Pacifics are worth photographing, and by dint of good fortune No 30707, a T9 class 4-4-0, comes through.

The next train should be the 7.41 Nottingham–Plymouth due out at 14.45. Wonderful, a Star, No 4056 *Princess Margaret*, from Bath Road shed, runs in. The guard explains this is a relief (that accounts for the scruffy stock) and that the main train 'must be well down'. This is now the old GWR holiday line and No 4056 picks up speed once past Exeter St Thomas and drifts nicely along the Exe estuary past Exminster through Starcross to Dawlish Warren over the sea wall to Teignmouth slowing for the station, then once past the Teign estuary turning west up river.

Newton Abbot in the early 1950s is still a very important place on the Western Region, home of a divisional locomotive superintendent whose sway ranges from Taunton to Penzance: the shed boasts a repair works similar to that at Tyseley and Caerphilly. As the Nottingham has eleven on there is a wait for a pilot up to Dainton and over the south Devon banks to Plymouth, this time No 7812 *Erlestoke Manor*, grimy and still with the letters GWR on its tender sides. The pair make a fine sound as they bark their way towards Aller Junction. The enthusiast stays at the end of the down platform and gazes wistfully over towards the shed thinking of happy times when he was here as a boy, when for example 31XX tanks piloted expresses over the Dartmoor foothills.

THE NAMED EXPRESSES

This lists named trains running in August 1956, those picked out in bold type being continuations (or restorations) of those running in 1939.

Name	Running between	Date of inauguration (or naming of existing train) and Post-War Restoration
The Flying Scotsman	London Kings Cross and Edinburgh Waverley	Popular use from about 1862
The Aberdonian	London Kings Cross and Aberdeen	1 January 1927
The Night Scotsman	London Kings Cross and Edinburgh Waverley	1 January 1927
The Queen of Scots	London Kings Cross, Edinburgh and Glasgow (Pullman car train)	October 1927. Suspended 2 September 1939. Resumed 5 July 1948
The Heart of Midlothian	London Kings Cross, Edinburgh Waverley and Perth	3 May 1951
The Yorkshire Pullman	London Kings Cross, Hull, Harrogate and Bradford Exchange (Pullman car train)	30 September 1935. Restored 4 November 1946
The Tees-Tyne Pullman	London Kings Cross and Newcastle (Pullman car train)	27 September 1948
The Northumbrian	London Kings Cross and Newcastle	26 September 1949
***The Scarborough Flyer**	London Kings Cross and Scarborough Central	11 July 1927. Restored 9 June 1950
†**The Norseman**	London Kings Cross and Newcastle (Tyne Commission Quay)	June 1931. Restored 5 June 1950
The Harrogate Sunday Pullman	London Kings Cross, Harrogate and Bradford Exchange (Pullman car train)	17 July 1927. Restored 11 June 1950
The Tynesider	London Kings Cross and Newcastle	5 June 1950
*The Elizabethan	London Kings Cross, Edinburgh Waverley and Aberdeen	As 'The Capitals Limited' 23 May 1949. Renamed 'The Elizabethan' 29 June 1953
The Fair Maid	London Kings Cross, Edinburgh Waverley and Perth	16 September 1957. An extension and renaming of the Morning Talisman, begun 17 June 1957
The Talisman	London Kings Cross and Edinburgh Waverley	17 September 1956. A successor to The Coronation, which was inaugurated on 5 July 1937, but withdrawn on the outbreak of war and not restored.
The White Rose	London Kings Cross, Leeds Central, and Bradford Exchange	23 May 1949
The West Riding	London Kings Cross, Leeds Central and Bradford Exchange	23 May 1949
The East Anglian	London Liverpool Street and Norwich Thorpe	27 September 1937. Restored 7 October 1946
The Broadsman	London Liverpool Street, Norwich Thorpe, Cromer and Sheringham	5 June 1950
*The Easterling	London Liverpool Street and Yarmouth	5 June 1950
The Norfolkman	London Liverpool Street, Norwich Thorpe, Cromer and Sheringham	27 September 1948
The Essex Coast Express	London Liverpool Street and Clacton	9 June 1958
†**The Hook Continental**	London Liverpool Street and Harwich Parkeston Quay for the Continent	2 October 1927 (Called the 'Continental Express' before the 1914 war, and the 'Hook-of-Holland Express' after). Restored November 1945
†The Day Continental	London Liverpool Street and Harwich Parkeston Quay for the Continent	14 June 1947 (Called the 'Flushing Continental' before the war)
†**The Scandinavian**	London Liverpool Street and Harwich Parkeston Quay for Esbjerg	15 May 1930 (Previously called the Esbjerg Continental). Restored December 1945
The Fenman	London Liverpool Street and Hunstanton	23 May 1949
The Irish Mail	London Euston and Holyhead	1 August 1848 (as a description)
The Emerald Isle Express	London Euston and Holyhead	20 September 1954
The Royal Scot	London Euston and Glasgow Central	11 July 1927. (Naming a train which had run from 15 February 1848, and became known popularly as the Ten O'Clock in 1862)
The Caledonian	London Euston and Glasgow Central	17 June 1957. A successor to 'The Coronation Scot', which was inaugurated on 5 July 1937, but withdrawn on the outbreak of war and not restored
The Mid-day Scot	London Euston and Glasgow Central	26 September 1927. Restored 26 September 1949. Unofficially known as 'The Corridor' from July 1893
***The Lakes Express**	London Euston, Keswick, Workington, and Windermere	11 July 1927
The Ulster Express	London Euston and Heysham	11 July 1927. Restored 26 September 1949
The Royal Highlander	London Euston and Inverness	26 September 1927. Restored 17 June 1957
The Northern Irishman	London Euston and Stranraer Harbour	30 June 1952
The Comet	London Euston and Manchester London Road	12 September 1932. Restored 26 September 1949.
The Red Rose	London Euston and Liverpool Lime Street	17 May 1951
The Shamrock	London Euston and Liverpool Lime Street	14 June 1954
The Mancunian	London Euston and Manchester London Road	26 September 1927. Restored 26 September 1949
The Lancastrian	London Euston and Manchester London Road	January, 1928. Restored 16 September 1957
The Midlander	London Euston, Birmingham New Street and Wolverhampton High Level	25 September 1950
The Merseyside Express	London Euston and Liverpool Lime Street	1 March 1928. (London-Merseyside Express from 26 September 1927). Restored 26 September 1949
***The Manxman**	London Euston and Liverpool Lime Street	11 July 1927. Restored 18 June 1951

THE NAMED EXPRESSES

Name	Running between	Date of inauguration (or naming of existing train) and Post-War Restoration
***The Welshman**	London Euston, Llandudno, Bangor, Pwllheli and Portmadoc	11 July 1927
The Thames-Clyde Express	London St Pancras and Glasgow St Enoch	26 September 1927. Restored 26 September 1949
The Waverley	London St Pancras and Edinburgh Waverley	17 June 1957
The Palatine	London St Pancras and Manchester Central	February 1938. Restored 16 September 1957
The Master Cutler	London Marylebone and Sheffield Victoria	6 October 1947
The South Yorkshireman	London Marylebone and Bradford Exchange	31 May 1948
The Cornish Riviera Express	London Paddington and Penzance	1 July 1904
The Torbay Express	London Paddington and Kingswear	23 June 1923. Restored May 1946
The Red Dragon	London Paddington and Carmarthen	5 June 1950
The Cambrian Coast Express	London Paddington, Aberystwyth and Pwllheli	11 July 1927. Restored 18 June 1951
The Inter-City	London Paddington, Birmingham and Wolverhampton	25 September 1950
The Bristolian	London Paddington and Bristol	9 September 1935. Name restored 18 June 1951. Full reinstatement 14 June 1954
The Merchant Venturer	London Paddington, Bath, Bristol and Weston-super-Mare	18 June 1951
The Pembroke Coast Express	London Paddington and Pembroke Dock	8 June 1953
The South Wales Pullman	London Paddington and Swansea (Pullman car train)	13 June 1955
Capitals United Express	London Paddington and Cardiff	6 February 1956
Cheltenham Spa Express	London Paddington and Cheltenham Spa	9 July 1923. Restored 17 September 1956
The Royal Duchy	London Paddington and Penzance	28 January 1957
The Mayflower	London Paddington and Plymouth	17 June 1957
The Cathedrals Express	London Paddington, Oxford, Worcester and Hereford	16 September 1957
The Atlantic Coast Express	London Waterloo and Plymouth, Padstow, Bude, Torrington and Ilfracombe	19 July 1926
The Bournemouth Belle	London Waterloo and Bournemouth (Pullman car train)	5 July 1931. Restored 7 October 1946
The Royal Wessex	London Waterloo, Bournemouth and Weymouth	3 May 1951
†The Normandy Express	London Waterloo and Southampton Docks (For Southampton-Havre service)	1952
†The Cunarder	London Waterloo and Southampton Docks	2 July 1952
†The Statesman	London Waterloo and Southampton Docks	1952
†The Springbok	London Waterloo and Southampton Docks	As 'Union Castle Line' 1953. Renamed 1958
†The South American	London Waterloo and Southampton Docks	1953
†The Holland American	London Waterloo and Southampton Docks	1954
†The Greek Line	London Waterloo and Southampton Docks	1954
†The Arosa Line	London Waterloo and Southampton Docks	1955
The Brighton Belle	London Victoria and Brighton (Pullman car train)	As the 'Southern Belle' 1 November 1908. Renamed the 'Brighton Belle' 29 June 1934. Restored 7 October 1946
*The Kentish Belle	London Victoria, Canterbury and Kent Coast (Pullman car train)	As the 'Thanet Belle' 31 May 1948. Renamed the 'Kentish Belle' 18 June 1951
The Golden Arrow	London Victoria and Folkestone/Dover (Pullman car train in conjunction with *Fleche d'Or*, Calais-Paris)	15 May 1929. (The name had been used for the Calais-Paris Pullman train from 12 September 1926). Restored 15 April 1946
The Night Ferry	London Victoria and Paris and Brussels (international sleeping cars) via Dover-Dunkerque	14 October 1936
The Man of Kent	London Charing Cross and Sandwich	8 June 1953
The Cornishman	Wolverhampton and Penzance	30 June 1952
The Devonian	Bradford Forster Square, Torquay and Paignton	26 September 1927. Restored 23 May 1949
The North Briton	Leeds City and Glasgow Queen Street	26 September 1949 (naming an old-established train)
The Pines Express	Liverpool Lime Street/Manchester London Road and Bournemouth West	26 September 1927. Restored 23 May 1949
The Bon Accord	Glasgow Buchanan Street and Aberdeen	5 July 1937. Restored 23 May 1949
The Saint Mungo	Glasgow Buchanan Street and Aberdeen	5 July 1937. Restored 23 May 1949
The Granite City	Glasgow Buchanan Street and Aberdeen	17 July 1933. Restored 23 May 1949
The Irishman	Glasgow St Enoch and Stranraer Harbour (for Northern Ireland)	17 July 1933. Restored 23 May 1949
*The Fife Coast Express	Glasgow Queen Street and St Andrews	23 May 1949. (The name **'Fifeshire Coast Express'** was used from 1 July 1912, until suspension in 1939)

NOTES *Summer only. †Run in connection with sailings of ships of various shipping lines

Pre-war named trains not restored include LMS: Coronation Scot (Euston-Glasgow), Thames-Forth Express (St Pancras-Edinburgh Waverley), Sunny South Express (Liverpool/Manchester-Brighton/Eastbourne/Hastings) and Blackpool & Fylde Coast Express (from Euston); LNER: Silver Jubilee (Kings Cross-Newcastle), Coronation (Kings Cross-Edinburgh).

All aboard. Paddington station around 1949/50 with the 2.10pm to Birmingham and Wolverhampton in platform 1. The clock shows 1.59 and by now most of the passengers are on board. The stock carrying roof destination boards appear to be in GWR livery but on a black and white photograph this is hard to discern; some may be in the new BR red and cream. The picture is taken from the steps of the footbridge adjacent to the booking office looking down towards the 'lawn' and 1950 dress is apparent; 'new look' skirts and striped blazers! In the background is a set of Hawksworth coaches. The 2.10pm is one of the regular interval ten past the hour services to Birmingham and the north and will almost certainly be King hauled.

Breaking the Rules

January 1955 was darkened by a disaster at Sutton Coldfield which killed seventeen, including three enginemen. The 12.15pm York–Bristol, headed by class 5 4-6-0 No 45274, had been diverted via Lichfield and Aston because of engineering work at Tamworth. Inexplicably, the conductor driver, who was actually driving, because the rostered driver had broken the rules and retired to the train – entered the sharp 30mph restricted curve into the station at nearer 60mph and the engine and first few coaches were strewn about the platform ends. The men on the footplate were killed.

Sheer recklessness caused the year's second serious derailment through excessive speed, at Wormit, Fife on 28 May. A tender first class 5 4-6-0 No 45458 took the sharply curved approach to Tay Bridge at 40–45mph instead of the prescribed 10mph and spread itself plus the first four coaches of a packed return excursion from Tayport over the platforms. Evidence showed that the driver had an irresponsible record; he had been drinking between out and home legs of the run; moreover he was entertaining an unauthorised adult and child passenger on the footplate. Both gatecrashers and the fireman were killed.

Sutton Coldfield disaster. A scene after the tracks had been cleared.

3
THE ANATOMY OF THE EXPRESS TRAIN

YOU can look at an express train in many different ways. It is, for example, a major profit (or loss) centre in its own right yet, far from running in isolation, is part of a complex overall pattern and provides connections for a multitude of other services. It is a social institution, and over the years carries many people making journeys that are the turning point of their lives, as well as countless others travelling in a more humdrum way. Each day its safe passage is noted by many people along its route. At least two-thirds of the year it runs with clockwork regularity, but at summer weekends it perhaps changes its character, indeed becoming two (sometimes three) separate trains, and at times of bad weather it is specially prone to delay. Then it is, of course, hardware, and very lovely hardware too. The most prestigious train on the route, it normally has at least the second-latest carriages and a

Holiday Journey. Manchester London Road (now Piccadilly) station around 1950. The Wymans (now John Menzies) bookstall is on the right – a relic of LNW/LMS days. There was (and still is) a second bookstall – W. H. Smith – dating back to GC and LNER times. Presumably the contracts have not yet run out.

powerful locomotive in good trim. The locomotive depot responsible for the allocation sees to that; though it is a double-home duty, it is specially popular with the footplate men, indeed taking them further from their base than any other service. The train is also something that needs rostering, given an appearance in the working and public timetables. And finally it is a piece of history. It has already been running to much the same schedule for several decades, almost since Brunel's broad gauge was abolished, in fact, and though we are now in the 1930s most of what is said will remain equally true (after the interruption of the war) from the late 1940s into the early 1960s.

Requiem for a Star. One of Churchward's masterpieces, No 4031 Queen Mary *runs along the Devon coast between Dawlish and Dawlish Warren on 20 August 1949. The train is the 08.45 Plymouth to Manchester (with through coaches from Torquay) which will run via Bristol Temple Meads and the old GWR/LNWR joint line through Hereford and Shrewsbury. No 4031 was then a Wolverhampton Stafford Road engine, rather off course on that train.*

Much planning has taken place before the day on which the train runs. Each season the commercial people take another look at the loading, and note that it continues to increase. Over the years the number of coaches, at least in the summer, has steadily increased from eight or nine to thirteen or fourteen, occasionally the maximum of fifteen that the most powerful locomotive that can be sent on this important cross-country link can haul. Because of its popularity, substantial party travel is discouraged on this service, but since it links two great ports there are ever unpredictable numbers of naval and merchant sailors on board. They indeed make it necessary to run a relief service before and after Christmas as well as to divide the train in summer.

Over the years much discussion has taken place about the stations at

which the train should stop, but little has changed in recent years. Discussing things is one thing; actually changing them quite different. Many of those responsible for the timetable firmly believe that if an entirely new team had to start from scratch, logic would inevitably drive them back to exactly what is now provided. There has, however, been a recent addition to the through coaches. Let us not get too bogged down in the precise example, for most remarks in this chapter will apply to any major train anywhere in Britain, but to be specific we are talking about the 8.45am from Plymouth. The main train with restaurant car goes to Liverpool (Lime Street) but also from Plymouth there are through coaches to Birkenhead (Woodside) and Glasgow (Central), while between Newton Abbot and Crewe through coaches from Paignton to Manchester (London Road) are also carried. Newton Abbot provides the Castle, the Devon men taking pride in handing their train over to the LMS men at Shrewsbury punctually. Of course they are sure their Castle is the better.

Each year the authorities also review which depots should be responsible for what, but see little need to meddle. It is as though some higher authority than man has decreed that this is a Newton Abbot duty, and so it will remain until the last days of steam. Again, the rolling stock is never exactly the newest but always respectable. Though mainly GWR, there are always LMS coaches, the Paignton–Manchester as well as the Glasgow through coach currently being composed of them and giving the train its distinctive cross-country appearance. The restaurant car is of course GW, slightly older than the adjoining coaches, and naturally the Plymouth–Birkenhead coach is also chocolate and cream since it will never leave the GW system (if you allow that that includes the joint route from Hereford and of course the joint stations at Chester and Birkenhead).

Other matters that have been much discussed over the years are what seat reservations should be provided, the order in which the train should be marshalled, how to restrict the amount of bulk mail and parcels carried. Though the two vans are always well used, and in the Christmas rush much time is wasted at principal stations waiting for loading and unloading to finish, the district offices keep up their reminder that this is a prestigious *passenger* service.

The processes by which passengers make their decision to travel are almost as complicated as the railways' own methods of putting the train together. By the mid 1930s, people are travelling around more than they used to, but for most a journey from the West to the North or vice versa is still a major undertaking. Northcountry people with successful businesses or careers are increasingly sampling the delights of Devon for their holidays, and not surprisingly the demand for seats on the Torbay section increases more sharply than on the rest of the train in high summer. There is already growing two-way holiday traffic between the West Country and Scotland, too. But outside the few busy holiday months (when anyway most of the traffic is at weekends) the train has no one obvious category but carries passengers on an incredibly wide range of journeys. A few commercial travellers are still going by train;

Apprehension

While express train journeys were something that in later years many people planned with eager anticipation, nearly all earlier and many later travellers faced them with apprehension.

The loss of landscape ('visual perception is diminished by velocity'), a feeling of captivity ('the traveller finds himself condemned to idleness as he enters the carriage . . . impatience engulfs the unfortunate traveller, pulled along by the machine like a piece of baggage') were only two of the lesser fears. Others included being separated from luggage, left hungry, becoming very late.

More serious worries were whether the locomotive boiler would explode (just occasionally it did) or the train would run off the line (as happened much more frequently). Most people such as Charles Dickens escaped from accidents unharmed but for ever after realised it might have been different . . . fire spreading from gas lighting being a real killer. Then there was always the chance of being molested (a real risk if you were alone in a non-corridor compartment and someone suspicious jumped in just as the train was leaving) or being murdered (very rare indeed, though the handful of Victorian and Edwardian railway murders naturally were given headlines).

In the days when everything depended on the family's sole wage earner, buying insurance at the station was fairly normal. However most people realised that the risk of life and even limb was scant, and were again more concerned about domestic matters, especially on long runs whether they could hold out till the next stopping (and toilet) place.

But then some passengers were born worriers. If they admitted the train was going in the right direction at a reasonable speed,

continued on page 37

West to North Express. Reboilered Patriot class 4-6-0 No 45536 Private W. Wood VC *climbs the 1 in 82 bank from Abergavenny to Llanvihangel near Llantilio Pertholey at the head of the 08.45 Plymouth to Manchester train (with through coaches from Torquay) on 11 September 1952. The stock appears to be mainly ex-Great Western. The engine is a Longsight (9A) locomotive working home – with a Western crew as far as Shrewsbury.*

some use the service to catch a ship from Liverpool to Canada or Belfast or just the Isle of Man; inevitably there will be some visiting distant relatives, especially if there is a new-born baby or illness, and most days you will see a couple of women in mourning.

Every day the train carries people going to new jobs, often moving home and hoping that their belongings are making safe progress at the same time as they are. Certainly there will be merchant sailors going to join new ships at Liverpool, or in the reverse direction young sailors going for a stint in Plymouth, the more fortunate even to the Royal Naval College at Dartmouth. Beginnings and ends of school terms also have their effect, though more usually bringing extra passengers travelling fifty to a hundred miles than transferring from South to North. But then at any one time the train will throughout its journey always be carrying more passengers on short than long journeys. South Devon people will be going to Exeter to shop, Exeter people to do business in Bristol, and so on. Many of those who use the train along its picturesque route along the Welsh borders may never get to even one of (leave alone all) the towns listed on the destination boards. And for Torquay people, a train journey even to Bristol is still quite an event.

The day comes. The big case may already have been sent off PLA, but there is still more than can be comfortably carried to the station. In some towns a porter with barrow – the old Town Porter – will oblige for a few coppers; otherwise it will be the unfamiliar use of a taxi for many people. The taxi was of course booked several days ago and checked up on again last night, but there is great anxiety among the whole family if it is fifteen seconds late. Though only mum is travelling today, the whole family climb into the taxi and buy platform tickets to see her off. The departure of an express train brings two or three times as many people to the platform than are ever going to board it.

Meanwhile all has gone smoothly behind the scenes, the booked engine men arriving promptly, the locomotive coming off shed ahead of time, and both the Plymouth and Paignton sections are running well, so that the combined train should be away just as the timetable promises. The cleaners of course did their bit last night, the smokebox emptied of ash, fires re-lit on all the locomotives concerned, seat reservations labelled . . . and a whole world of activity has been taking place to ensure the restaurant car is stocked with the dishes on the menu, fresh linen, drinks. Meat and fish are of prime quality bought by the department in the early hours of this very morning. For years the restaurant car people have been taking their pick of the best boys at a famous Plymouth school, and this train is a popular assignment even though the overnight accommodation in Liverpool is nothing to write home about.

Let us say we are joining the train at the first stop it makes as a combined affair: Teignmouth. Passengers start arriving soon after half past nine. Regulars know that the booking office will be busy since there is this important up service departing only minutes before the down train after the longest gap in the day in that direction. In between many demands for day returns to Exeter and singles to Dawlish could be the occasional request for a ticket to almost anywhere in Wales, the North of England and Scotland. It makes you realise that trains like this succeed by combining the carriage of numerous small minorities, with nothing in common at all except they sit close to each other for an hour or two. Ten minutes to go, the moment the train should be leaving Newton Abbot all hooked up together in the right order, the stationmaster asks those waiting for the down train to step out of the queue at the booking office so they can concentrate on those going up.

Several porters have pushed luggage over the crossing while passengers pay a ritual visit to the bookstall and go by the bridge. Now the stationmaster also crosses and answers questions about where to stand for which part. Those going to Birkenhead and Glasgow (if there are any; it is certainly not an everyday event from Teignmouth) are advised that their coaches will not pull up at the platform and so they will have to walk through the corridor.

Tension rises. The young enthusiast hears two bells telling that the down stopper has left Dawlish, but only moments before the up West-to-North Express is heard and seen does Teignmouth Old Quay give two bells to Teignmouth's main signalbox, train entering section. The gleaming Castle enters the station at impressive speed and shoots out beyond the platform edge, but the fireman is watching for the stationmaster's instruction to stop and instantly passes it on to the driver on the other side of the cab.

continued

and that the tunnels and viaducts were safe, it was all too easy to complain about the dirt in steam days. Maybe the sun was fading your new hat and, darn it, where had you placed the ticket. If you had children, how would they behave. Open the window quickly for that man wants to spit. Must we be exposed to such language? The list of things that could make you unhappy was endless, and some passengers literally were bundles of nerves.

Passenger comfort. The LMS was well to the fore in providing high quality accommodation for third-class passengers. This photograph shows a typical third-class compartment of the early/mid 1930s with individual armrests, four courtesy lights as well as a ceiling light and double sliding doors. The sliding window is of the earlier single shallow type which were soon superseded by the deeper double sliding windows.

Mouth watering! The interior of the LMS kitchen car showing the chef at work. These cars used oil gas for cooking. The picture shows the cramped conditions under which the crews had to produce perhaps up to 180 meals on a long journey.

There is the usual rush for corner seats. The family going to Hereford hear that the lady opposite is getting out at Exeter and arrange to take her place then. They're off . . . along the Sea Wall as the down stopper passes. They pass each other, these two very different trains, only yards different ninety-five days out of a hundred. Shortly the ticket inspector will be through, and then the chief steward asking us if we would like to take our place for morning coffee and biscuits and proffering the luncheon menu lest we might be tempted to first or second sitting. Even ensuring there are the right number of tickets on board for each of the restaurant car sittings is a detail that has to be remembered.

Getting the train out on the road with everything in its right place is a daily miracle of organisation. It of course requires paper work, some of it – like the guard's list of the vehicles, the chef's supplies – even on board, though the brunt of the writing and printing was done earlier and well out of sight of the train. Keeping the train running punctually of course still requires great teamwork. The passengers would have a fright if they could see how many slow passenger and freight trains were on the route ahead; connections have to be made; and the engine won't steam well unless she is in good condition and given quality fuel. Dozens of signalmen will be involved in the train's smooth passage, each of them of course recording her times in their logs, as will the guard along with passenger headcounts at prescribed points.

If there are any delays the operating people will want to know why; if they become regular, they will want extra minutes inserted in the schedule, while the commercial people will hope that good punctuality promises an earlier arrival at Crewe next year. No question of changing the departure time since that is cast in tradition.

There is never a day without a minor hitch. Yet again we are stopped outside Bristol Temple Meads waiting for signals and so arrive a minute late and leave two late because of slack platform work. But the footplate crew work hard on the long haul up to the junction with the trunk Paddington–South Wales route, and for once the Severn Tunnel is clear. The fireman hoses gently down to prevent dust being blown everywhere by the tunnel's draught. A broken signal wire at Abergavenny is another irritant, but the hand-over to the LMS on time at Shrewsbury. 'Pity they can't do the same for us,' mutter the GW men to themselves. They love this long run, though time passes slowly once they have shedded the Castle and next morning they fear the LMS will be late again. But then, from what they have heard of Crewe being a kind of railway hell on earth, what can you expect.

At one time our train also carried through carriages from Cardiff to Manchester, and complex indeed were the shunting movements at Crewe, especially for the Glasgow passengers who were apt to find themselves parked on a track without a platform edge for a couple of hours waiting attachment to the Mid-Day Scot from Euston. Think of the planning that went into that! Each year there would be renewed discussions between the GW and LMS as to what through coaches were desirable. In the mid-1930s you could get them via Crewe from Newquay and Carmarthen as well as more obvious starting points, and while half the Manchester services ran to London Road the rest ended on the other side of the city at Victoria.

But back to our train. Passengers heading miles away from home are contemplating the reason for their journey and wondering what will be the outcome – especially perhaps of a love affair. It has been an expensive train to provide, but once more justified itself. Though really its own business, and not so small a one at that, nobody will know exactly how much it earned in fares, and even less would it be known what revenue would have been lost had there been fewer through coaches or what might have been gained had there been more stops – at Newport for example, bypassed at this time though in the 1960s a stopping (and reversal) point. The train does have a very distinct identity of its own, yet it is judged as part of the overall service. Only the restaurant car takings are precisely known, and since it would be unthinkable to turn out so prestigious a service as this without full meal service even that is not a matter of great commercial concern (except that perhaps the chief steward's request for an extra pair of hands is justified).

They are already working on next year's timetable. As soon as it is circulated in proof, stationmasters the length of the route will see if any change has been made. In the excursion offices that are part of each district set-up, even a minute's difference in one station timing will have to be reflected in all those leaflets and advertisements that use this train for some kind of special offer. When the timetable is printed and sold first at the booking office and then on the bookstalls, the enthusiasts will check to see that things remain as they should. Should a station stop be taken out, there will bound to be letters to the Press. For many people care about individual trains like this as much as they do about their favourite charities.

Wanderers

Football excursions brought some unusual workings. For example during 1953 SR light Pacifics made occasional Saturday appearances at Watford to turn there after taking specials from their home territory to Wembley Central. On 7 February there were a couple of other unusual workings, an ER class L1 tank No 67739 and a B17 No 61664 brought specials from Walthamstow via the Tottenham & Hampstead and North London lines and Harrow & Wealdstone. On 14 February three Royal Scots, Nos 46131/44/6 felt their way over the ex-L&Y main line with excursions from London for an Arsenal cup tie with Burnley. Each paused for a banker – a WD 2-8-0 at Todmorden – for the 1 in 65 climb to Copy Pit. A couple of weeks later Rose Grove shed had no fewer than nine NER B1s as a result of an influx of Sheffield supporters. Winter Saturdays could be really fascinating; one did not need to be a football supporter to await the results of the draws for the games with some interest.

Llandudno Excursion

'Five shillings and sixpence return' said the handbills hanging in bunches threaded on bits of string outside the booking office windows. Half-day excursion to North Wales shrieked the billboards outside, and on the platforms of the stations all the way from Coventry, through the Black Country to Wolverhampton. Relief No 737 said the special traffic notice. 9.12am off Aston shed, 9.48 Vauxhall carriage sidings, 9.56 arrive New Street station, 10.03 depart for Llandudno with stops at Smethwick, Dudley Port, Wolverhampton (High Level), Rhyl, Colwyn Bay, Llandudno Junction and Llandudno.

It's a Sunday morning in the summer of 1933 and the day-shift foreman at Aston checks through the notes left by his night colleague. There's a Walsall 18in goods stopped with a collapsed brick arch and it's needed for the early Lichfield local on Monday. Some idiot has put the blower on when the fire has run down on a Webb coal tank leaving a number of stays to be tightened. And there is that blasted 'Halfex' to Llandudno which is booked for one of the shed's Prince of Wales class 4-6-0s, just out of a valve and piston exam. This needs a crew who know the road right through. He checks with his clerk and finds that the driver is a near neighbour in Alma Street and yes he has signed for Holyhead but not for the three miles from Llandudno Junction to Llandudno terminus – well they will just have to get a pilotman over that section; that's *not* going to be his worry this morning. In any case they have wired Llandudno Junction shed accordingly. What about the young fireman who is only in the goods link – has he any experience in picking up water, as they are theoretically non-stop from Wolverhampton to Rhyl? At least the driver is a good man and he'll keep him right – and they won't be all stations to Wolverhampton either as that will have been taken care of by the 8.20 to Holyhead. That's yet one more worry as this is booked for one of the shed's three elderly Experiment class 4-6-0s which are not even superheated. Ah well, it's just another ordinary Sunday!

The Prince is No 5673 *Lusitania*, one of the regular engines used on the fasts from New Street to Manchester via Stafford and Stoke, and is in fair enough condition so they roll into the station about right time with the

Progress?

Years ago, when the fastest route to Australia was by the Suez Canal, great express trains set out on far longer journeys than anything you will find in today's timetable. Paddington to Plymouth and King's Cross to Edinburgh were at different times the world's longest non-stop runs and much commented upon, but there were numerous other non-stops that have become rarities or clean disappeared: Paddington to Taunton, Newport, Kemble; Euston to Preston, Carlisle; King's Cross to York; Liverpool Street to Lowestoft.

Not only were the trains kept continuously on the move for two, three, four and even more hours, but many of them were much heavier than anything normally run by day passengerwise on BR.

The commercial men have demanded greater frequencies which means more stops. A much larger proportion of Western expresses thus call at Reading and Swindon, for example, while on the Berks & Hants the HSTs serve Newbury, Pewsey, Castle Cary and Tiverton Parkway (Junction) all totally ignored by the prestiege services of pre-Jumbo Days. The further you fly non-stop by air, the more frequently you stop by train! Great has been the loss to human kind, for nothing was more soothing than a four-hour train journey uninterrupted by people getting in and out, and nothing developed the character and responsibility of the train crews more than being totally on their own all the way from one part of the country to another. No wonder the drivers loved their jobs, disagreeable though conditions might be in some of the lodging homes. No wonder the train journey was regarded as the highlight of the holiday. No wonder that village folk watched in awe as powerful locomotive and fifteen coaches flashed by not stopping anywhere even vaguely in their locality.

A Prince indeed. Ex-LNWR Prince of Wales class 4-6-0 No 25725 at platform 3 of Birmingham's New Street station in the late 1930s. At the time Aston shed had several of this class including No 25673 Lusitania *for use on secondary expresses, reliefs and excursions.*

During most of the period covered by this book colour photography was either non existent or in its infancy, certainly not capable to recording moving trains. In addition the atmosphere of the railway is often better captured by evocative paintings hence the use on the following colour pages of reproductions from some of those excellent railway postcards so common in the days of their issue but now collectors' items and modern day artists whose expertise has brought earlier post war scenes to life dramatically.

The Locomotive Publishing Company Limited was, perhaps, the premier firm in the railway postcard business, their cards being based on photographs usually overpainted in oils and signed with the pseudonym F. Moore; their atmosphere and sense of accuracy was first class providing today's historians with an excellent record of the Great Days of Express Trains past. Those reproduced on this and the following pages illustrate such trains in the pre-grouping era just prior to World War I; the Golden Years.

The down Irish Mail, Euston to Holyhead behind one of the LNWR's then crack express locomotives, a 4–4–0 Precursor. The picture was painted over a daylight scene probably round 1909. This was one of the company's prestige express trains making connection with the overnight boat to Kingstown (now Dun Laoghaire).

The Caledonian Railway at about the same time. The train is the 2pm from Glasgow Central made up of West Coast Joint Stock as it is a London express. Engines will be changed at Carlisle. The pilot is Connor 2–4–0 No 40 and the train engine one of McIntosh's fine Dunalastair 4–4–0s. Note the CR route indicator set at 'quarter to three' for the main line to Carlisle.

The Great Northern main line, the East Coast route to Scotland about 1910 with two of H. A. Ivatt's large boilered Atlantics about to pass. That on the left is an up Scottish express, the second train a down Leeds. Note the somersault signals introduced shortly after the Abbots Ripton disaster.

A north bound express leaving St Pancras probably just prior to 1914 when the station was re-signalled but a picture which would have been similar well into grouping. The pilot is a Johnson class 1 4–2–2 No 672 and the train engine a Johnson class 2 4–4–0 rebuilt by Deeley with a class H round top boiler. Both are spotless as one would have expected from the Midland Railway at that time.

Another F. Moore card this time published by Tuck in the 'Oilette' series showing the Cornish Riviera Express behind one of G. J. Churchward's experimental Atlantics No 171 Albion. *Originally built as a two cylinder 4–6–0 No 171 ran as a 4–4–2 between 1904 and 1907. The blurb on the rear of the card states that the Cornish Riviera Express is equipped with every modern convenience including valets and ladies maids. The fourth coach is one of the new 'Dreadnought' dining cars.*

An LPC card showing one of Holden's fine Claud Hamilton 4-4-0s complete with train describing discs leaving Liverpool St station, the cast metal company coat of arms is on the leading splasher. The period is probably 1910–14 and the train the Norfolk Coast Express. On the left is a 2-4-2 tank for the suburban lines and a reboilered 2-4-0.

There were fewer cards issued of the Big Four as the older ones in their bright colours were reissued time after time in the 1920s and 1930s. Both LPC and Salmon produced a number however most of the former were still based on photographs and using the F. Moore pseudonym. The Salmon cards appeared to be paintings per se *and not, perhaps, quite so appealing to those whose aim was total accuracy.*

An LPC card showing a typical GWR roundhouse interior. Although this is certainly a pre-World War I picture apart from the Dean Single on the right it could well apply into the 1920s. The photograph on which the painting is imposed was probably taken at Old Oak Common with a Saint, a Bulldog and a Star to the fore. Note the boarded turntable and the generally spotless condition of both the shed and its occupants.

Two Tuck 'Oilette' cards of the 1920s. The first is a Continental Boat Express from Victoria to Folkestone Harbour between Bromley and Bickley. The engine is a Maunsell rebuild of one of the SE&CR E class 4–4–0s designated E1 and numbered 67. These were superheated long valve travel engines which were immensely successful lasting on some Kent Coast expresses into the 1960s. The second is a Bournemouth express with a Urie 4–6–0 No 737 prior to 'Maunsellisation' and the fitting of nameplates. It later became King Uther *of the King Arthur series. Both trains have typical stock for the period.*

An LPC card taken from a photograph by The Times *but credited also to F. Moore. It was probably issued round 1927/28 to show off the new Royal Scot class 4–6–0s then introduced for the Anglo Scottish services. The train is probably the down Royal Scot passing Leighton Buzzard judging by the formation and the number of roof boards.*

The Flying Scotsman near Hatfield. Another LPC card showing the new Gresley Pacific No 1471 Sir Frederick Banbury *with its train of teak rolling stock with white roofs built in 1924. The locomotive still carries its Great Northern number but is lettered LNER.*

One of Salmon's cards, a Great Western scene with a westbound train at Teignmouth behind No 6929 King Edward VIII *– or so the legend on the rear of the card reads. The date of the picture must be post May 1936 before which it was named* King Stephen. *The coaches are the luxurious 'Centenary Stock' introduced in 1935.*

typical tinkle, tinkle, tinkle, tinkle of the vacuum pump and pull up past the calling-on arm at the end of platform 3. The load is 12 for 352 tons, and the punters are going to be lucky as they are all LNWR corridors displaced from main-line duties by newly introduced LMS stock. No problems for the children or the old folk today. Some of the lights may not work mind, but who's going to worry too much on the way home? The crowd is five or more deep on the platform so there is much pushing and shoving, but access is generally easy as each compartment has its own door on the non-corridor side. There is a rush for the corner seats whilst the children (who have been this way before) thump the button-backed bench-type sprung seats to see how much dust flies out; there's plenty and they get a clip over the ear for their trouble.

As they settle in there is a whistle and an arm outstretched from the platform foreman. Within a couple of minutes they are away under Hill Street bridge blasting up towards the exit tunnel and the 1 in 77/100. The driver thanks his Maker there is no stop at Monument Lane and that he was wise enough to jump on that fireman when he said 'won't she want to be blowing off to take 12 out of No 3?' 165 on the clock should be quite enough to curb that tendency to slip in the tunnel. 'Leave that fire until we get away. Then rake it level as fast as you can and shut the door until we are at the top of the bank.' Little time is wasted at Smethwick and Dudley Port, where the two-coach push and pull behind a superannuated Webb 5ft 6in 2-4-2 tank has done the honours from Dudley, but it is knocking 20 minutes from New Street before the train is away. Another 11 minutes and they are at Wolverhampton High Level stopping carefully by the water column for a quick top up – and it *is* quick, the fireman is off before they actually stop, grabs the waterbag chain and immediately climbs back on to the tender tank. 4 minutes later they begin the sharp drop down to Bushbury, past the shed with its new allocation of Baby Scots to replace the compounds on the Londons and an easy road to Trent Valley Junction enabling them to hit a good 70mph through Penkridge.

The fireman has had experience on the Super D 0-8-0s so is used to the long narrow box with a good thick fire which is just as well as No 5673 tends to roll more than somewhat when running hard. They are checked by signals at Trent Valley: what else do you expect on a Sunday when there is not supposed to be much about? So the driver takes it easy up to Whitmore – about 15 miles steady climb but on a good four-track main line and not a bit like that Fred Karno's back yard between Birmingham and Wolverhampton. But after some 10 miles of steady climbing the engine doesn't seem to be liking it very much. The driver checks the fire which looks thick enough but a bit patchy so his mate is instructed to put no more on until they can see what is happening. As they pass Whitmore the feed is shut off and the scoop goes down but an inexperienced fireman is a bit late coming out and water showers over the front

North Wales express. A Llandudno–Chester–Birmingham (New Street) train on the viaduct at Old Colwyn. The locomotive is a named Prince of Wales class 4-6-0, probably in red as it carries the early LMS livery of the company crest on the cabside. The tender has LMS on its sides which means that it is black – a real hybrid not unusual for the livery changeover period of the early 1930s. The coaches are one hundred per cent LNWR.

coaches drenching those passengers looking out and washing any sparks out of their eyes to boot. Another look at the fire with the front damper closed, blue flames appear in places showing that clinker is stopping the air coming through properly. So they have some bad coal, surprising when one thinks of the engine's normal turns on expresses to Crewe, Liverpool and Manchester. The fireman opens the damper again and riddles the fire right down to the bars in the blue patches and they run at about 70 down Madeley Bank. Slow past Basford Hall with every board on until they get to it but they don't actually stop at Crewe. In theory there is no problem from there on as it is 50 miles of downhill and level to Abergele, if everything is all right, with the engine that is. But it isn't. The driver keeps her pulling pretty hard over the next 8 miles to Calveley and from there *Lusitania* runs easily to Chester, the driver using a short burst with full open regulator every now and again to lift the fire; this saves the fireman's hands. He already has a hand cloth round his left wrist, and makes light work of a nasty job. But by the time they reach the edge of Chester the pressure is down to 130 instead of 175.

They are all ready to slip through Chester and get going on the coast road but stick at the next signal for 10 minutes, keeping the fire hot with the blower hard on; at least that keeps the clinker soft. At last the signal arm comes off and they run through the station dead slow, then round the bend into the rock cutting. For the first mile or two they take it easy, the driver helping out by raking the fire again and firing little and often all round the box, carefully one in the middle of each of the four sides two at the back to right and left of the door and one on each side a quarter of the length ahead of the corner. He tells the fireman to open up and she pulls quite smartly and keeps going at a fair speed but steam pressure comes down to about 120; there is a lot of dirt in that coal and a lot of clinker on the bars.

Flint is passed without picking up water and at Prestatyn they drop the scoop again but the Rhyl distant is 'on' and they almost come to a stop once more. Four minutes in the station as half the train empties here, kiddies with wooden spades and tin buckets left over from last year's trip (no paid holidays then), with dad and mum fussing them up the steps from the platform. The crew has the blower hard on once more so the pressure rises to 140 before they have finished the station work. From here it is a few miles on the level before a mile of 1 in 100 between Llandulas and Llysfaen – something to laugh at in the normal run of events but not today. With a dirty fire and down in steam, you can't afford to laugh at anything. So they make a smart start out of Rhyl, take it easy to Abergele, opening her up to make a run for the bank; but they only just get over the top having dropped her nearly into full gear on the steep bit. Down then through Old Colwyn and along the coastal embankment past Colwyn Bay wishing that they were on the beach with the bathers or fishing off the pier; the regulator is shut and the blower full on.

By now the fireman has had a pretty rough time of it and says so, but the driver tells him there is only another 8 miles to go. He keeps his thoughts to himself for if pressure drops much below 120 they may have trouble in getting the brakes off at the Junction. A quick stop to pick up the pilotman and they make it, but it has been touch and go as the fire which has been white hot, and fluid is settling into a solid cake with the clock only registering 90. By now they are some 20 minutes down and as the passengers walk by there are a few dirty looks. They uncouple from the train which is heaved out by the station pilot. The old Prince then drops back to the Junction shed where they hand over to a disposal crew who water, turn her and put her on a line where they can clean the fire when they get round to it. In six more hours the Aston men will be on their way back. This is supposed to be a rest period and does not count in their time booked on the job.

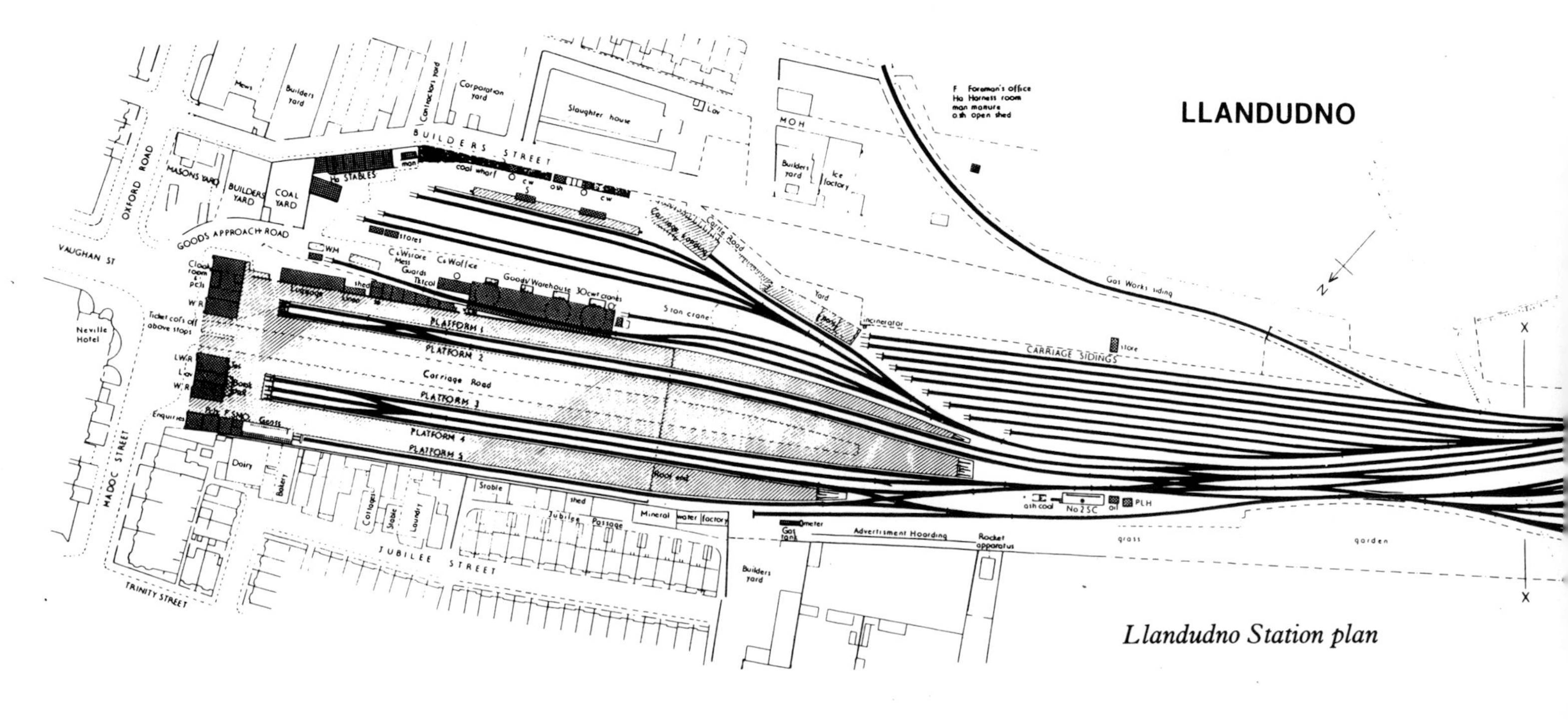

Llandudno Station plan

4
SLEEPERS AND NIGHT TRAINS

THE Aberdonian in the late 1950s pulled out of Kings Cross behind an A1 or A4 Pacific at 19.30. You could go along to the restaurant car for an aperitif and leisurely dinner as the summer evening light began to fade. The Scots steward, if he saw that you were hesitant about the choice of main course on the menu, would somewhat confidentially mention that 'we *also* have home-made steak and kidney pie', which those with a taste for it were strongly advised to accept. It was made in a very large dish, succulent Aberdeen Angus beef and kidney topped with a mouth-watering pastry. It was a splendid foundation for a nightcap before retiring to your sleeper, a Gresley or Thompson vehicle with beds carefully made up (not the easiest of tasks) by one of a small group of bedmakers at Hornsey depot.

Whisked unconsciously through the night, you might just be aware

Western Mail. A night scene at Paddington in the late 1930s showing the 10.10pm (22.10) Penzance postal, made up entirely of mail vans, behind Castle class No 5059 Earl St Aldwyn. *This was the principal GWR down mail train for the West of England.*

of the Dundee stop about five o'clock when a few early risers left the train. By the time the attendant knocked discreetly on your door with coffee and biscuits after leaving Montrose, you could wash and shave to an unfolding panorama of broad strath and mountain. From Stonehaven it was all spectacular granite cliffs pounded by a steely grey sea until the final curving sweep into Aberdeen just before seven. The sharp salty breeze off the North Sea, overlaid with the aroma from the fish market where sales were just starting, stimulated the nostrils. Alternatively, if you had made your sleeper reservations correctly in the rear two cars, you could wake to the sight of Dumbarton Rock bathed in sunlight and the small boats bobbing in the Gareloch, take breakfast in the buffet car as your plucky K1 pounded up Glen Falloch and round the Horseshoe Curve, and settle back to take in the views of moor, loch and mountain before reaching Fort William in mid morning.

The sleeping car had been slow to become established in Britain. The first examples could better be described as dormitory cars, with separate sections for ladies and gentlemen, of course, but did not prove popular; the late Hamilton Ellis likened them to 'sleeping in close-packed rows like recumbent cod on a fishmonger's slab', which was only a modest exaggeration. The Midland Railway's dalliance with the Transatlantic Pullman car in the 1870s, with passengers sleeping in upper and lower berths arranged longitudinally either side of a central aisle behind the 'privacy' of full length curtains, also cut very little ice with its users.

The forerunners of the modern sleeping car appeared on several railways in the 1880s featuring two-berth compartments with side

Two Favourites

The good traveller has his favourite trains. They are rarely the fastest available. There is, for instance, really no doubt which is the best train from Manchester to London. It is the one which leaves Manchester Central at 7.20am and arrives in St Pancras at 11.27. The connoisseur prefers it in the winter. He gets up in the chilly dark, unwarmed by morning tea, and drives to the station. The platforms are filled by early suburban trains arriving and de-

continued opposite

Overnight from Kings Cross. Sir Nigel Gresley's A3 class Pacific No 60046 Diamond Jubilee *waits for the right away at the head of an Edinburgh-bound express towards the end of the 1950s. In a few minutes the heavy sleeping cars will swing out past the colour lights and, gathering speed northwards through the night, into the dawn of a Saturday morning in Scotland.*

corridor access to lavatories. They were for first-class passengers only; lesser mortals endured more upright night travel. By the turn of the century single-berth cars were in use and have remained the standard ever since, except during World War II when, to meet demand on an unprecedented scale, they were fitted with upper berths also. The modern Mark 3 sleeper may have air conditioning, give a smoother ride and incorporate special fire precautions and modern decor, but the practice is still based on those pioneering cars of ninety years ago. It has survived despite ingenious attempts to get more berths into each coach, of which the LNER concept in 1947 of interlocking compartments with alternate upper and lower berths was but one. The third-class traveller was lulled to sleep much later however. The Midland ran a composite sleeper on its through service to Inverness introduced in 1901, but it was only composite in that, besides its first-class berths it had two conventional third-class compartments of extra width for sleeping. The hire of a pillow and blanket, at 6d (2½p) each, later a shilling, from a trolley on the platform was considered adequate provision for the lower orders at this period. Not until 1928 were third-class sleeping cars introduced on Anglo-Scottish services. They were, in modern parlance, *couchettes* with four-berth compartments providing pillow and rug only. The LMS built massive twelve-wheeled composite sleepers at this time with six first-class single-berth compartments in the centre, flanked by two four-berth compartments at each end (where the ride over the bogies was both rougher and noisier) for third class. The modern two-berth compartment third-class sleeper had to wait for its introduction until after World War II, inspired by the wartime modification of first-class cars.

The overnight sleeping-car trains have always been a mixed lot. The three Anglo-Scottish routes – we must not forget the Settle & Carlisle line in its heyday, linked to both the Sou'West and Waverley routes in Scotland – were always naturals on a late-night-to-breakfast-time schedule, though shorter hauls as from Liverpool, Manchester or Leeds have always been of more limited appeal and dubious economics. Similarly, the long route from London to Devon and particularly Cornwall could be attractive. But there have long been oddities; the night Irish Mail leaving Euston at around 20.45 and conveying sleeping cars since the 1880s offered the dubious pleasure of being decanted from your berth on arrival at Holyhead soon after two o'clock to face a raw wind off the Irish Sea as you transferred to the mailboat for an 03.15 departure. And in its last years, before withdrawal in 1969, the Edinburgh Waverley sleeper(s) to St Pancras were advertised as not taking throughout bookings, ostensibly so that such passengers should not crowd off those for the Midlands cities. The all-sleeper train is a post-war phenomenon, a product of brisk demand on the routes between London and Glasgow, Edinburgh, Aberdeen and Inverness, though as this book goes to press BR have announced that from 1990 only one all-sleeper Anglo-Scottish train will survive.

Quite the most exotic sleeping-car train to operate in Britain was inaugurated in 1936, ceased during the war, was reinstated in 1947 and

parting. But one is leisurely and quiet, and at it the lordlier London train waits. He enters the breakfast car, and there his morning tea awaits him. Then, as he eats his breakfast – much the best meal in a train – he can watch the sun rise over the Derbyshire hills, and, if he has wisely chosen a seat on the right, all the Peak District is specially lit up for him, little by little, until, in the neighbourhood of Matlock, daylight has at last driven the last remnants of darkness away. The 7.20 is a happy train at all times; but in winter it has no peers.

Another good train for those who like to travel with sensuousness is the 12.59am mail train from Cambridge, due at Liverpool Street at a quarter to three in the morning. This, emphatically, is a summer train, and at its best about the end of June. Then mountains of baskets await it at every station, filled with strawberries, fruit, and cut flowers for Covent Garden. The train is mostly made up of guards' vans, and all of them are crammed with all the produce of the soil of East Anglia, so that this train has a very distinctive earthy scent, which is all its own. – Roger B. Lloyd.

Overleaf: *South West-North East Mail. The time is approaching 7.20pm (19.20) at platform 12 when Jubilee class No 45626* Seychelles *of Derby shed (17A) will move out of Bristol's Temple Meads station into the rain and head north with the fast Royal Mail express for Newcastle. The date appears to be around the mid 1950s. On the right is an Avonmouth or Severn Beach local.*

45626

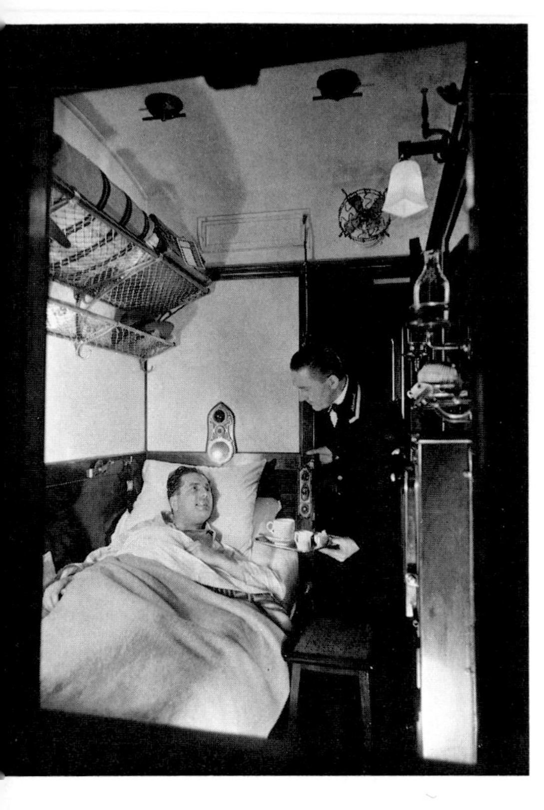

Good morning, sir. A first-class passenger in one of the late 1930s sleepers is called by a smart stiff-collared attendant with a cup of tea and biscuits. Note the LNWR-type steam-heating control lever on the wall to the left of the pillow, the male 'uniform' of the period – a trilby hat on the rack and the LMS publicity people making their point with the label on the suitcase – LMS Hotels.

Opposite: Sleepers for all. In 1928 three of the four railway companies introduced third-class four-berth sleeping cars, for which an Act of Parliament was necessary. This LMS period III vehicle shows the rather Spartan accommodation with blanket and pillow for each berth.

lasted until 1980 when it was withdrawn. It was, of course, the Night Ferry between London (Victoria) and Paris (Gare du Nord). The dark blue Wagons-Lits sleeping cars, with their French attendants, brought the Continent into the heart of London, courtesy of the Dover–Dunkerque train ferry ships. The passenger from London cleared Customs and immigration checks before boarding, and the French controls were carried out on the train invariably without the passenger being conscious of them; passports were handed to the attendants who cleared them with the French authorities before returning them next morning. The all-steel sleeping cars were very comfortable, though the shackling down on the ferry's train deck could often wake the light sleeper. In 1957 the train was augmented by one or two cars for Brussels, and at its peak in the early 1960s was the heaviest passenger train in Britain, running to nineteen vehicles of well over 800 tons. Alas, airline competition and the unwillingness of the Wagons-Lit Company to replace the life-expired cars killed it off.

Not all trains than ran at night were of this calibre, of course. Two at the other end of the scale come vividly to mind. The first was a wartime utility model, which set off from York at the back of ten o'clock and wandered on to the Great Central line at Doncaster with several passenger coaches and a retinue of vans. After a night out among the fleshpots of Nottingham, this dowdy, unhurried express would uplift you from the echoing Victoria station at a nominal 01.15 and, calling at Loughborough, Leicester and Rugby, make its pedestrian way to Banbury and disappear into the maw of the Great Western. Its timekeeping under wartime conditions was abysmal – an hour late was nothing exceptional, three hours not unknown – and, devoid of any facilities for satisfying the inner man, the journey had to be accepted stoically with as much sleep as the available space allowed. Then there was an express from Perth to Glasgow Central in the early 1950s, leaving at 22.15 and getting by a circuitous route to its journey's end a little after the witching hour. 'Limited passenger accommodation,' said the timetable. How right they were; it consisted of a Stanier corridor brake composite, all three third-class and two first-class compartments of it, trailed by twenty or more fish vans from Aberdeen and the Buchan for Clydeside and the Ayrshire coast. It was in effect the proverbial Scottish mixed train running with express headlights.

There was always a market for overnight long-distance travel without the luxury of a sleeping berth and the supplementary charge it incurred – particularly amongst the young. It is perhaps worthy of note that of the trains involved in the 1895 Race to Aberdeen by the West and East Coast partners, the West Coast train, the 20.00 Tourist express from Euston, conveyed no sleeping cars; at the speeds which were achieved in the later stages of the Race little sleep would anyway have been possible. But in general it was catered for by conventional trains at standard fares.

By the 1950s, with competition arising from the private car, the overnight coach and the growing menace of air travel, new thinking was necessary. It took two forms. April 1953 saw new services introduced between London and Glasgow/Edinburgh, marketed as 'Starlight Specials' at a fare of £3 10s return, which was little more than the current coach fare. The Glasgow service ran from St Pancras via Leeds and the Sou'West route to St Enoch, while the Edinburgh train left from Marylebone, running via Sheffield and York. There were all-night buffet cars (some were extensive conversions of older coaches) which served breakfast for 3s 6d (17½p)! The service initially prospered, but became less attractive with the years and ceased in 1963. Two years later came the first car sleeper service, between Kings Cross and Perth, the cars being conveyed in vans. The charge for car and driver was £15 return, with special low rates for additional passengers. The idea caught on to some extent with other routes opening up, and was extended to some day services. But hard economics caught up with the concept and after flowering it has withered to a few of the longer hauls on which passengers and cars are mainly conveyed on regular trains.

Trains conveying passengers, with or without cars, sleeping or sitting, were of course not the only ones during the hours of darkness carrying express headlamps. Newspapers and mail trains competed for paths on the trunk routes with passengers and express freight, and both required express transits. Few things are more perishable than the morning newspaper.

Until the end of the 1970s, virtually all except local mail found its way on to a train at some stage in its journey, and the railways in conjunction with the Post Office provided for the conveyance of mailbags on passenger trains. In some cases this provision was quite extensive; the Irish Mail from Euston, for instance, took a full stowage van and two Post Office sorting vans. Indeed, a whole network of dedicated mail trains and feeder services was established to handle the principal flows. Quite unknown to many regular travellers, their operation and punctuality were matters of prime importance to railwaymen: a delay to the Great Western Travelling Post Office mattered even more than one to the *Cornish Riviera Limited.*

The most important of the mail trains were the Down and Up Special Travelling Post Offices (to give them their full title) or TPOs for short, between Euston and Glasgow/Aberdeen, better known as the West Coast Postals. These were most impressive trains, immortalised in W. H. Auden's poetic commentary for the 1936 film 'Night Mail'.

> This is the night mail crossing the border
> Bringing the cheque and the postal order,
> Letters for the rich, letters for the poor,
> The shop at the corner and the girl next door.
> Pulling up Beattock, a steady climb –
> The gradient's against her, but she's on time . . .

The down train, at 20.30 from Euston, left as a fourteen-coach formation behind a Royal Scot, Jubilee or occasionally a Pacific; it stopped at Rugby, Tamworth, Crewe, Preston, Carlisle and Carstairs where it divided into Glasgow, Edinburgh and Aberdeen sections of two, six and

Value For Money

Complaints about BR's prices in their diners are far from new. Take 1950, for example. There was an outcry over the increase from three shillings and sixpence (17½p) to four shillings (20p) for a full breakfast, lunch and dinner going up from four shillings (20p) to five shillings (25p). Full afternoon tea was unchanged at one shilling and sixpence (7½p) but for a shilling (5p) you could now get a 'simpler service' – tea, bread and butter or toasted teacake, sandwich, cakes or biscuits! As a sop, a plain breakfast was introduced at two shillings and sixpence (12½p). Mind you, it was then still possible to get a Friday night excursion from Glasgow Central to Euston and back the next night for five pounds three shillings and sixpence (£5.17½). For this the excursioners got their return rail journey, breakfast, lunch and high tea in London, a sightseeing tour by coach and a seat either at the Hippodrome or Casino theatre.

Letter sorting on the move. The down special TPO, leaving Euston at 20.30 for Glasgow and Aberdeen, was the *overnight postal train with a normal formation of fourteen vehicles of which five were sorting vans. In these vans, sorters worked to a vast rack of destination pigeon holes (right) the sorted mail being transferred to sacks hanging on the wall behind (left). Note the high level of illumination in this 1960s picture. Many of the sorting vans and some stowage vans, were fitted with nets for picking up and traductor arms for setting down mail 'on the run'. This practice ceased in October 1971.*

four vehicles respectively. With the exception of Carstairs the stops were the opportunity for heavy pickups or setting down of sorted mail to and from feeder trains, and in some cases to drop or attach whole vans.

There were two 'Irish Mails', the 'Day Mail' and 'Night Mail', both of which carried passengers including a restaurant car and on the 'Night Mail' sleeping cars. One of the more interesting cross-country journeys was that made by the mail train which left Newcastle on Tyne for the south including sorting vans painted in LMS colours but bearing the mysterious legend M&NEJPS, a service established back in pre-grouping days by the Post Office in agreement with the Midland and North Eastern Railways to run through to Bristol. Another unusual route was from Lincoln and Derby to the High Level station at Tamworth where bags were dropped down a chute to be bundled up for collection by the West Coast Postal. This train was regularly worked by a 2-6-4 tank engine. The Tamworth mail was not much of a train but to Lincoln it was second only in importance to the LNER's boat express. The single Post Office van stood on the middle road at Lincoln Midland, later St Marks, until it departed every evening. The 'Eight O'clock

Mail' was known to everyone locally and was an institution, perhaps because it had been running so long and was just that much out of the ordinary. Newcastle also connected to Ireland by a postal van which ran over the direct route to Carlisle and then through southern Scotland to Stranraer where a company ship took them on to Belfast.

The Post Office sorting vehicles, going back to the first conversion from a horsebox on the Grand Junction Railway in 1838, have always been specialised hives of industry. Many traditional features (including the 'late box' accepting letters posted on the platform sometimes hours after they would have missed the mail placed in a pillar box) are retained on the modern fleets – but not the retractable nets for 'catching' mail pouches at speed or the traductor arms for delivering pouches to the lineside nets. On the West Coast Postals, transfers were once effected at upwards of two dozen locations. Earlier generations of vehicles were unique in having off-centre end gangways for ease of access between them by sorters carrying sacks and to avoid disturbing the busy sorters, also to the stowage vans to prevent unauthorised access when worked in passenger trains. However the events of 8 August 1963 proved that this precaution was not infallible; £2½ million was lifted in the Great Train Robbery from the up West Coast Postal south of Leighton Buzzard by the simple expedient of exhibiting a false red signal aspect.

Picture the scene just south of Carnforth at half past one on a clear night that brings a chill wind off Morecambe Bay. The two postmen, their van parked alongside the A6, are huddled in their lineside hut, a leather pouch containing mail from the Furness area for the north already hanging on the 'gallows' but not yet turned into its pickup position. They can see the signal lights of Carnforth No 1; a down freight rumbles past, slowing for the No 1 Goods Loop, and they watch the flickering tail lamp swing left under the bridge and disappear. Now the main-line signal clears to green and the phone rings for the bobby to tell them that *their* train will be the next along. They hurry out and turn the arm to swing out the pouch for delivery, then extend the catching net, a heavy rope affair on steel frame. In the distance they can hear the hurried beat of a big engine working hard, and two pulsating headlights appear; further back on the train an aura of white light from lamps mounted at solebar level confirm that this is indeed the Postal. The engine goes by in a welter of steam and sound, water still sloshing from the back of the tender after overfilling on Hest Bank troughs, and is followed by the regular clickety-click of the coach wheels. Silhouetted in the light they can see a pouch hanging from the sixth vehicle. Then – Wham! Thud! as it lands like a live thing in the catching net and their own pouch is torn off the arm at 65mph; by Carlisle its contents will have been sorted and rebagged. They replace the apparatus to its standby position and return to the van with their new prize.

The last ground/train interchange 'on the run' was made in 1971. The division of mail into first and second class has made the use of air travel attractive for some first-class long-distance mail. Yet while the TPOs have long disappeared in North America, their number here was considerably increased in a 1988 reorganisation. For example, a new service

Night Scene

It is a winter's night soon after World War II and the boat train from Manchester to Heysham has made its booked stop at Lancaster's Castle station. The little platform work is completed but, as no attempt has been made to start, a passenger opens the off-side window and looks out. There are four tracks with platforms only at the outer ones. At the north end, the through line starter on the signal gantry shows green. The sky is clear and frost sparkles under a full moon. The silence is emphasised rather than broken by the few faint sounds of escaping steam from the waiting 5X and an occasional clink of metal as the fire is cleaned and made up, an orange glow reflects back from the open firebox door.

This peace is ended by the sound of an approaching train and amidst a cloud of steam a rebuilt Scot bursts from under the south end bridge and roars past at high speed. A long line of lighted windows flash past and then in *decrescendo* the sound and fury passes northwards. Peace comes again and shortly the slow six beats to the revolution of the 5X disturbs it once more. An everyday scene with nothing remarkable about it yet there is an indelible impression left on the mind of the observer.

was introduced between Dover and Manchester via Reading and Birmingham, thus linking South-East England with the north without the hassle of handling in London. The West Coast Postals run via Birmingham also, making interchange between trains easier, and the Aberdeen section is a thing of the past. But always the emphasis on sharp station work, punctuality and reliability remains. Derby instead of Crewe is the Midland hub and here and at Bristol Temple Meads where various TPOs connect there is great activity starting before midnight.

If mail trains have adapted to changing demand, the other long-established night traffic, newspapers, has sadly disappeared from the railway scene. The dedicated trains for national newspaper distribution have fallen victim to the dispersal of printing from the traditional Fleet Street and Manchester bases to new plants in green field areas (that is if Wapping can ever be so described!).

The great newspaper trains are no more. Few were more dramatic than the 02.32 from Marylebone, getting the London editions to the East Midlands towns and cities. After the seeming chaos of the loading, with newspapers' vans milling about on the centre carriage roadway at Marylebone came the extremely hard locomotive work involved in running this heavy and tightly timed train down the Great Central main line. Before the war it was Sandringham 4-6-0s that took the strain; they gave way to Gresley Pacifics. The train would roll into Rugby a few minutes after four, invariably needing to draw up twice, and be away with the usual Great Central verve in ten minutes for its next stop at Leicester. The engine would be blowing off as if impatient to be on its way, and many were the complaints from local residents of the nightly disturbance to their slumbers. Other trains, some with limited passenger accommodation or even sleeping cars, radiated from London in the small hours to get the morning papers to the Midlands and the far corners of Southern England and Wales.

Serving the north, Manchester saw at least four dedicated services to transport its own editions. The first left Exchange station at 23.20, loading on the long through platform from Victoria and with a Patricroft Jubilee at its head, bound for Glasgow. It was always a difficult train to get away to time, its early departure time constantly at odds with news deadlines and printing delays. The next two, 00.12 and 00.20 from Victoria, left for Leeds and Newcastle behind a Newton Heath Jubilee or Class Five. Perhaps the most modest of the entire genre was a diminutive train from London Road (now Piccadilly), often no more than a couple of vans, which was wont to arrive at Crewe about three o'clock for further distribution; in the fifties it was often a job for Crewe North's Class 2P 4-4-0 station pilot, and seldom did the engine get a greater chance to get some speed out of its elderly limbs. Now it is all a memory, and the name of TNT reigns on the motorways.

For passengers, thin in numbers, with life at a low ebb and ever reluctant to be away from their own beds, night travel is at best an adventure but can become an occasion for annoyance and discomfort. But for the railway it can be a time of intense effort. O. S. Nock noted, during a night spent in Carlisle signalling centre in 1977, no less than

Car Sleepers

The first car sleeper ran from Holloway to Perth. The working was complex, unique. At the start cars were conveyed in double-deck vans with a power lift at the centre, two cars being conveyed between the van bogies and four on the higher level. This was a clever design, but caused many problems.

Only low cars could go down the lifts, so a booklet was produced of every imaginable model showing those excluded. On arrival cars were parked in groups of six, four for the top deck and two for below. A close watch had to be kept if drivers were late and other cars switched to their vans. The loaders could all too easily find, just before the train was due away, that they had one small space and one large car left.

If a lift failed, there was an emergency pump. But this sometimes did not work either. Top Shed came to the rescue with a very old jack with an extremely low foot which could just be inserted under the roof of the bottom deck (floor of the top deck) so that the two cars could be jacked out. It was finally decided to convert to GUVs, conventional covered bogie vans.

Loading was performed by railway motor drivers, normally employed on collections and deliveries. One night one of them put a groove down the roof of a Rolls-Royce hired by a Canadian.

The passenger list in those early days contained many VIPs. It was the start of something big. Continental railways did not think the idea was worth adoption until they saw the success BR made of it. Then they exploited their much greater distances.

twenty-one northbound trains coming into the panel area just north of Carnforth between 23.13 and 02.57, of which ten carried express headlamps. Eight were passenger expresses, there was the Down Postal, the Manchester–Glasgow newspapers, six Freightliners and five parcels or express freight trains. The dark hours may be the natural time to stretch out but they conceal parts of the railway working at full stretch.

A special comradeship often developed between staff working at night, the postmen working on the TPOs clearly enjoying the challenge of interpreting incorrect addresses and always remembering special occasions like one of their lot retiring. Up and down the land for well over a century clusters of postmen have gathered on wind-swept platforms, exchanging gossip before spreading out, each exactly in position for the door of the right mail coach to be opened by the very same travelling postman often decades in a row. Two minutes to load and unload and continue the conversation perhaps started three weeks ago; the men share thoughts they would be shy to let on to their wives, and then – to the second – the doors slide close, the guard gives his green light, and away the train goes.

Letter collection. Three heavy leather pouches, each containing up to 30lb of mail, are about to be transferred from the lineside apparatus at Harrow & Wealdstone (note the DC electric lines on the right) into the net on the Down Special TPO passing at 55mph. The net was extended just before reaching the apparatus and retracted immediately after. This transfer point, being only eleven miles from London, no provision was necessary for setting down pouches; the traductor arm on which such pouches hang can be seen folded back against the van side. The photograph was taken in 1947 when double summer time was still in force.

Enginemen often enjoy night hours to the full. Of course, who would not prefer to be in bed, but this is real men's work, socially useful if any were, and noting the trains pass in the opposite direction usually with clockwork precision brings its own joy. The weather of course affects the mood far more by night than by day. Many a driver has said that his most memorable journeys were on crisp moonlight nights and in the very early hours of summer mornings when foxes and other wildlife but little human activity abound.

A very special type of person has always been attracted to work on the sleeping cars. Whatever changes are made to the rest of the crew en route, the sleeping-car attendants both welcome their passengers and help them out with their bags having served early morning tea or coffee. It is lonely work and means spending many days resting up in a second home, but at least there is a feeling of belonging, being needed, and good wages because of the long hours. And ever interesting passengers, and a chance to get close to them. A case of alleged rape of a third-class passenger in a first-class sleeper not only hit the West Country headlines but showed how peculiar were the lives of these travelling hotel porters cum room-service attendants.

Two fifty-six from Fort William. During BR days locomotives began to appear on what prior to 1948 would have been 'foreign' lines. An LMS class 5 4-6-0 No 44974 doubleheads (with class K2 2-6-0 No 61788 Loch Rannoch*) the 13.00 Mallaig–Glasgow Queen St over the former LNER West Highland line in 1959. It is shown here at Tyndrum summit. This service also conveyed the Fort William–Kings Cross sleeping cars.*

Claughton in the rival camp. The ex-LNWR 4-6-0s may not have shone during the 1923 Leeds–Carlisle comparative trials, but with new Royal Scots taking over the principal West Coast trains twenty-five Claughtons were transferred to Midland Division sheds at Kentish Town, Leeds and Carlisle. For clearance purposes it was necessary to cut down the cab roofs, and many, including No 6025, were fitted with Great Central-type tenders taken from ex-ROD 2-8-0s bought after World War I. Here unnamed Claughton No 6025, a Kentish Town engine in gleaming crimson lake, awaits departure from St Pancras with an evening express in 1929.

The Search for Improvement: Tests and Trials

The directors of the Liverpool & Manchester Railway had a simple task in 1829. They wanted locomotives not exceeding six tons in weight and capable of hauling twenty tons at ten miles per hour, and were prepared to put up prize money for a contest. The Rainhill trials that year tested the three engines offered by private manufacturers and found *Rocket* the clear winner. But over the years, as conditions became more demanding, coal more costly and a preponderance of locomotives were built in railways' own shops, more widespread testing (including some interchange of locomotives between railways) became common. In the event, not much of this activity achieved worthwhile results.

There were, however, two notable exceptions. For some time in 1909 the London & North Western and the London, Brighton & South Coast railways pooled the working of the *Sunny South Express* between Brighton and Rugby. On alternate days the train was worked by a highly competent LNWR 4-4-0 Precursor (using saturated steam) and an LBSCR 13 4-4-2 tank (recently built with a superheater boiler). The tank engine showed such a marked economy in coal consumption over the saturated engine that even the lordly LNWR sat up and took notice; thenceforward superheating became the accepted standard for all except engines on shunting and other intermittent work.

The other important comparative trial took place some sixteen years later. It arose from the adjacent display at the 1924 British Empire Exhibition at Wembley of two recent locomotives, the Great Western Railway's 4-6-0 No 4073 *Caerphilly Castle* and the London & North Eastern Railway's Gresley Pacific No 4472 *Flying Scotsman* – and the GWR claim that their Castle was the most powerful express passenger locomotive in Britain. In terms of tractive effort this was irrefutable, but in boiler

Teaching them how. A large and interested crowd on the platform end at Kings Cross awaits the departure of No 4079 Pendennis Castle *for Leeds in April 1925 during the LNER/GWR exchange, while driver Young from Old Oak Common climbs aboard after a last look round his engine.* Pendennis Castle *impressed observers by its energetic and sure-footed starts from stations, it also beat the LNER engine hollow on its own home gound.*

Foreigner on the Great Western. During the 1925 LNER/GWR locomotive exchange, an apple-green Gresley Pacific No 4474 Victor Wild *passes Sonning signalbox near Reading at close on 70mph while working one of the Great Western's prestige trains, the 1.30pm from Paddington to Plymouth. This picture taken on 22 April 1925 on one of the familiarisation runs in the week before the tests proper. A difficult task for Kings Cross driver Pibworth over this very complex route.*

power the Gresley engine was undoubtedly superior. The issue was put to the test in April/May 1925 with No 4474 *Victor Wild* working between Paddington and Plymouth and No 4079 *Pendennis Castle* between Kings Cross and Leeds. Suffice it to say that the GWR engine handled the trains easily and with greater economy. The LNER authorities were quick to learn the virtues of long travel, long lap valve gear and applied it to all new construction and to a number of rebuilds.

Not all trials were so realistically interpreted. On the formation of the LMS in 1923, comparative trials were arranged over the difficult Leeds–Carlisle line using Midland Compounds and 990 class simple 4-4-0s, LNWR Claughton and Prince of Wales 4-6-0s, and a Caledonian Railway Pickersgill 4-4-0. It was a classic 'rigged' operation; one Compound out of the five which were tried was head and shoulders in economy over the others, which were no better than the Prince of Wales, while the Claughton was a dud but no other member of the class was offered a chance. Having 'proved' what the motive power authorities wanted, the Compound was approved for large-scale production, a decision which set back locomotive development on the LMS for some years. In further trials in 1925 using the also difficult Preston–Carlisle route, two new types entered the fray, the L&YR Dreadnought 4-6-0 and the rather effete Caledonian 60 class 4-6-0. In this case the Compound did prove eleven per cent more economical on coal than the Claughton.

Nigel Gresley, chief mechanical engineer of the LNER, clearly foresaw the need for more scientific testing of locomotives, away from the random disturbing influences of on-line travel, and in this he was soon supported by William Stanier, his opposite number on the LMSR. As a start Gresley despatched his new Class P2 2-8-2 *Cock o' the North* to the French stationary test plant at Vitry-sur-Seine in 1934 for comprehensive testing under controlled conditions. World War II intervened before the resultant joint LNER/LMSR Rugby Testing Station could be opened in 1948. Meantime, in 1935 the GWR's obsolete test plant in Swindon works was also modernised and uprated. Under BR control these two plants tested a wide range of steam locomotives (and one gas turbine locomotive), establishing performance characteristics subsequently confirmed by controlled testing at constant steam rates out on the line. These could be used both for design improvement and for timetabling purposes. Much valuable work was

Watching Princess Elizabeth *at work. During the high-speed tests from Euston to Glasgow and back in November 1936, when No 6201 covered the 401¼ miles southbound in 344.1 minutes, at an average speed of 70mph, the crew of the LMS No 1 dynamometer car study the engine's performance data unrolling before them on the Amsler recording table. These tests were the precursor to the introduction of the streamlined Coronation Scot service in July 1937.*

A King in the east. During the spring of 1948 a series of locomotive exchanges was arranged to evaluate current locomotive design prior to building BR standard locomotives. Most classes were able to run over lines of the other three railways but due to clearance problems the GWR Kings were restricted to their own lines and between Kings Cross and Leeds. Here No 6018 King Henry VI *leaves Gas Works Tunnel with the 07.50 ex-Leeds Central on 11 May 1948.*

also done on the design of the blastpipe/chimney combination to bring out the full steaming capabilities of boilers; this was particularly valuable during the 1950s as the availability of good quality locomotive coal declined.

Until these stationary plants came to full fruition, most testing was done on service trains, using a dynamometer car to produce a continuous record of distance, speed, drawbar pull and horsepower, and coal and water consumption. The results were variable, though lessons could be learned if interpretation was skilled and honest. Between 1933 and the outbreak of war the lead was taken by the LMS, whose two dynamometer cars were in almost continuous use, firstly to identify and overcome design weaknesses in the new Stanier locomotives, and then to demonstrate how their abilities could be exploited in the acceleration of express passenger and freight services. Typical of this work were the trials of Jubilee 4-6-0 No 5660 *Rooke* on the Bristol–Leeds–Glasgow route in 1937 and the heavy haulage tests of 4-6-2 No 6234 *Duchess of Abercorn* with a 600 ton train between Crewe and Glasgow fourteen months later, when maxima of 2,511 horsepower at the drawbar and 3,348 indicated horsepower in the cylinders were recorded.

Another facet of this testing in the 1930s was to establish the feasibility of high-speed services – not just in being able to reach and sustain such speeds, but perhaps more important being able to stop from them within the existing signalling system. The LNER progressively pushed the maximum speed of its Pacifics from

Going nowhere fast. Merchant Navy Pacific No 35022 Holland–America Line *was tested on the rollers at Rugby Testing Station between March and October 1952. While comparatively uneconomical due to erratic cylinder performance it did sustain an extremely high boiler output which required the ministrations of* two *firemen but which could not be taken to its limit because of fear of slipping. The test fittings alongside the chimney were part of the cylinder indicating equipment while smokebox vacuum at several positions was measured through the small-bore piping installed below the cab.*

100mph with No 4472 *Flying Scotsman* in 1934 to 126mph with No 4468 *Mallard* in 1938, the all-time record with steam. On the other side of England a trial in 1936 preparatory to the introduction of a new high-speed *Coronation Scot* service between Euston and Glasgow saw No 6201 *Princess Elizabeth* setting new standards of sustained speed and hill climbing. The Press run before introduction of the new train in 1937 produced a then speed record of 114mph with No 6220 *Coronation*.

These exceptional speeds were of course largely publicity stunts, and with the onset of World War II were soon only memories. Peace in 1945 brought a desultory resumption of on-line testing, the most notable and visually interesting being the Interchange Trials of 1948 involving engines from all four pre-nationalisation companies. A4s and a Duchess appeared in Plymouth, a King in Leeds, Bulleid Pacifics in Carlisle and Inverness. Ostensibly it was to provide information on which the design of new BR standard locomotives would be based, though the running conditions were decidedly slack. In practice the BR range was already on the drawing board before the results were announced.

Swindon Road Test. Following the post-war fitting of self-cleaning smokeboxes to Gresley's class V2 2-6-2s, the steaming deteriorated badly, maximum continuous steam production with grade 2 coal falling from 24,000 to 14,000 pounds per hour. No 60845 was therefore tested on the Swindon stationary plant, where blastpipe and chimney alterations increased output to over 30,000lb/hr. She is seen here passing Hullavington on one of the subsequent road proving tests between Stoke Gifford and Didcot in March 1953 with shelter on the front platform to protect the men taking cylinder indicator cards and linked to the ex-GWR dynamometer car. During these tests No 60845 worked a maximum train of 25 coaches, 762 tons.

Thereafter, locomotive testing went all scientific.

Lickey licked? The two miles of 1 in 37.7 from Bromsgrove to Blackwell demanded banking assistance for everything except passenger trains of under 90 tons. In March 1955 unassisted tests were made with a Jubilee No 45554 Ontario, *hauling eight coaches; stopped near the foot of the bank it was unable to restart. Class 5 No 44776 seen here with seven coaches soon after the Bromsgrove start managed with a mighty effort to reach the top. But it tore the fire about making things all too chancy; the banking rule was left unchanged.*

There were memorable performances in confirmatory road testing: one thinks of the little Ivatt class 2 2-6-0 No 46413 with a *fifteen*-coach train on her tail, working up to and sustaining 40mph up the eleven miles of 1 in 300 from Stoke Gifford (now Bristol Parkway) to Badminton, and at the other end of the scale Duchess 4-6-2 No 46225 *Duchess of Gloucester* pounding up the 1 in 100 from Appleby to Ais Gill with a 442 ton train (including the Mobile Test Units working against the engine to give *an equivalent load of 900 tons*) at a steady 30mph. What a magnificent sight – and sound – both must have been.

Such things are now in the past. The haulage characteristics of the diesel and electric locomotives which have supplanted them can be calculated in the drawing office before ever they reach the shop floor. In the process the romance of the struggle against the forces of nature has gone.

5
SAUNTERING AT LONDON TERMINI

ON a September evening in 1935, a small crowd gathers at the 'country' end of No 6 platform, Kings Cross. By no means all are railway enthusiasts. This crowd is a cross section of businessmen and others who have delayed their journey home to enjoy a new London spectacle. Under the station roof the still unfamiliar front end of a Gresley steamlined Pacific shows where the *Silver Jubilee* is waiting for departure. Compared with the smokebox door of an A1 or A3, the unadorned cowl which hides the smokebox of the A4 has an austere, even haughty look. On the platform the passengers are going to their reserved seats, guided by smartly uniformed attendants. Doors slam as the clock approaches half past five. Then there is a short blast on the whistle to acknowledge the guard's signal from the rear and the *Silver Jubilee* swings into its stride for the four-hour journey to Newcastle, surprising the onlookers at the platform end by the speed of its departure. For some the most memorable feature will be the soaring white plume of the exhaust, looking as if etched against the darkening sky. The fading light emphasises the glow from the cab as the engine sweeps past. There is some waving, even a spontaneous burst of applause, before the watchers disperse.

The *Silver Jubilee* went into service at a time when the German diesel *Flying Hamburger* seemed to be making the running in railway speed. But while the then two-car German train seated only 102 passengers, limited to a cold buffet, the *Jubilee* seated 194 with first- and third-class accommodation and full restaurant car service.

The best place from which to watch operations at Kings Cross was platform 10. One might see the locomotive for the next departure disengage itself from the others in the locomotive sidings, or enter the station slowly from the tunnel, its identity remaining hidden until it had backed on to the coaches. There was uncertainty and expectation when a locomotive loomed up in the darkness of the tunnel on its way in from Kings Cross shed. The shed was on the down side between the Copenhagen and Gasworks tunnels. A locomotive from the shed moved first on to the down slow line at the mouth of Copenhagen tunnel. It then reversed at Copenhagen Junction on to the down fast line and into a siding between the down and up lines. When a clear road was obtained it moved on to the up carriage road and through the centre Gasworks tunnel into Kings Cross.

The late Cecil J. Allen once called the footplate 'a jealously guarded stance'. In later years as steam neared its end, the barriers came down a little and with them some of its exclusiveness when viewed from

Contemplation
There was once an ardent religious neophyte who was troubled to find that he could not meditate. The trouble, he thought, was that he had not discovered the church with the precise atmosphere of suggestive peacefulness. So he went to his spiritual director, an old, wise priest, famous for his powers of rapt contemplation. 'Father,' he said, 'I cannot meditate. Will you tell me what is the best church to go to?' 'Marylebone station, my son,' came the answer, 'it is the best place in London for meditation.' – Roger B. Lloyd.

Overleaf: Kings Cross departures. With a squealing of flanges and a thunder of exhaust the Norseman departs from platform 10 behind A3 Pacific No 60054 Prince of Wales *whilst an arriving train runs into platform 7 behind A4 No 60010* Dominion of Canada. *The date appears to be around 1954/5.*

Kings Cross arrivals. A familiar picture to most travellers and enthusiasts, main-line expresses at rest after arrival. The A3 Pacific with German-type smoke deflectors is not known but the A4 is the now preserved No 60010 Dominion of Canada. *The date is May 1961. All expresses are 'on time' on the arrivals board.*

platform level. Previously a very small boy, devouring the footplate with his eyes, might be invited on board by a kindly driver, even allowed to pull the whistle chain, but that was a rare experience.

Until the first diesel sets let passengers in the front seats look ahead, the driver's view of the railway was unknown to most travellers. Looking backwards from the observation car of the *Coronation* or the *Devon Belle* was the nearest thing, but lacked the fascination of watching the landscape ahead unfold after each bend in the track, and identifying signal aspects at long range.

In 1930 Gresley's high-pressure locomotive, No 10000, made a return trip to Kings Cross on the *Flying Scotsman*, varying its normal duties from Gateshead. Towards the end of the decade a new No 10000 appeared with a standard-pressure boiler but keeping the same wheel arrangement. The LNER referred to No 10000 as a 4-6-4 but this was not strictly correct, as the erudite have never ceased to point out in letters to the railway press. The two trailing axles were not in a bogie. The front one was carried in Cartazzi axleboxes as in the Pacifics but the rear axle was in a separate Bissel truck. This made the locomotive a 4-6-2-2.

Kings Cross long retained a Great Northern flavour. The large-boilered Atlantics, already between twenty-four and thirty-two years old in the mid 1930s, were to be seen on the Pullman trains. Kings Cross shed had six of them for these duties, and as far as possible they were always worked by the same drivers and firemen. Other duties for this class were the Cambridge buffet car expresses, known to the university as 'Flying Pubs'. The earlier small-boilered Atlantics appeared on stopping trains and were rarely to be seen in London but by the 1930s they had been rebuilt by Gresley with larger boilers and extended smokeboxes. N class 0-6-2 tank engines bustled in and out of the suburban station with trains to main-line suburbs and to branches now served by London Transport or closed.

St Pancras, only the width of a street from Kings Cross, offered less to the observer unless he was a devoted admirer of Derby locomotive practice. Suburban trains provided more locomotive variety than the expresses, with Kirtley 0-4-4 tanks hanging on into the thirties, Johnson 0-4-4 tanks, and for a brief spell at the end of the previous decade a Whitelegg 4-6-4 tank transferred from the London Tilbury & Southend section. But how could one distinguish a Compound of genuine Midland descent from one built by the LMS, or identify the various classes of simple 4-4-0s?

At St Pancras the huge arch of the roof dwarfed the trains. The clerestory windows overlooking the concourse seem to have provided the viewpoint for many an artist who painted the station with miniature trains and passengers. Towards the end of the 1920s some Claughtons appeared on the Carlisle expresses but there was no large scale change of motive power until the Stanier era with its Black Fives, Jubilees, and 2-6-4 tanks, joined later by rebuilt Royal Scots and Patriots. There had

St Pancras 1959. The great arch dominates the scene at the Midland Railway's one-time terminus in London making the waiting trains seem almost like models. Stanier classes predominate with Black Five No 44984 leaving on a Bedford local, Jubilee 4-6-0 No 45628 Somaliland *on the 16.25 for Manchester Central and a sister engine No 45565* Victoria *on the 17.05 for Bradford. A sign of the times is BR standard class 5 4-6-0 No 73137 at the head of the 16.45 to Nottingham. This was the last possible year such a scene could be witnessed. The St Pancras–Bedford locals went over to diesel multiple units in January 1960 and diesel locomotives came to main-line trains in the same year.*

Morning arrival. Euston as it was, with much more character (even if it was scruffy) than the present concrete monstrosity. The up Irish Mail arrives at platform 1 in April 1948. No doubt the overnight service running late due to lengthy customs examination of passengers' luggage at Holyhead. The railway was still a universal carrier, witness the barrowloads of parcels obstructing the platform and awaiting removal to the parcels office for sorting and delivery. The locomotive is converted Royal Scot No 6147 The Northamptonshire Regiment *still in the final LMS livery; it was rebuilt in September 1946.*

been a break with convention in 1928 when the Beyer-Ljungstrom condensing turbine locomotive worked for a short time in regular passenger service between St Pancras and Manchester. The Midland section was also chosen for the first main-line workings of the LMS three-car streamlined diesel train after it had shown its paces on the Oxford and Cambridge branches. On 20 March 1939 it began working a diagram which brought it from Bedford to St Pancras, then to Leicester, on to Nottingham and back direct from Nottingham to St Pancras. It returned to Luton in the late evening and then provided a new service at 11.45pm from Luton to Bedford. This was the first regular diesel service to a London terminus.

On days when P&O liners were sailing from Tilbury, St Pancras took on a different aspect. Suburban travellers alighting from their trains found themselves picking their way past cabin trunks and other large impedimenta on their way to the Underground. Small groups of travellers stood chatting to friends and relatives who had come to see them off. On the bookstall postcards of the ship were displayed alongside the usual London and local views. The locomotive at the head of the train would probably be an ex-Midland Fowler 0-6-0 and in later years this would be fitted with apparatus for the Hudd automatic warning system installed on the Tilbury line. After passing Kentish Town the train would cross the main lines on a flyover taking it on to the Tottenham & Hampstead Joint. It would then circumnavigate London to the north to join the LT&S section at Barking. The number of junctions on the route precluded high speed: Kentish Town Junction, Junction Road Junction, South Tottenham East and West Junctions, Woodgrange Park Junction, and several others at Barking.

St Pancras only had a short life as a terminus for the Continent. At the beginning of the decade trains were run to Tilbury to connect with steamers sailing between Tilbury and Dunkerque. The boat train had a restaurant car and included through carriages from Glasgow and Manchester between 1927 and 1932. The overnight service provided by the shipping company did not attract the patronage hoped for and after a year or two was quietly dropped.

Among the London termini, Marylebone was unique for its atmosphere of repose. A. G. Macdonnel teased the station gently in *England, Their England* with a description of a train departing for the country after driver and guard had exchanged a quiet word or two, with no shrilling whistles or waving of flags. Until the first 'Football' Sandringhams appeared in 1935 the station was pure Great Central as far as locomotives were concerned although the Atlantics and 4-4-0 Directors had lost their green livery and been endowed with flowerpot chimneys spoiling their former elegance. The massive 4-6-2 tank engines with side window cabs framing the footplate slipped in and out on local trains. Services to Aylesbury were shared with the Metropolitan, and to High Wycombe with the Great Western, for access to Marylebone was over two joint lines.

There was no main-line departure from Marylebone between 12.15pm and 3.20pm but at 3 o'clock the 10am from Bradford arrived and there

Train Aesthetics

Once a man spent his retirement and the money he had saved in endless travelling on the Great Western Railway. When he died, it is good to remember, his body was borne to the grave on the shoulders of railway porters, and the company, whose system he had travelled over so many times, furnished a guard of honour and a wreath to the honoured memory of so good a traveller.

Perhaps, on a day which we all hope is yet very far off, they will do the same for the last remains of Naomi Royde Smith, who, in her series of sketches, 'Pilgrim from Paddington,' discovered a vital truth, that for gentle, restful meditation there is no place quite so fruitful as a comfortable railway compartment. The rhythmic pattern of the wheels, and the flow of the countryside past the window, are the very stuff of an easeful meditation; and they contain the hypnotic magic which, unlike the blacker arts of hypnotism, does not stupefy the mind but lulls it only to set it racing like a highly bred horse on new and ever fruitful journeys of spiritual and appreciative adventure.
– Roger B. Lloyd

Morning departure. Euston station c1935 with a Manchester express on the right in platform 13. The locomotive is class 4P Compound No 1161 allocated to Manchester Longsight. On the left is a tank filler – used for topping up toilet tanks and restaurant cars. Note the corridor end boards stacked against the signal post.

Paddington. The red tail lamp is in position on the buffer beam as No 5040 Stokesay Castle *waits to back out to its home shed Old Oak Common (81A) in April 1957. The alighted passengers can be seen on the left waiting in the taxi queue.*

Banquet and Speeches

In connection with the opening of a new coal distillery at Glenboig (Glasgow), the LMS arranged what is probably one of the world's most luxurious special trains. It left Euston at 12.15am and was made up of 10 of the latest LMS sleeping saloons giving accommodation for approximately 120 passengers. At Lanark (Race Course Station), on the way down to Glenboig, passengers were transferred to a luxurious day train in which breakfast was served, and this was used also for the return journey from Glenboig to Euston. In addition to restaurant cars the train was equipped with two cinema cars, a lounge, and observation saloons.

The journey from Glenboig to London, a distance of 395½ miles, was made without a stop. During the journey a banquet was held and speeches were made which were broadcast by means of loud speakers throughout the length.

Euston was reached at 7.30pm, six minutes before time; the journey having occupied eight hours altogether. – *Railway Magazine*, 1929.

Victoria. A Bognor Regis train makes ready behind express types from two of the Southern's pre-grouping constituents, ex-LSWR Class L12 No 416 and an unknown LBSC Class H2 Marsh Atlantic. The train carries headboards on the coach roofs and the reporting number suggests that it may well be a Saturday afternoon through working. Normally connections were made out of Portsmouth trains at Barnham. Likely times are 13.04 or 13.20 ex-Victoria. The disc 803 is a shed duty number.

was brief activity at the barrier. The 3.20 was the Marylebone 'classic', descended from the Great Central's *Sheffield Special* in the early days of the London main line. A through LMS carriage for Halifax was attached to the rear of the smart five-coach LNER set. Through carriages provided a little variety in a timetable consisting mainly of trains to Manchester or Bradford. A service which disappeared shortly before World War II was a through coach to Marylebone from Stratford upon Avon via the Stratford upon Avon & Midland Junction line and the spur from Byfield to Woodford & Hinton (later Woodford Halse). It arrived on a train from Mansfield and returned as a slip on the 6.20pm to Bradford.

Until the mid 1930s the LNER seemed to be taking little notice of its Great Central constituent but in 1934 the first Sandringhams from the Great Eastern lines appeared, to be followed by the Football series built specifically for the GC main line. The first Pacific was seen at Marylebone in 1935, a prelude to the widespread use of these engines and V2s on GC London line services. The only six-coupled tender engines seen regularly at Marylebone before the arrival of the Sandringhams were the mixed traffic version of Robinson's Lord Faringdon class. Three of the original Lord Faringdons were rebuilt with Caprotti valve gear and were to be seen most weekends on Sunday half-day excursions.

The period of greatest activity at Marylebone was when the station was used as a relief for Kings Cross in handling cheap fare overnight trains to the north east. Thus was fulfilled an aspiration of the Great Central to extend its services northwards. A direct line had been proposed from Beighton to Rotherham to shorten the distance to York, with an Anglo-Scottish service in collaboration with the North Eastern in view. Not surprisingly the idea was strongly opposed by the other companies and the Great Central decided that it had more immediate projects on which to spend its money.

After World War II when normal services were restored, two named trains, the *Master Cutler* and the *South Yorkshireman* gave promise of possible further developments. Hopes were disappointed and a service curtailed to semi-fasts to Nottingham foreshadowed Marylebone's end as a trunk-line terminus. But at the end of the express service Marylebone saw a greater variety of locomotives than it had before known, with standard classes and rebuilt Scots appearing as they were stepped down from more exacting duties. A Britannia Pacific was seen at Marylebone but what would once have been greeted with jubilation now seemed rather sad.

Marylebone was a friendly station. Platform tickets were punched without the suspicious look one encountered elsewhere when presenting oneself at the barrier unaccompanied. Its luncheon and tea room was well patronised, drawing some of its clientele from office workers in the area. There was little to disturb the calm of the waiting room.

One cannot write with similar affection of Euston. Arrival and departure platforms were on opposite sides of the Great Hall, and reaching the departure side involved picking a precarious way through a swarm of luggage trolleys to the accompaniment of warning shouts as

9
5040
45
803
Nº 416

Liverpool Street. Reunited – February 1946.

Liverpool Street. Britannia Pacific No 70001 Lord Hurcomb *leaves with the down Norfolkman made up largely of BR Mk 1 stock but with a Gresley brake as the leading vehicle. The train is in the short-lived red and cream livery nicknamed 'blood and custard' by the frivolous. This may well have looked smart on the steel-panelled coaches but Gresley teak did not respond well. The Britannias revolutionised the Norwich trains and greatly improved the locomotive rostering. On the left is one of Thompson's dreadful L1 2-6-4 tanks, No 67724, on the empty stock of the up Hook Continental.*

Waterloo. The handsome rebuild of Merchant Navy class Pacific No 35030 Elder Dempster Lines *waits to depart with the down Atlantic Coast Express in June 1959.*

what looked like a congealed mass suddenly stirred into movement in the manner of ice floes in the Arctic Spring. As for the Great Hall, the poet who dreamed of marble halls might have seen his vision materialise there, but functional it was not. Memories recall a distant age when shoppers relaxing before taking the train home were served at their tables by waitresses bearing trays of the traditional tea, cakes and buttered toast. In due course they would catch one of the rather sparse suburban trains to Tring or Bletchley. As so often happened in those days, the motive power of Precursor 4-4-2 tanks or the Bowen-Cooke 4-6-2s was made familiar by the pictures in the Bassett-Lowke catalogue. Two platforms on the arrival side of the station were used by the LMS electric trains to Watford. It was a tedious all-stations journey relieved by the opportunity of seeing expresses on the adjacent main-line tracks between Wembley and Bushey. The original stately Oerlikon stock with sliding doors rode smoothly, apparently as a result of some secret of design which was subsequently lost.

In the early 1930s the idea of a Pacific at Euston was hard to grasp. Then the wonder came to pass. Seen in an evening in the subdued light of an arrival platform, a Princess Royal looked immense. But the most impressive memory of Euston dates from after World War II when a passenger who had chosen his seat wisely in an outgoing local could enjoy the panorama of the *Midlander*, the *Mancunian* and the *Merseyside* at adjoining departure platforms, each locomotive standing proud with its own headboard. With luck the *Midlander* would later

70001
70001

35030

sweep past between stations, a Jubilee at the head.

The Great Western Railway and Paddington station survived grouping unaltered as far as one could see. For those who lived outside Great Western territory, impressions of the line were dominated by the Westbury route and the main line to Birmingham and Birkenhead. In the centenary year, 1935, the introduction of the *Bristolian* was a reminder of the roots of the railway. Platform 1 was a good place from which to view trains leaving for all the Great Western main lines. W. G. Chapman's book *The 10.30 Limited*, did much to imprint the idea of the supremacy of the Westbury route, but the variety from Weymouth to Birkenhead was considerable. And the comprehensive destination boards carried by the coaches, such as 'Paddington, Westbury, Frome, Yeovil and Weymouth' made their point. A headboard that intrigued those not familiar with the intricacies of the system in the West Midlands read 'Paddington, Worcester, Droitwich Spa, Kidderminster and Stourbridge Junction'.

Paddington combined the traditional with the innovative. The 'Lawn' had been tidied up in 1930 but retained its former name, associated in legend with the early years when wallflowers grew there and a child was arrested by a railway policeman for picking one, thereby stealing the company's property. In 1935 there was a sign of things to come when a 'Quick Lunch and Snack Bar' was opened on platform 1, with twenty-seven bar stools for the clients who were served by 'chefs dressed in white'.

Of the Southern termini, Victoria is associated with the anxieties of going abroad. The nonchalance with which staff slapped labels on registered luggage and handed out counterfoils did something to reassure the nervous traveller that he would be re-united with his belongings albeit in less homely surroundings. It was always a pleasure to watch boat trains departing. If working near Victoria the 2pm Continental departure might just be squeezed into an extended lunch hour. From October 1936 there was just a chance of watching the *Night Ferry* arrive in the morning rush hour with two 4-4-0s – perhaps a Wainwright class L and a Maunsell L1 – heading the train of blue Wagons-Lits sleeping cars from Paris. This train was liable to delays in the rush hour traffic and its appearance was unpredictable. On the Brighton side of the station electrification began taking toll of main-line trains in 1933, but the Newhaven boat trains retained their Atlantics and steam continued to Bognor via the mid-Sussex line until 1938. On these trains towards the end one was as likely to see Drummond 4-4-0s from the Western section as a Marsh B4X. In those days most people worked on Saturday mornings and a pleasant way of starting the weekend was to take a cheap return to Oxted and travel behind one of Marsh's celebrated I3 4-4-2 tanks.

Neither Liverpool Street nor Waterloo offered vantage points to compare with Paddington or Kings Cross, and the habit of indicating through portions on Liverpool Street trains by means of notices on the platform seemed an inelegant substitution for destination boards. There was, however, a fascinating enquiry office facing the approach road, with

Mini Excursions

See the *Empress of Britain* go down the Clyde was the invitation from the LMS to the citizens of Glasgow for 5 April 1931. It was a unique opportunity in at least three respects. First to be able to view the latest enterprise in British shipping as she passed on her way from the shipyard to the sea. Second the distance travelled by the excursion was unusually short, as Langbank, the chosen vantage point was only sixteen miles from Glasgow. Third the terminal point itself, only a small station on the coastline to Gourock serving only a one-street village. Perhaps there was a fourth point which was long remembered by the LMS authorities; they sadly underestimated the response.

The two trips were booked to run out of Central station at 12 noon and 12.15pm, each behind elderly Caledonian 0-6-0s carrying express lamps even for this short non-stop run. In the event there were actually *twelve* of them carrying 11,000 and more people who appeared in huge queues at the booking office windows from 11am. It was a credit to local organisation that locos and stock were provided to move the crowd, but they did. The trains were booked to run to Langbank in twenty-eight minutes with an intermediate stop at Paisley to collect tickets and that must have been a heavy day for the normal Sunday staff; most trains took at least ten minutes longer.

So up to 15,000 people in all saw the gigantic white Canadian Pacific Railway ship glide down the river with five attendant tugs.

George Heiron's painting of a scene at Ais Gill in the late 1930s. The train is a southbound express from Glasgow (St Enoch) to London (St Pancras) headed by Stanier Jubilee No 5593 Kolhapur *and is nearing the summit under a mile short of the signalbox.*

L M S
5593

34017

Near journey's end. Southern Region West Country Pacific No 34017 Ilfracombe *opens up for the final run into Padstow as it clears the girders of Little Petherick Creek bridge with the down Atlantic Coast Express. The final section of the former LSWR route from Waterloo, between Wadebridge and the terminus at Padstow, alongside the Camel estuary, has been turned into a walkway. Little Petherick Creek bridge has been retained. The Creek used to serve a tidemill. The painting by Don Breckon forms part of his collection for the forthcoming* Country Connections *to be published by David & Charles.*

L.M.S

literature on Continental connections via the Hook or Antwerp, and on weekend trips to Flushing by the Zeeland Line. These included a night at the company hotel and a motorcoach trip round the island of Walcheren the next morning before embarking for home. Waterloo trains were best seen away from the terminus, as in the Byfleet cutting, but the seeker of antiquities could visit Waterloo for the sight of Adams Jubilee 0-4-2 tender engines on outer suburban trains.

All the great London stations had bookstalls displaying a range of reading matter which seemed greater than that in the average bookshop. An invariable purchase for a schoolboy before a long journey was the *Wide World Magazine* with its supposedly true accounts of exploration along the Amazon, where giant anaconda lurked in the still impenetrable rain forests or of rigours of life in the French Foreign Legion. When this began to pall one could turn to *The Happy Mag*, which adopted the slogan:

Forget your ticket, train or bag
But don't forget your *Happy Mag*

Two paintings taken from frontispiece to the Railway Magazine *by courtesy of the editor. These show LMS No 6203* Princess Margaret Rose *(now preserved) on a southbound express on Dillicar troughs and an unknown Great Western King with a down Paddington to Birkenhead express at the summit of the 1 in 100 Hatton Bank. Both show typical express trains of the mid to late 1930s.*

Excursions Ever Further

The 'school train' was the 4.42pm all stations from Warwick to Snow Hill usually behind a Tyseley Saint, more often than not No 2902 *Lady of the Lake*. Kept late and the next train was not until 5.59 with all the explaining that meant. On race days, however, there was the excursion special. Leaving immediately after the last race, it was first stop Snow Hill – and on to Shrewsbury usually behind Star No 4051, *Princess Helena*. It was an introduction to the world of card-playing men with alcoholic breath and also to some of the GW's more unusual coaches. Third class you travelled in what was technically described as a nondescript saloon. It had a side corridor leading to a large central compartment with comfortable settee-type seats round the sides and a table in the middle (just right for cards) plus four single well-upholstered seats which, being isolated were not always taken by the booked parties. To these were added a number of first-class coaches, sometimes saloons. It was experience coupled nicely with expediency.

Excursions were of course run to race meetings all over the country. Those for the Grand National were handled at three stations at Aintree, two LMS and one Cheshire Lines Committee. The Liverpool Overhead Railway used to organise a special race day electric service with LMS stock, using a short spur line between the LOR and the ex-L&Y electrified line via Linacre Road and Ford. Main-line trains came from all over the country. In 1934 the starting places included London (Euston, St Pancras, Kings Cross and Marylebone), Carlisle, Workington, Preston, Glasgow, Edinburgh, Blackpool, Peebles, St Albans, Newcastle, Nottingham, Bristol, Gloucester and Market Harborough. Between 11am and 1.30pm a train arrived every two minutes. Half the trains were double headed.

The first event of the flat race calendar was the Lincolnshire Handicap, then held on the Carholme course at Lincoln, followed two days later by the great steeplechase at Aintree. The LNER used to organise high-class trains from Kings Cross to Lincoln (a great day for local railwaymen because they were usually Pacific hauled) and after the last race on via Sheffield, the Woodhead route and Manchester to Aintree. The passengers, many of them first class, were mainly professional gamblers and bookmakers.

Doncaster Race Week in September, especially St Leger Day, generated an unusual volume of excursion traffic. Its handling was made more difficult by the fact that Doncaster has always been a very busy junction between the East Coast main line and several important cross-country routes. A high proportion of the specials before the war came from west and north of Doncaster and the main-line station could handle only a few of them. Most of the trains consisted of loads of coal miners carried in anything that would run, bogie or not, and they had to be dealt with at St James Bridge and in sidings at Hexthorpe and between the station and loco works.

From 1923 the LNER kept a complete set of first- and third-class Pullman cars for special workings on the Great Eastern section. During race weeks the train was

Holiday express. In the 1950s and early 60s BR organised excursion trains for town holiday weeks visiting a different resort each day Monday to Friday at an all-inclusive fare – with the same reserved seat every day. The Manchester Holiday Express returns from Stratford upon Avon in 1954 hauled by an LMS class 5 4-6-0 and banked by a GWR 2251 class 0-6-0. The train of ten LMS coaches includes a cafeteria car and no doubt was fully booked.

used to and from Newmarket. On Sundays it became the *Clacton Belle*, giving London people a day at that resort. This developed into the *Eastern Belle Pullman Limited* which ran from Liverpool Street on different days to Cromer, Sheringham, Yarmouth, Lowestoft, Walton-on-the-Naze, Hunstanton and Skegness, at cheap fares and high speeds, an idea copied elsewhere in Britain for many cities' holiday fortnight in the 1950s, passengers having the same reserved seat each day.

Perhaps the human activity which has caused the running of more special trains than any other has been football. The district excursion officer had to keep a close eye on the fixture list and gauge what support for away matches would be. If the team reached the FA Cup Semi Final or the Final, he had to be prepared to run a large number of trains to the Semi Final venue or to London for Wembley. When English teams played in European competitions much longer and very complicated excursions were involved. Liverpool in the European Cup Final resulted in several trains to the Channel ports and from French ports across Europe to Rome. So far as the FA Cup Final was concerned, it being a national event trains converged on London termini or Wembley from all parts of the country. (See snippet 'Football Traffic at Marylebone' on page 169.)

International football matches were also hectic occasions for the railways, particularly those between England and Scotland at Wembley or Hampden. Unfortunately even in those days there were many problems with drunkenness and vandalism; great operating difficulties occurred when communication cords were pulled, often several times in one journey. Similarly many trains were run for the Rugby International matches, often at good express speeds. Hundreds of thousands of people first travelled to a different part of the country on such trains at bargain fares.

Some collieries used rail trips for various bonanzas, entraining and detraining sometimes taking place by portable steps in the colliery sidings. One example was Firbeck, on a freight-only branch south west of Doncaster.

Then there were the public day and half-day excursions taking people ever further afield – London and

BRITISH RAILWAYS

LIVERPOOL RACES

FIRST RACE 2.0 p.m. LAST RACE 4.45 p.m.

GRAND NATIONAL

AT 3.15 p.m.

SATURDAY, MARCH 21st

LIMITED RESTAURANT CAR EXCURSION

TO THE

GRAND NATIONAL

(AT AINTREE)

FROM	DEPART	RETURN FARE (Including bus conveyance to and from Aintree)		ARRIVAL ON RETURN
		First Class	Second Class	
	a.m.	s d	s d	p.m.
PADDINGTON	8 5	68/6	48/0	10 48
HIGH WYCOMBE	8 40	61/3	43/3	10 16
READING GENERAL	7A 13	68/6	48/0	11C 56
MAIDENHEAD	7B 47	64/9	45/6	11B 11
SLOUGH	7B 25	66/6	46/9	11C 34
WEST RUISLIP	7B 54	65/9	46/3	10B 53
DENHAM	7B 59	65/0	45/9	10B 48
DENHAM GOLF CLUB	8B 2	64/9	45/6	10B 45
GERRARDS CROSS	8B 9	64/3	45/3	10B 41
SEER GREEN & JORDANS	8B 15	63/6	44/9	10B 35
BEACONSFIELD	8B 20	62/9	44/3	10B 31
	p.m.			
BIRKENHEAD (Woodside) ... ...arr.	12 57	BIRKENHEAD (Woodside) dep.		6 7

Notes:—A—Change at Maidenhead and High Wycombe.
B—Change at High Wycombe.
C—Change at High Wycombe and Maidenhead.

Tickets at the same fares as from Paddington may also be obtained at the following Stations: Westbourne Park, Acton Main Line, Ealing Broadway, West Ealing, Hanwell & Elthorne, Southall, Hayes & Harlington, West Drayton & Yiewsley, Uxbridge (Vine Street), Cowley, Staines West, Colnbrook, Iver, Langley and Greenford. Passengers may, with these tickets, travel by Ordinary Trains between these Stations and Paddington in order to connect with the special excursion.

If these Races are cancelled, and notice is given to The British Transport Commission in time to cancel these facilities, the fares paid by intending passengers will be refunded on application.

THE ACCOMMODATION IS LIMITED AND BOOKINGS WILL CEASE AT 12.0 noon, FRIDAY, MARCH 20th

TICKETS MUST BE OBTAINED IN ADVANCE FROM BOOKING STATIONS OR ANY OFFICES OF THE FOLLOWING TRAVEL AGENTS:— AMERICAN EXPRESS COMPANY, THOS. COOK & SONS LTD., DEAN & DAWSONS LTD., FRAME'S TOURS LTD., AND PICKFORDS TRAVEL SERVICE.

BREAKFAST AND LUNCHEON ON THE FORWARD, AFTERNOON TEA AND DINNER ON THE RETURN JOURNEY, OBTAINABLE ON THE TRAIN

Notice as to Conditions.—These tickets are issued subject to the British Transport Commission's published Regulations and Conditions applicable to British Railways exhibited at their Stations or obtainable free of charge at station booking offices. Luggage allowances are as set out in these general notices.

Further information will be supplied on application to Stations, Agencies or to Mr. N. H. BRIANT, District Operating Superintendent, Paddington Station, W.2; or to Mr. E. FLAXMAN, Commercial Officer, Paddington Station, W.2 (Tel.: Paddington 7000, Extension "Enquiries"; 8.0 a.m. to 10.0 p.m.).

Paddington Station, W.2.,
November, 1958.

LpD. 770 P. Printed by W. A. SMITH (Leeds) LTD., Carlton Printeries, Leeds.

Aintree for the Grand National soon after the grouping. Very large numbers of passengers were handled at three stations, two belonging to the LMS and one to the CLC; excursions arrived in the area at the peak period every two minutes. Consequently many trains had to be handled away from platforms, passengers detraining by use of portable steps, which can be seen in this view. Many other things have now passed into history, such as the row of roof ventilators along the old rolling stock, and the leather straps to raise and lower the door lights.

Peak Forest excursion. Class 4F No 44470 leaves Chee Tor No 2 tunnel, near Miller's Dale with an excursion (possibly from Mansfield to Belle Vue as the engine was allocated to Kirkby in Ashfield) on Easter Monday 2 April 1956. The junction signal is off for the main line, the other arm indicating the junction for the Buxton line.

L M S
1182

CADBURYS
IX60

Portpatrick branch. Double-headed LMS-built Compounds (1182 and 1180) climb the 1 in 57 for two miles from the terminus to the summit at Colfin. D. S. Barrie in the Railway Magazine *for January 1939 speaks of a 'seasonal half day excursion from Glasgow sometimes run in duplicate. It provides a stiff task even for two Compounds when twelve or more heavy bogie coaches have to be hauled up the grade out of Portpatrick'. This would have been aggravated by the curvature, and if strong winds were blowing salt spray would have made the climb impossible. The platform at Portpatrick only held about six coaches, with two or three more back in the shunting neck so there must have been some intriguing moves to assemble a twelve-coach train! There is no sign of steam sanding in use in the picture. David L. Smith says these excursions started in 1927, but the Stanier coaches date this one mid–late 1930s. The leading vehicle appears to be a kitchen car.*

Birmingham to Weston-super-Mare being a popular half-day jaunt. The LMS and LNER, especially the latter, made cheap evening excursions a speciality. During the winter of 1934/5 the LNER ran 781 such trains, mainly to such places as Manchester, Sheffield, Nottingham, Leeds, Hull and Newcastle. About 300,000 people travelled on them. Evening excursions were also run in the summer from cities such as Lincoln to resorts like Skegness, arrival being timed after the day excursions had started to leave the coast. The fare for the ninety-mile trip was a princely 1s 6d (7½p). Especially popular on Saturdays was 'Belle Vue' at Manchester. From Lincoln, for example, the return fare for almost 200 miles was 2s 6d (12½p). Passengers could enjoy the zoo and amusement park, see the speedway and finish up with the firework display. Where can such an evening out be obtained now at a comparable price?

Lincoln usually used GC engines on these trains, a 4-6-0 if one could be found. One of the most popular was No 5424 *City of Lincoln* (GC class 1, LNER B2). Passengers and young enthusiasts were not at all interested in pounds of coal per mile satisfaction, if it looked and sounded the part it was a real engine, and the GC 4-6-0s met these criteria. In fact they looked as if they would last for ever. The return from busy Belle Vue on the GC & Midland Joint along a generally complex and hilly route included the three-mile climb inside Woodhead Tunnel. When working hard a GC 4-6-0 could make more smoke than a wartime destroyer in a tight corner. Beyond the tunnel they often opened the

Chocolate excursion. The three big chocolate manufacturers, Cadburys, Rowntrees and Frys, were always very publicity conscious and from the 1920s until the early 1960s regularly chartered trains to enable the public to visit their factories. Here is one bound for Cadburys, Bournville c1961 headed by an unknown Jubilee 4-6-0 passing Ashchurch (Gloucestershire). Many of these trains carried headboards on the smokebox proclaiming their destination.

CITY OF

BIRMINGHAM

HOLIDAY EXPRESS

WILL RUN

1st WEEK - Monday to Friday 29th July to 2nd August

2nd WEEK - Monday to Friday 5th to 9th August

FROM

BIRMINGHAM NEW STREET

TO

1st WEEK		2nd WEEK
SOUTHPORT	MONDAY	SOUTHPORT
PEAK DISTRICT	TUESDAY	PEAK DISTRICT
NORTH WALES	WEDNESDAY	NORTH WALES
LONDON	THURSDAY	BLACKPOOL
BRIGHTON	FRIDAY	WINDERMERE

FIVE DAYS TRAVEL

INCLUSIVE FARE **70/-** EACH WEEK

YOUR SEAT RESERVED IN A SPECIAL CAFETERIA CAR TRAIN TO A DIFFERENT RESORT EACH DAY. ACCOMMODATION LIMITED. BOOK EARLY

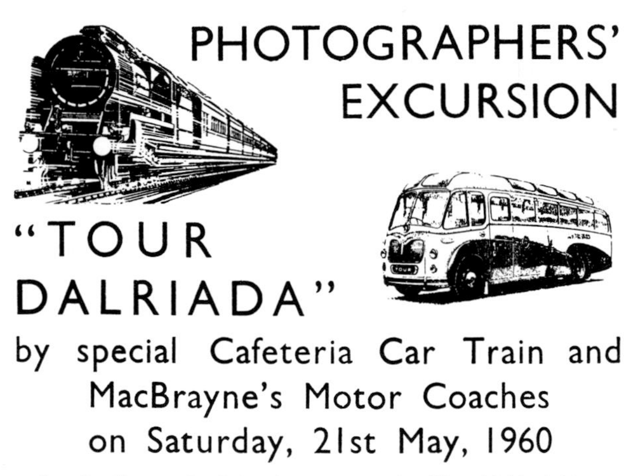

PHOTOGRAPHERS' EXCURSION

"TOUR DALRIADA"

by special Cafeteria Car Train and MacBrayne's Motor Coaches on Saturday, 21st May, 1960

fare for the round trip **35/-** (Rail and Motor)

Children (three years and under fourteen) half fare

Going by train via the West Highland Line to Crianlarich thence to Oban. Thereafter by Motor Coach to Kilmelford, Kilmartin, Ardrishaig, Lochgilphead, Inveraray and back to Dalmally. Returning by train from Dalmally to Glasgow via Callander.

Tickets obtainable at GLASGOW (QUEEN STREET) STATION ONLY.

LIGHT REFRESHMENTS AVAILABLE ON THE TRAIN IN EACH DIRECTION. Packed Meals—Price 2/6d. and 3/6d. can be supplied, but must be ordered at Queen Street Station Booking Office, **prior to Saturday, 21st May.**

NOTICE AS TO CONDITIONS—These tickets are issued subject to the British Transport Commission's published Regulations and Conditions applicable to British Railways or to any other body, company or person upon whose property or premises the tickets may be available.

Accommodation limited - early booking recommended

ash ejector and proved that the LNER could equal Belle Vue in an exhibition of fireworks.

Blackpool has always endeavoured to lengthen its season by its famous illuminations. Apart from the people booking for long weekends or for a week in autumn, numerous day and half-day excursions were organised, some from 300 miles away. In the admittedly long season Blackpool welcomed almost 22,000 excursion trains in 1938. Over 3,000 had restaurant cars. Excursion offices throughout the kingdom attracted the passengers by advertisements, posters and those handbills once so prominent at even small stations.

Some more enlightened companies organised annual trips for their workers, the bigger ones needing several trains. Engine headboards were frequently used. Good service earned valuable prestige for the railway. Canvassing for freight traffic after a successful trip almost a joy! But one small incident could throw the train working completely out of gear. On one particular Sunday in the 1930s the platforming of return trains at Skegness was so delayed that the passengers almost rioted, occupying any train rather than their own and refusing to move. It was well into Monday before the staff could relax.

Before the war Sundays in Glasgow were dry with alcohol only available to 'bona fide travellers', an encouragement for the excursion business of no mean proportion. The more adventurous might crowd the summertime excursion to Keswick, an attractive day out with a dining car. The enthusiast walks down the long platform of the old G&SWR station at St Enoch and waits; nothing on the shed in the triangle beyond the platforms, as this is only for the coast-line trains boasting no more than half a dozen class 2P 4-4-0s and some tanks, so the train engine will need to come from Corkerhill. Before long the familiar sight of a red-painted LNWR tender comes into view, behind it a large-boilered Claughton. The fact that it is a Claughton causes no surprise as these are now regular engines over the Settle–Carlisle route but a big-boilered engine is rare. Excitement number one. As the engine backs down on to the train it becomes clear that even this rare variety proves a comparative stranger, No 6017 *Breadalbane*, a Patricroft engine more often seen on holiday on the North Wales coast; it has probably come in with the newspaper train and been borrowed for the weekend. They leave prompt on 9.55 taking the Glasgow & South Western route via Kilmarnock and along the shore of Solway Firth to Carlisle. Excitement number two comes at Carlisle. *Breadalbane* is unhooked and makes off for Durran Hill shed and all is quiet for a few minutes. Upperby depot officially houses all the CK&P engines though there is a sub shed at Penrith; all in all there are eleven LNWR 18in goods or Cauliflowers and for a few more weeks a small number of Mr Webb's 2-4-0 Jumbos – the 6ft 6in Precedents famous in the Races to the North of 1895. There are three of them, Nos 5001 *Snowdon*, 5027 *Franklin* and 5050 *Merrie Carlisle*.

Two engines back down, sharp plumes of steam shooting up into the clear air from their safety valves . . . and, yes, the train engine is 18in goods No 8387 and, hardly believable, the pilot Jumbo No 5027 *Franklin* – perhaps on her last express working. They run quite fast to Penrith though rarely exceeding 55mph, slowing for the station and the crossing of the down main line to reach the branch. It is hard to make a real run at the bank but the drivers have a go and the noise is deafening, sparks raining down on the coach roofs like hailstones. At Keswick some make for the comfortable hotel via the long covered way from the platform, others in hiking dress, open-necked shirts, shorts and a walking stick, take a few deep breaths and head for the countryside.

In the twilight of a long July evening they set off at 6.55pm. After Penruddock it is a lively ride down to Penrith and the wooden brakeblocks on the tenders are smoking well. As the horse is heading for the stable the sprint from Penrith to Carlisle produces 67mph so *Franklin* goes out proudly – and the boxes on the eighteen-inch goods are warm to say the least. In those days you did not need an enthusiasts' special to score something special.

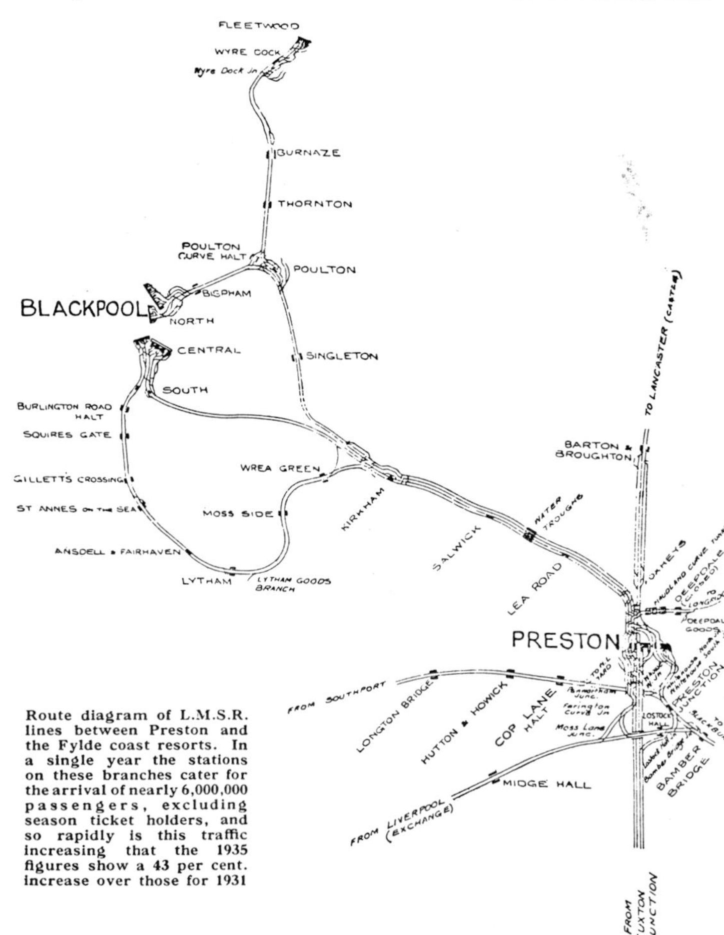

Route diagram of L.M.S.R. lines between Preston and the Fylde coast resorts. In a single year the stations on these branches cater for the arrival of nearly 6,000,000 passengers, excluding season ticket holders, and so rapidly is this traffic increasing that the 1935 figures show a 43 per cent. increase over those for 1931

Sunday excursion. A return half-day Glasgow–Keswick excursion stands behind one of the last 'Jumbos', Precedent class 2-4-0 No 5027 Franklin *and an unknown Webb 'Cauliflower' 0-6-0 at Keswick station around 1928–30. The CK&P line was the last haunt of both these classes, the latter lasting until the introduction of the LMS class 2 2-6-0s in 1950. The leading van is ex-Glasgow & South Western.*

Heading for home. The 'Halfex' has left Keswick at 6.55pm (18.55) and nears the summit of the CK&P east of Troutbeck, both engines working hard at the head of ten corridor coaches including a diner. Alcohol was only served to bona fide travellers in Scotland at that time and these trains were very popular. The fifth coach is the LNWR diner

Devil's Seats

In 1933 the LNER put tourist stock into service for excursion and similar expresses. Apart from a livery of green and cream, it was mainly notable for the bucket seats in 2+2 formation in the all-open cars. They were designed by the Devil for the punishment of sinners, though the official blurb opined that 'this type of seat will raise the standard of travel comfort considerably.' If so, heaven help passengers in what had gone before!

By 1940 some of this stock was in use on a Saturday afternoon train which I picked up each week at Nottingham Victoria on the way home to Rugby. It came from York or somewhere further north, and took the Banbury line to somewhere on God's Wonderful Railway. Even for a journey of 44 miles it could be writhing purgatory.

One day, watching a clean V2 come on to the train at the Leicester engine change, either my suffering showed through or I looked especially wistful, for the driver asked how far I was going and invited me to join him for the twenty miles. The fireman was busy on the long 1 in 176 climb to Lutterworth, and waved me into *his* bucket seat, where I could watch the road ahead and his dexterity with the shovel, all the time listening to the burble of the fairly even exhaust with the reverser showing 18 per cent and the regulator up to the stop.

Who shall say if it was more comfortable; but certainly a lot more interesting. – A. J. Powell.

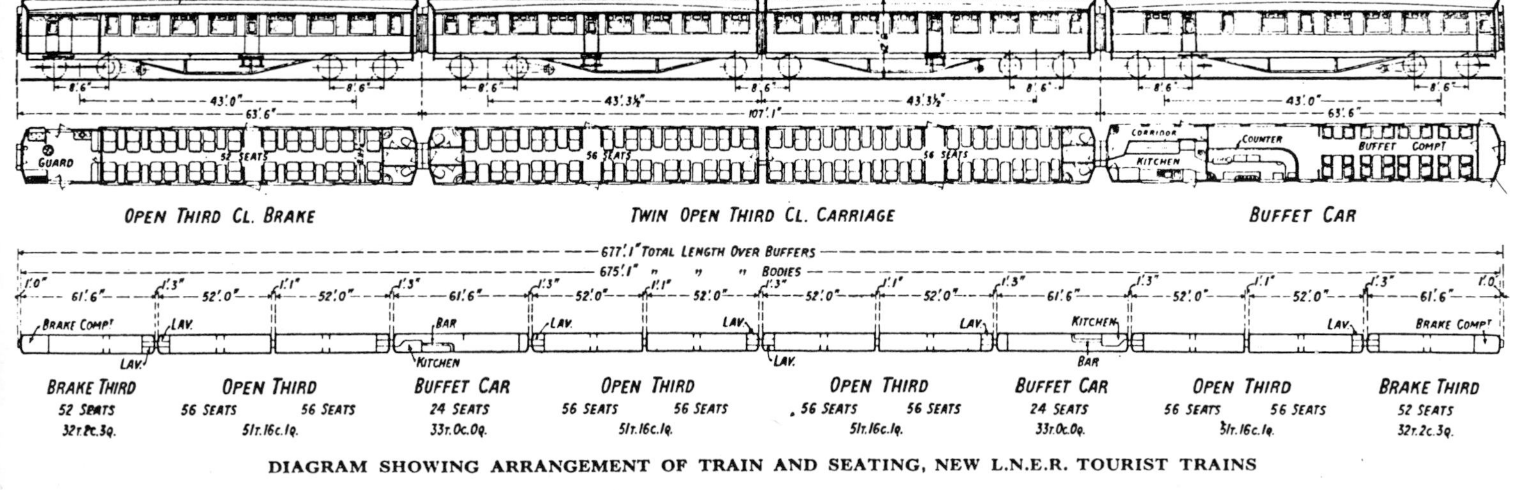

DIAGRAM SHOWING ARRANGEMENT OF TRAIN AND SEATING, NEW L.N.E.R. TOURIST TRAINS

COME ON
BARROW
P F T CUP LETS MAKE IT OURS
W536
026
84G

6
CHANGE HERE FOR JOURNEY'S END

SNAPPED the Charing Cross booking clerk: 'Bexhill return? change at Crowhurst, thirteen and sevenpence.' The Southern Railway's travelling ticket collector had a kinder thought. Scratching his head, he muttered: 'Might be better to change at Hastings, though don't say I said so.' And yes it was a dilemma if one wanted a private hotel or digs close to the centre of the town or near the beach, for Bexhill Central on the ex-LBSCR Eastbourne–Hastings route was *much* more convenient than the remote old South Eastern's Bexhill West.

For the enthusiast West could be fun, a Schools or L-class 4-4-0 on the express which dashed down via Tonbridge and Robertsbridge (change for the Kent & Sussex Railway), and a push-pull service from Crowhurst; or if one went on to Hastings an old F1 class 4-4-0, or a diminutive Brighton 0-4-2 tank with a seemingly huge auto-trailer on the coast line. But for the unwary traveller just wanting to get there (and without the local knowledge to bend the rules for his own convenience) it was a trap, a long – unnecessarily long – way out of the town.

Normally, of course, there were no such options. One changed at Penrith for Keswick, Ruabon for Barmouth, Brent for Kingsbridge, and Crewe for Chester, North Wales, Shrewsbury, Liverpool or Manchester. Learning these and many more was part of every intelligent boy's progress to manhood.

Fan trip. Thirty-five or more years ago many excursions were run for sporting events including cup finals at Wembley. Rebuilt Royal Scot No 46144 The Honourable Artillery Company *is leaving Stonebridge Park sidings for Wembley Central to work a return Rugby League excursion to Barrow in Furness on 30 April 1955.*

To the Western from Wembley. A clean No 6964 Thornbridge Hall *heads a return schoolboys' football international excursion out of Wembley Hill station en route for Shrewsbury on 26 April 1958. The engine comes from Shrewsbury (84G) shed and the train will run via Northolt Junction and GW&GC Joint line. There is a nice set of Great Central signals on the left.*

Change here for Bexhill West. Crowhurst on the ex-SECR main line to Hastings with Schools class No 30900 Eton *on the 8.25am (08.25) Charing Cross–Hastings express and H class 0-4-4 tank (ex-SECR) on the 10.37 Crowhurst to Bexhill West push and pull service – withdrawn 15 June 1964. Bexhill was served by both the SECR and the LBSC (via Lewes) to Bexhill Central.*

Making the connection. Trains classed as 'Express Passenger' were not confined to the main trunk routes. LNWR Precursor tank, LMS No 6787, is leaving one of the north bay platforms at Rugby in 1937 with the 17.47 SX to Warwick calling only at Leamington Spa. This was presumably rather ineffective competition with the GWR for Leamington traffic although it made a good connection out of the 16.10 ex-Euston. There was a corresponding up service in the morning, 08.32 from Warwick, although this was a 'Motor Train' in LMS parlance and had conditional stops at Marton, Birdingbury and Dunchurch to pick up for London.

Summer Saturdays, with their enormous range of through services, disturbed the pattern. There were whole express trains booked right through to and from branch termini and through coaches (some by slips). But usually the non-holiday traveller to destinations off the main through routes had to change. How evocative is that very word change. It meant horror to old ladies, interludes of great variety to those interested in the railway scene. The contrasts could hardly have been greater between huge junctions, such as Crewe or York or Reading, and small ones like Lostwithiel for Fowey, Miller's Dale for Buxton and Holywell Junction for Holywell Town, with a multiplicity of medium-sized ones like Ipswich for Bury St Edmunds and Haywards Heath for Lewes via Plumpton in between. Each had its own ambiance, smells, sounds, peculiarities.

Reading was (and still is for that matter) very much an exchange point with passengers scurrying across platforms to connecting trains once headed by Halls or 43XX Moguls, or tank engines serving intermediate stations missed by the expresses. One of its peculiarities was the army of travelling ticket collectors it housed. Their raison d'être was the need to collect tickets from several hundred passengers in half an hour on the numerous non-stops to Paddington, but in Great Western days they were ever watchful if not positively suspicious on their august employer's behalf. You could scarcely do what you were *told* to do, CROSS the LINE by the SUBWAY, without having to *shew* the appropriate ticket: GW tickets were always shewn not shown.

Often however the appearance of a travelling ticket collector (in the days when a guard was always in his van) would reassuringly give the traveller the chance to check he was 'all right'. You might, for example, be pleased to see him on the 2.15pm express from Shrewsbury to Paddington because at Birmingham Snow Hill it split itself in two, becoming both the 3.55pm for Paddington direct and the 4.05pm semi-fast. This stopped at Hatton (for Stratford upon Avon), Warwick, Leamington Spa (for LMS stations to Coventry, Daventry or Weedon – these could just about be called connections), Banbury (for the Cotswold line to Kingham), Oxford (for Fairford), and Reading (for Basingstoke, Southampton Central, Bournemouth Central and Portsmouth) before ending up at Paddington at 7.28 – almost an hour and a half after the fast. Travelling in the wrong part or not knowing where to change could have serious consequences. The 4.05, by the way, was the preserve of a 'Star', often in the form of No 4017 *Knight of Liege* (*Knight of the Black Eagle* until this was considered inappropriate in World War I) or No 4018 *Knight of the Grand Cross* – an exciting engine even if it was by then stripped of the brass beading over the splashers. What memories of just managing to see both trains despatched before having to rush off home in time for tea.

Similarly, if you wanted to reach certain branch-line stations on the way to the West you had to travel in that part of the *Atlantic Coast Express* that was detached at Salisbury and followed the main train much more sedately. But other branches had their own through coaches. Much more knowledge was required than on today's much more standardised services. Passengers joining the *Atlantic Coast Express* indeed sometimes had sections going to nine different destinations from which to choose. Well might it be called a 'portmanteau' express. On ordinary days most sections were a single coach, with van, first and third smoking and non-smoking, so for a through journey you might have little or no choice. But then at busy times, of course advertised on summer Saturdays, but sometimes unadvertised, the East Devon resorts or just Bude or Padstow, would have whole trains to themselves. Waiting to catch the fourth or fifth train calling itself the *Atlantic Coast Express* required determined patience.

Shrewsbury was one of those busy junctions that were a great challenge to timid old ladies travelling by themselves and a joy to the enthusiast. For here, in addition to the comings and goings of both LMS and GW trains, there were running-in turns for locomotives just out of Crewe Works, sparkling red Duchess Pacifics or Scots, mixing with equally pristine Jubilees or Compounds. The West to North expresses from South Wales or Bristol could boast 'Saints' or 'Black Fives' or in later days Britannias or Castles, the Londons glistening green Kings, the Chesters Saints or Moguls and the Staffords LNWR Prince of

Freeze

Railways do not like cold weather at all. Nobody would who depends on water for making steam. If it freezes we can't get it from the tenders into the boilers; we can't get steam into the heating pipes of the carriages.

On electric lines when there is a glazed frost – that is a quick frost after sleet or rain – it forms a thin sheet of ice over the conductor rails so that the train cannot pick up any current. It jams the doors of electric trains so that they won't open or shut. It jams points and signals.

All these things are extremely difficult to deal with once they have happened but they are fairly easy to prevent by an hour or two's work beforehand. If we light braziers and stoves by the water columns that fill the tenders; if men with lamps go round warming the injectors on engines which are not in steam; if we get our engines out of their sheds early to heat their trains for an hour before their first journey; if the signalmen and linesmen keep working their points and signals; if we keep ghost trains running on electric lines all night or use a special de-icing fluid – if we do all these things there is no reason for us to be frozen up. Always provided we get accurate weather forecasts and the strain of a long severe frost is not too much for us.

It means a lot of us getting up a lot earlier on beastly mornings to do beastly jobs. Sometimes of course we fail. Last Thursday *Britannia* herself, the first standard engine which the railways built in 1951, turned up at Liverpool Street with her tender steam heater pipe frozen. She took our 9.30 *Norfolkman* cold all the way to Norwich; and covered us with shame. – Gerry Fiennes in a broadcast to schools, February 1954.

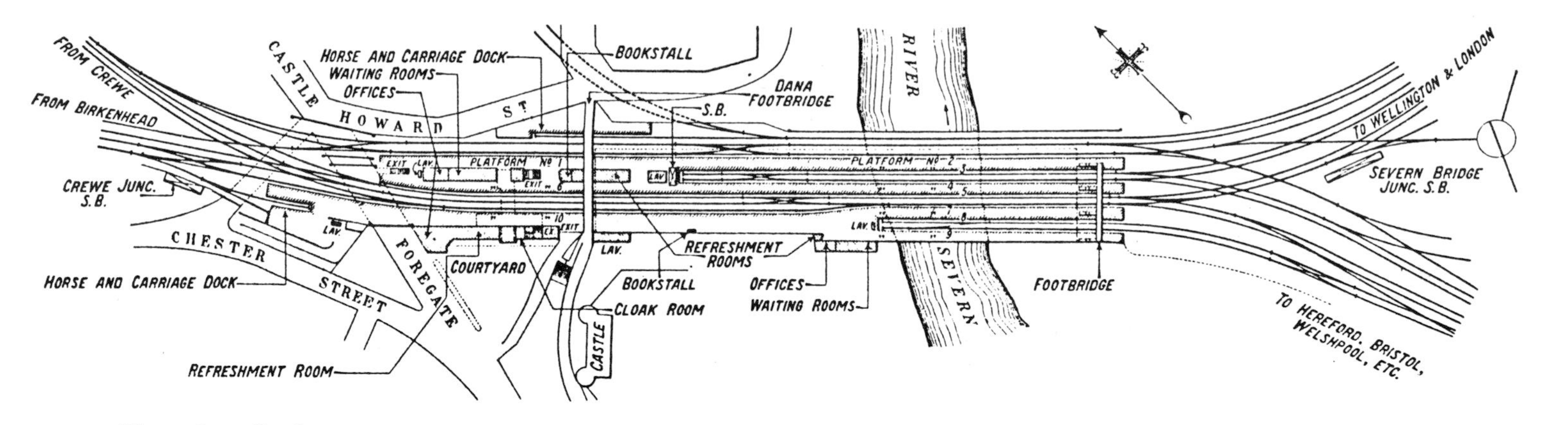

Shrewsbury Station

Wales class 4-6-0s in their ageing and declining years, not forgetting the Dukedogs or Manors off to Aberystwyth and the Fowler 2-6-4 tanks to Craven Arms and the Central Wales line. The stationmaster sported the gold braid and pork pie hat of the Great Western.

Going north west soon after leaving Rock Ferry the broad Mersey came into view, a particularly fine sight in the days when the huge four-funnel Cunard liners, *Mauritania* and *Aquitania* used the port of Liverpool before they were diverted to Southampton. Instead of docking between voyages, these great ships moored in the river – and a grand spectacle they were from the train. But a glimpse was all too short and tantalising for carriage sidings and a tunnel intervened to mark the approach of Woodside station.

There is the story of the stationmaster at Birkenhead Woodside (GWR passengers change here for Liverpool via the Mersey ferry!) spotting two separate gentlemen going round his station with tape measures looking at the advertisements and writing down details. They turned out to be from the publicity departments at Euston and Paddington respectively, one object being to see that 'my' company was getting a fair deal in advertising space. The stationmaster, Mr McNaught, tactfully invited both to lunch in the first-class refreshment room to put his own ideas forward. Rivalry between companies certainly did not end with grouping.

Birkenhead was not the only terminus where the Great Western's passengers had to change to reach their journey's end. Those on the *Torbay Express* leaving Paddington for their first holiday at Dartmouth had a nasty shock arriving at the buffer stops at Kingswear only to find the last leg of their journey was to be by a company steam ferry across the Dart estuary. But the Great Western being the Great Western did little by halves and Dartmouth had a proper 'station' with a large sign with raised metal letters declaring it to be just that. There was a full booking office, parcels office, waiting room . . . sufficient for the GW at one time to have destination boards proclaiming 'Paddington–Dartmouth'!

Although the popular image of East Coast main-line expresses was reflected in the evocative non-stop or limited-stop named trains, in reality more business was done in a humdrum manner at the many intermediate large market towns with their branches (and sometimes other railways or joint lines) providing a multitude of connections. Grantham was typical: a busy but not especially large town in itself, it had much greater railway status. It was home to a bevy of well-kept Pacifics and a place for crew changes as well as junction for Nottingham, Lincoln and Boston.

The very last timetable sheet exhibited by the LNER on Grantham platforms in 1947 detailed seventy-nine departures between 12.26am and 10.46pm. Virtually all provided connections to others and the terminating arrivals from the west and east not included in the figure. There was perpetual activity and variety. One observer even saw a couple of Great Western Castles there. For many years Halls had worked through from Banbury to Nottingham but on 14 February 1937 two cross-country

Pendennis Castle

Perhaps the saddest failure in recent years was that of No 4079 *Pendennis Castle* at Westbury on the farewell high-speed run involving three Castles on 9 May 1964. They had just reached 96mph at Lavington when a watchful inspector noticed a trail of red hot pieces of metal on the track behind. He pulled the cord and they found that No 4079 had shed a large number of her firebars. Definitely a failure. They made their way to Westbury where the only available engine was No 6999 *Capel Dewi Hall* and the footplate crew transferred themselves fearing the worst. But they performed one of the outstanding feats of the day, running the 47.20 miles to Taunton in 43.09 minutes start to stop with a maximum of 86.5mph on the descent from Somerton tunnel to Curry Rivel Junction. A fine performance for a mixed traffic engine with only 6ft 0in driving wheels and completely unprepared for the job. As the great recorder Cecil J. Allen remarked 'It was quite a day'.

Only another Castle! BR-built No 7025 Sudeley Castle *stands at the head of the up Cambrian Coast Express in Shrewsbury station during the summer of 1961. The shed plate reads 89A (Shrewsbury) and the smokebox numberplate figures have been carefully machined in accordance with Swindon practice – the other regions left them as cast. The train will have come from Pwllheli and Aberystwyth – the two portions combining at Dovey Junction and will be further strengthened at Wolverhampton, probably going on to Paddington behind a King.*

specials from Bournemouth and Hastings (via Oxford) had been too heavy for the class and Nos 5006 *Tregenna Castle* and 5045 *Bridgwater Castle* were substituted. The engines could not be turned at Nottingham and ran through to Grantham! Only twelve years before *Pendennis Castle* had given the LNER Pacifics a lesson in economy on their own ground.

Grantham will always remain in the memories of RAF servicemen and women of World War II. It was the junction for Sleaford, the station for Cranwell, one of the largest RAF training schools in Britain. Just how many tens of thousands of extra passengers got out of those dimly lit, often very dirty trains, en route for this huge piece of the establishment is impossible to say but there was always a touch of blue at Grantham round the clock. Trains would come in from main-line stations, north and south disgorging airmen and women with gas mask cases slung over their shoulders watched over by vigilant service police corporals whose eagle eyes would spot anyone 'improperly dressed'. Other personnel came behind an elderly GN 4-4-0 from Nottingham through Bottesford and Sedgebrook to find a dirty large-boilered GN Atlantic waiting to take them towards their next place of posting.

Grantham was a great place for the enthusiast for as well as an excellent selection of main-line express classes and secondary-route engines which could be easily inspected from the platforms, the shed was close by – and a top-link one to boot. Yet in the days that the real expresses were great, and you could sense the atmosphere as staff

Watching trains in Lincolnshire. A down Leeds express headed by A1 Pacific No 60123 H. A. Ivatt, *still in blue livery with electric light and original chimney, leaves Grantham in 1951. It is a Leeds Copley Hill (37B) engine. The train coming out of the bay behind K2 No 61771 is a local for Nottingham.*

prepared for a major arrival or the passage of a non-stop, most activity was with more mundane traffic with a constant shunting of vans.

The West Coast route had many attractions for the enthusiast: Rugby and Crewe were major meccas . . . of course again just the kind of place many passengers hated changing. You still meet some who complain they spent the worst hours of their lives changing trains at Crewe. And it was not only 'Oh Mr Porter' that turned it into a music hall joke. But though on a smaller scale, Carlisle had unbeatable interest.

Three main platforms (one up, one down and one reversible) and five bays once saw trains of seven different railways. Until the Pacific era, many services were double headed; not one of the great Anglo-Scottish companies could escape the hilly country to the south and north. Back in pre-grouping days when their owners painted engines in glistening black, red, blue, brown and varying shades of green and their coaches in an equally colourful kaleidoscope, there was non-ending variety, and indeed even today there remains more variety of mood and movement than at many larger and more imposing stations. To change trains in style, make it Carlisle. And for most of railway history, it was not only passengers who changed but the engines. Even the vaunted non-stop *Royal Scot* went through the ritual of engine change – though hidden away from the bustle and crowds two miles north opposite the old Caledonian shed at Kingmoor northbound and at Carlisle No 12 box southbound, opposite Upperby shed.

Change for Blackpool, Southport and the East Lancs line. Preston at the end of steam on the London Midland Region in 1968 when the only steam power for passenger and parcels trains was the Black Five and an occasional Britannia Pacific. Class 5 No 45345 was then allocated to Lostock Hall shed. Note the lamp brackets – after the introduction of electrification that on top of the smokebox was moved on to the door but to the right. The buffer beam bracket was similarly altered to allow for the appropriate 'through freight' code – one lamp directly on top of the other. All the East Lancs (rhs) section of the station is closed and the fence is already in place.

Perhaps the greatest junction of them all. Carlisle station in the early 1950s with one of the later (and unnamed) Britannia Pacifics No 70051 (later named Firth of Forth) *from Polmadie shed (66A) backing down and following a down express. A stopping train for the Maryport & Carlisle line is about to leave No 2 bay platform.*

A Message for Home

One of the privileges (or pleasant duties) of a cadet was the possession of a footplate pass. I was riding up to Victoria on a gleaming Lord St Vincent in the incomparable Maunsell olive green livery with a very heavy boat train including four Pullmans. It was an autumn evening and we were on time as we ran through the junction at Herne Hill. And then the driver, close to retirement but

continued opposite

In railway folklore it was always the engine change which was the focal point of the story, or photograph. What could be more exciting than seeing a blackberry-black LNWR Claughton giving way to a sky-blue Caledonian 4-6-0 or pair of Dunalastair 4-4-0s, or in grouping days a North British Atlantic in apple green taking over from a newly commissioned Stanier Jubilee. Even in BR times the sight of huge Pacifics changing places was something to give a tingling sensation. But back to the passengers. From Liverpool they changed for Dumfries, from Leeds for Whitehaven, from Glasgow for Newcastle or Derby, and so on with non-ending permutations, some of them throwing up regular traffic, others used only spasmodically – all helping knit together the economic and social life of the northern half of our island.

Many more people passed through or changed at Carlisle than bought their tickets there, and again there was a constant topping and tailing of trains as horseboxes and vans were shunted while passengers changed platforms. There was such a distinctive daily pattern that without knowing the time of day you could quickly have guessed it. In the 1930s, for instance, the semi-fasts collecting passengers off the overnight trains had all gone by around nine o'clock and the station dozed for almost three hours before the next flurry of activity. One of the first of the bunched-up arrivals was the 9.30am luncheon-car express from Glasgow to Liverpool and Manchester due at 11.45am; it had to be got away

smartly at 11.51am not to delay the up *Royal Scot*. Worse still, before the *Scot* arrived the *Thames–Clyde* express from Glasgow (St Enoch) came in at 11.55am exchanging a *Royal Scot* for a Jubilee before it was due out again within five minutes. Then there were the semi-fast connections from the coast line out of Carnforth at 11.55am and Lancaster at 12 noon both using the main down platform. At 12.6pm the up *Royal Scot* behind a Princess Pacific pulled in to the single up platform, loco crews were changed before leaving at 12.10pm. Meanwhile an LNER train from Newcastle came into one of the south end bays at 12.18pm behind a Gresley Shire class 4-4-0 – always a Shire never a Hunt. All this was followed by a succession of up trains, the Glasgow–Birmingham (a through *Royal Scot* working from Glasgow to Crewe, 12.23–12.28) while an LNER connecting semi-fast left the other south end up bay for Newcastle at 12.20. At 12.32 the 6.45am express from Aberdeen to Euston arrived behind a Compound and three minutes later the *Thames–Forth* express from Edinburgh to St Pancras behind a Gresley Pacific. Both trains changed engines, the Compound for a Pacific and the Pacific for a Compound. The Aberdeen train with its five or six coaches may have looked odd behind a Pacific but had to pick up a number of through portions en route and was well up to thirteen coaches by the time it got to London. The Aberdeen train left at 12.40pm and the *Thames–Forth* at 12.44pm. In just on one hour important expresses

Change here for Windermere. Oxenholme c1960 with an express at the up main platform hauled by an LMS class 5 4-6-0 No 45032. The Windermere branch train is waiting in the down loop under the overall roof and a class 4 2-6-4T stands outside the station wall. Note the complicated track layout leading to the down loop lines.

continued
a splendid runner, left the regulator and brake to his fireman, got out an oil lamp, primed the wick a bit, lit it and crossed to the right hand side of the footplate, leaned out waving the lamp slowly up and down as the train approached Brixton. Then he blew it out and put it away and took over the engine again. 'Always does that,' said the fireman, 'to his wife. He's done that for nearly forty years.' – Patrick Stevenson.

From South to Southwest. West Country class 4-6-2 No 34048 Crediton *enters Salisbury from the east end with the Brighton–Plymouth through train. The three-disc headcode is described as Brighton–Salisbury so possibly the one over the right hand buffer (from the driver's viewpoint) was removed at Salisbury to give the normal West of England code.*

had come into Carlisle from the north at 11.45, 11.55, 12.16, 12.23, 12.32 and 12.38 with local connecting trains at 11.55, 12.00, 12.08 and a stopper from Newcastle at 12.39. There was then a slight pause until the morning luncheon-car express from Leeds to Glasgow drifted in headed by a brand new Jubilee which hooked off and dropped back to Durran Hill shed. The train split here with a Scot taking the Glasgow portion forward and a North British Atlantic (plus an LNER buffet car and extra coaches for passengers joining at Carlisle) the Edinburgh portion, running over the Waverley route. The first section left at 1pm, the second three minutes later. Last among the midday rush was the 1.12pm arrival from the south, a Crewe to Glasgow and Perth train leaving at 1.18pm.

Comparative peace now descended until the next intensive period which began just before 3.30pm with the succession of down trains arriving and departing. And all day long there were locals to Whitehaven, Newcastle, Silloth and indeed 'all stations' on both the two north and south routes. At times the local business reigned supreme . . . but not at night when the sleeping-car expresses, postals, newspapers and parcels once more imported a very different atmosphere. If you could stand the pace, each of the twenty-four hours on Citadel station in the 1930s was one to savour. And though we speak of the 1930s, in fact it was much the same right through to the end of steam.

Then, Perth, gateway to the Highlands. General station (one must not overlook the *other*, Princes Street, much nearer the town centre but closed in 1966) was another of those from which expresses radiated to all points of the compass – north to Inverness, north east to Aberdeen, east to Dundee, south to Edinburgh and south west to Glasgow, Carlisle and much of England. Remarkably, only two of these prime routes are no more, the direct Edinburgh line having been taken over in parts by the M90 motorway, and the Aberdeen trains diverted from the Strathmore line to run via Dundee. There were also sparse stopping trains on lesser routes to Crieff, Alloa, Ladybank and North Fife; only the Ladybank line clings tenuously to life. And we must not forget the country stations along the main lines, albeit there were seldom more than a stopping train in the morning and another in late afternoon.

The pattern of expresses had an almost God-given timelessness about it. And until the Beeching era their connections were similarly immutable. Travel overnight from the south, be you laird or sassenach,

Perth General Station

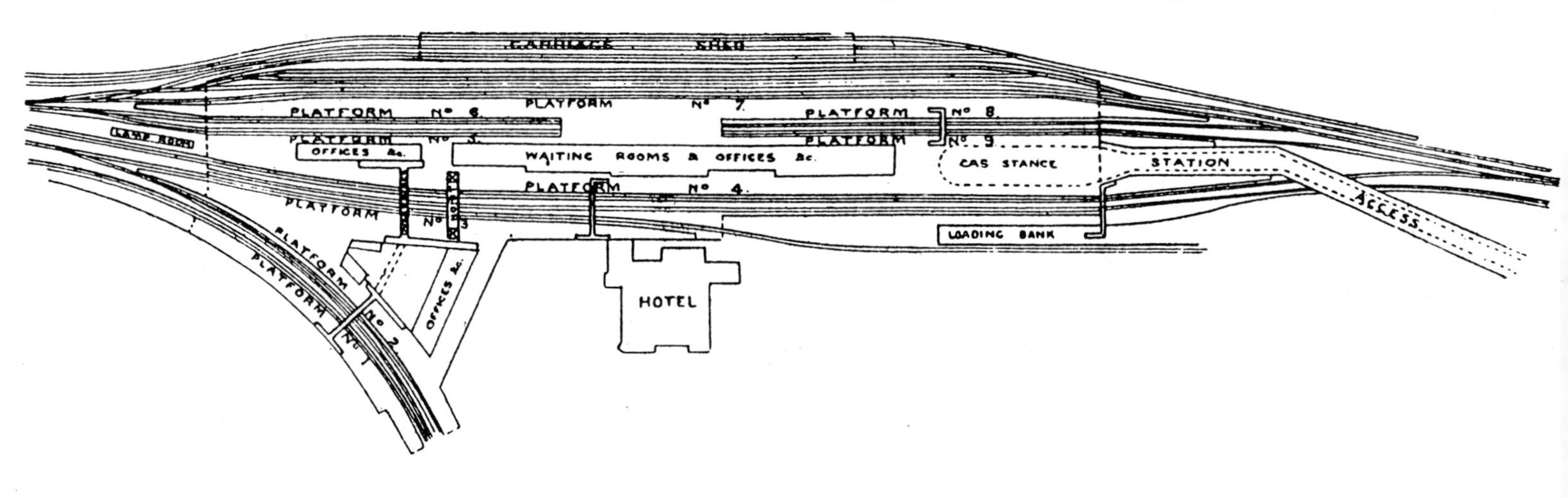

and you were important, someone to be pandered to. Step from your sleeper on the *Royal Highlander* on to the platform at five in the morning, and within half an hour you could even get a through local to Blairgowrie. It was the only one of the day! Arrive on the Perth sleeper an hour later, and before you had time to get breakfast you could be on your way to intermediate stations on the lines to Inverness, Aberdeen, Edinburgh, Dundee or Ladybank. But arrive by any other trains, and apart from the Dundee line your prospects were much less rosy. There was another curious omission; the direct line from Edinburgh Waverley offered little in the way of connections at Perth for north and north east. Perth had been a Caledonian station, and thirty years later it still showed; Edinburgh people were constrained to travel from Princes Street and get their connections at either Larbert or Stirling.

One concession to passenger convenience was made, however, and it caused mild operating headaches. Perth station is almost two separate entities, with the two long through platforms Nos 4 and 7, each with its loop, for the Aberdeen and Inverness trains, and the two Dundee line platforms Nos 1 and 2, curving away sharply from St Leonard's Junction at the south end. The LMS, ever frugal with their engine and train miles was wont to run certain expresses between Glasgow and Aberdeen with Dundee sections. Northbound, these divided on the main line at St Leonard's (for which two minutes was allowed) the Dundee portion pulling into platform No 2 and leaving the Aberdeen coaches to be rehorsed and drawn into platform No 7. Southbound it was a more cumbersome operation; the Dundee portion arrived first, was set back into a south end bay and in due course had the Aberdeen section set back on to it, leaving fifteen minutes after arrival of the Dundee coaches. That left the coaches right way round for the next working from Glasgow.

Wherever you went, you saw evidence of expenditure on the grand scale when railways had a monopoly and of economy caused by road competition and in the thirties the depression. It is one of the ironies that not merely were the expresses much faster and more luxurious but the local train services more frequent on many routes after the railways ceased to have it all their own way. At stations such as Shrewsbury, Grantham, Carlisle and Perth, not having things all their own way generally meant the railways steadily devoting more resources to long-

Quick Change

The *Atlantic Coast Express* would sweep fast and splendidly into the wide, curved down main platform at Salisbury. The moment it stopped, the fireman leapt down between tender and train and simultaneously the driver, spinning the reversing wheel, set back. Vacuum broken, coupling unhitched and let fall against the tender with a clang. Quick blow up of the brake with the reversing wheel spun again as the fireman got out from under, and the King Arthur was already moving forward as he rejoined it. Instantly, the regulator was opened wide and in full fore gear the engine absolutely tore off down the main line as if going non-stop to Exeter. About 600yd away it braked sharply and swung left into Salisbury Loco. The moment it was clear of the crossover at the platform end, the replacement Arthur, often with a Drummond water cart eight-wheel tender, would move back on the adjoining road, over the crossover and gently set back on the train. Coupled at once, the new engine blew up the train brake – thirteen coaches, which took rather longer! And then right away to Sidmouth Junction, Exeter, Ilfracombe, Torrington, Bude, Padstow and Plymouth! And this operation from stop to re-start was allowed exactly four minutes; an observer once saw it done in a little over three. – Patrick Stevenson.

Car sleeper. Stanier class 5 4-6-0 No 45178 leaves Perth at the head of the 5.16pm (17.16) for Marylebone on 6 July 1957, a service that would well be appreciated if it were still in action today. On the right is a Perth–Edinburgh local behind an unknown V2 class 2-6-2.

distance passengers. Even in 1900 those going more than a couple of hundred miles were an elite few. They provided the glamour, of course, but only very thin icing on the cake. The proportion of revenue they contributed rose steadily, though even in the 1930s and 1950s the number of day-time expresses on routes now boasting an hourly service could be counted in most cases on the fingers of one hand, in nearly all on two. The variety was of course greater: Leicester for example boasted two day-time Anglo-Scottish expresses. So whereas today the arrival of an HST causes little more stir than that of a commuter train, *every* express was once a major institution, met by a small army of railwaymen from stationmaster to wheel-tapper, refreshment trolley operator to porters anxious to serve and earn coppers.

Only on Southern lines did the passage of expresses as well as more humdrum trains have anything ordinary about it. To North, East and West, but especially in those great cathedrals of steam in the North and Scotland, the arrival and departure of major expresses was each one a great occasion. See the enginemen changing over, the vans being opened and worked at lightning speed, passengers anxiously watching over their mountains of luggage, the platform inspector glancing at his watch ready to urge the pace with the first blast on his whistle. Of the two hundred passengers on board (perhaps fifteen enviously glanced at eating their lunch in the diner) well over three-quarters will use at least one connecting train to complete their journey, and some will need two or even three. Very few of them regard their journey as other than an important, exceptional event whose timings they have carefully rehearsed. The local passengers at the next platform are less likely to visit all the towns listed on the destination boards than they are to emigrate.

Third Hymn, Second Lesson

The first hymn was always over and the ministers at the churches on either side of the main line were just starting prayers when the 11.5 express to Paddington ran into Teignmouth, because of the shortness of the platform the locomotive stopping well forward, right between the churches. Occasionally it would stop on a dead, and the congregations could tell the pressure the driver must be under from the general hissing and puffing. Once one of the ministers even included him in the prayers . . . no doubt hoping he'd be on his way the sooner.

Then one Sunday the engine would not budge at all. Prayers, second hymn, first lesson, third hymn, second lesson . . . wasting steam was lifting the safety valve and making concentration difficult. And two enthusiastic members of the congregation could restrain their curiosity no longer, slipping out to see help coming in the form of a second loco.

The express incidentally ran via Bristol and at Swindon stopped one side of the up island while on the other side was a York train with its LNER loco, at certain periods the only one in the week to work beyond Oxford.

North Cornwall junction. Wadebridge on a spring Saturday, 18 May 1959 with U class 2-6-0 No 31809 (once the 2-6-4 tank River Dart*) backing down on to the 12.58 Padstow–Waterloo. This portion would have been attached to the main Plymouth–London train at Okehampton. The 2-6-0 was probably an Exmouth Junction engine outstationed at Wadebridge and/or Okehampton on a daily basis, changing every day or so: it would have worked the train to Okehampton. Note the paper number D2 on the coach corridor window. This would almost certainly have been a reserved-seat train. The Padstow section was worked in by T9 class No 30711.*

Luxury Trains and Streamliners

Take your chance. A finely panelled high-backed mahogany-framed armchair, deeply sprung and well-padded with leather upholstery, set in pairs at tables astride a central carpeted passageway, with ornately timber-panelled walls often in walnut or rosewood decorated with inlaid patterns, clusters of 'electroliers' suspended from the finely moulded ceilings. Or a low-back sofa-style armchair with loose cushions, upholstered all over in pastel moquette, with wall-to-wall carpeting, lighting hidden behind cornices, pressure ventilation and stainless steel or aluminium door and window fittings providing relief to the all-over single or twin colour areas of rexine or painted surfaces. Whatever the style, the railways provided the luxurious best during a period of innovation that World War II brought to a close.

It was the era of the 'crack' express, one or two expresses out of the handful of daily trains singled out for special treatment in speed, comfort, and amenities. They were invariably named services, the title often reflecting destinations or characters or events associated with the route.

Of course, what was 'luxury' in one decade was often the norm in the next. In the 1890s, when the conventional express train on most routes consisted of non-corridor six-wheelers, bogie stock with corridors and restaurant facilities was luxury indeed. But ten years on into the new century when bogie coaches were becoming commonplace, 'luxury' called for electric instead of gas lighting, better seats and end doors to prevent passengers being bothered by others scrambling across their knees. There were better standards of decor with (as in our opening examples) fine timber panelling and mouldings instead of plain deal boards.

The Great Northern's Sheffield sets of 1906 certainly raised luxury standards, but the LNWR trains of 1907/8 for the American boat specials between Euston and Liverpool Riverside connecting with the great Atlantic liners (and the broadly similar stock for the afternoon Anglo-Scottish trains between Euston and Glasgow/Edinburgh) then led the luxury field. They were the railway companies' response to the advances in luxury train travel evolved by the Pullman Car Company in Britain from the mid 1870s. George Mortimer Pullman, whose name would for ever be associated with luxury, appalled by the poor standards of accommodation on American railroads in the 1850s, had already made his mark across the Atlantic by producing his own luxurious trains for hire. Pullmans were not immediately successful in Britain but they made more of a mark after the UK concern had separated from its US parent. In 1907, for example, was built a new train of cars for what was to become a daily *Southern Belle* between London and Brighton. During World War I third-class cars were added and for the modest supplement of just 9d. Third-class cars usually had fixed seating, tables for two on one

West coast glory. An official LMS Publicity photograph of the down Royal Scot, 10.00 Euston–Glasgow on Bushey troughs c1934. The locomotive is No 6200 Princess Royal, *the first Stanier 4-6-2 built in 1933; it is shown with the original straight-sided tender.*

High-speed trial. The Silver Jubilee set on a trial trip to Scotland on 26 September 1936 (it was a Saturday as this was in use on weekdays) with the LNER (ex-NER) dynamometer car at the front of the train. It is headed by No 2511 Silver King *and is passing through Morpeth. The run was between Newcastle and Edinburgh and was one of several in preparation for a new high-speed service leaving London at 12.15 and going on to Aberdeen arriving at 21.30 with Newcastle, Edinburgh, Kircaldy, Dundee and Montrose stops. In the event the train became The Coronation running only to Edinburgh and leaving Kings Cross at 16.00.*

The trial that almost came to grief. The LMS (possibly reluctantly) followed the LNER's example in 1937 of building a streamlined train for its Euston–Glasgow service. Strictly speaking it was only the locomotives that were streamlined, the coaches were standard LMS vehicles which were painted blue with white stripes and given pressure ventilation. A test trip was run on 29 June 1937 from Euston to Crewe which nearly came to grief when it hit the curves at the south end of Crewe station at 56mph after attaining 114mph on the descent from Whitmore. This is seen here passing Kilburn High Road hauled by the first streamlined class 7P 4-6-2 No 6220 Coronation.

The LNER was to the fore in introducing high-speed streamlined trains consisting of specially constructed coaches in articulated pairs. The down Coronation, 16.00 Kings Cross–Edinburgh is near Hadley Wood in 1937 hauled by No 4489 Dominion of Canada.

Southern luxury. Of all the express trains with luxury connotations the Golden Arrow was certainly one of the first as well as the best known. Providing a service which cossetted first-class passengers between London and Paris (including their own reserved section on the cross-Channel steamer) it lived up to its name until 1972 when it became impossible to justify the allocation of one set of coaches, now some forty years old, for only one trip daily to and from the Channel coast. The locomotive is No 21C140 (later named Crewkerne)

side of the passageway and tables for four on the other, while first-class cars had single moveable armchairs at tables for two on each side of the passageway. Some of the cars had kitchens, and meals and refreshments were available to all at their seats. Personal service was a Pullman hallmark with the attendants at the doors to help passengers on and off at stations and to show new passengers to their seats, and taking charge of luggage during the journey.

In the 1920s Pullmans were steadily introduced on more routes especially in the East and South, such as what was at first called the *Harrogate Pullman* and later renamed the *Queen of Scots* running through to Glasgow, the *West Riding Pullman* between Kings Cross and Leeds (later with other Yorkshire starting points retitled the *Yorkshire Pullman*), and the *Thanet Belle* from Victoria to Ramsgate. The *Bournemouth Belle* followed in the early 1930s when the Southern also used single or pairs of Pullmans on many ordinary services. Doyen of the Southern Pullmans was undoubtedly the *Golden Arrow* boat train providing the British end of the Paris route with something worthy of the patronage of the rich and famous.

With electrification, the *Southern Belle* was replaced by a multiple unit *Brighton Belle*, also used by the famous, particularly many of the acting profession living on the South Coast. It was also the only luxury service in Britain which the working man, if he could afford to travel at all, could for a small supplement use for a day out to the seaside. It and the *Golden Arrow* came to an end in 1972.

The *Flying Scotsman* (and its predecessors) had always been the leader on the East Coast route. New stock was built by the NER and GNR in 1914. In 1924 the new LNER upgraded it again with the latest type coaches, though hardly in the luxury bracket. And in 1928, when it was to be booked to run non-stop between Kings Cross and Edinburgh, it was time for a further rethink. Competition for the Scottish traffic was hotting up and, since there was still a longstanding agreement not to cut the schedule (running non-stop actually meant going slower) the emphasis had to be on luxury. Outside designers were called in to devise the decor of the restaurant cars. The first-class cars were finished in what was described as Louis XIV style with low-backed loose armchairs blending with painted wall panels in stone picked out with blue mouldings. The moulded panels on the ceiling were highlighted by lights hidden discreetly behind the curtain pelmets, and the spaciousness of the interior was enhanced by the elimination of luggage racks. What might be called gimmicks were added in the form of hairdressing saloon, ladies' retiring room and cocktail bar.

The LMS answer concentrated on the basic hardware of luxury stock. The principal features were the adoption of end-only entrance doors; indeed they were soon standard on LMS side-corridor stock which became familiar for its large picture windows with rotating glass vane ventilators above them, and a high standard of seating comfort. The first design, introduced to the *Royal Scot* in 1928, was semi-open first and a first-class lounge brake, seating respectively just 30 and 10 passengers. The semi-open first had three side-corridor compartments seating just four passengers each in deeply sprung well-padded seats with loose cushions; everybody had a corner seat. A large toilet compartment in the vehicle centre with space for a loose chair divided the compartment end from the open saloon dining end, laid out in three bays of seats, in pairs on one side and fours on the other. Additional coaches were built in following years and added to other services but the lounge brakes with leather-upholstered armchairs and sofa were not repeated.

The LNER also developed end-door designs for some of its stock from the early 1930s (but continued to build large numbers of side-door stock until World War II) and it too, built some first-class coaches for the *Flying Scotsman* in 1930 with four-seat compartments but with the added refinement of pressure ventilation. Then, five years later it embarked on the ultimate luxury train, the first streamliner, the *Silver Jubilee* between Kings Cross and Newcastle. It was not the light seven-coach formation (with two articulated twin sets at each end, a triplet dining car set between) that was remarkable: what made this train stand out were the interior decor and the leap forward in insulation. Certainly the first-class compartments seated only four to a compartment but compartments that were very much akin to a private drawing room. The seats were fixed but were deep and welcoming and the upholstery was carried round to the walls on each side and below the windows. Windows themselves were double glazed and every bodyside space was filled with insulating material to deaden sound and to form a heat-loss barrier. Pressure heating and ventilation meant that fresh air was introduced without the need to have windows open although all the large bodyside windows had sliding window ventilators in the top quarter. Visually the outside of the set was remarkable for the train was finished in silver grey Rexine covering the steel body panels. Third-class compartments were less ornate but still a vast improvement on ordinary LNER stock. The train was so popular that an extra third-class coach had to be provided and in two years the supplements (5s first and 3s third) had returned the whole investment.

In 1937 the LNER expanded its streamlined train fleet with two more services, the *Coronation* between Kings Cross and Edinburgh and the *West Riding Limited* between Kings Cross and Leeds. Four sets were built, two for the former, one for the latter and one standby, all basically similar. The eight-coach trains were arranged as articulated twins (brake third and third, third and kitchen third, two firsts, and kitchen third and brake third), all open saloon stock foreshadowing BR practice of 30 years later. Meals were served at every seat. To overcome resistance to the open saloon arrangement each

Holiday named train. The up Torbay Express on the Devon coast between Teignmouth and Dawlish on 9 August 1956. The engine, carrying a new headboard, is No 5038 Morlais Castle*; it is heading a recently painted chocolate and cream set of BR Mk 1 coaches. Almost a generation earlier, in 1929/30, the GWR ran an experimental Torquay Pullman but this was not an economic proposition.*

first-class bay was screened by partitions to give four-seat alcoves, while the two-plus-one seating in the thirds was divided into pairs of seat bays. Interior decor was in pastel colours with a mainly green theme relieved by aluminium fretting trim. Insulation standards were even higher than in the *Silver Jubilee* sets. Externally the sets were finished in two shades of blue. The *Coronation* trains were also graced in summer with a streamlined observation car which included rotating armchairs. The LNER also built new train sets with interiors of much the same standards and decor as the streamliners, but with conventional teak bodies, for the *East Anglian* service and the *Hook Continental*.

The LMS answer was the Euston–Glasgow *Coronation Scot*, hauled by the new streamlined Coronation Pacifics. The LMS coaches, though, were not all new and most were refurbished from existing stock of the then standard Stanier type with steel flush-sided bodies dating from the mid 1930s. The third class was largely of open saloon pattern though with two-plus-one seating at tables of four and two, but the first class was mainly side-corridor compartments with an open first for dining. The first-class compartments seated only four passengers. Decor was not remarkable and continued the 'Empire timbers' tradition for partitions and bodyside internal finishes. The coaches had pressure heating and ventilation, an obvious feature by the large ducts mounted along the coach roofs.

Just two years later the LMS embarked on a new *Coronation Scot*, mostly formed as articulated twins, initially for exhibition at the New York World Fair and including a sleeping car and cocktail bar. After World War II two more trains were built, but alas the *Coronation Scot* was never revived. The post-war coaches

with their spacious and non-standard seating did not fit in with seat reservation charts for the heavier patronage of the time and were allocated to Manchester area commuter services, relief and excursion trains, giving many passengers a pleasant surprise.

The years following World War II were not conducive to further luxury services except for Pullman, with which the LMS and GWR would have nothing to do. But early in the acceleration of the mid 1950s modernisation programme came a great step forward in luxury travel and again under the Pullman banner, though by then within the BR orbit. This was in the form of the Blue Pullmans – diesel-electric multiple-unit trains with streamlined power cars at each end including passenger accommodation, six-car first-class-only trains for the *Midland Pullman* between St Pancras and Manchester, and eight-car bi-class units for the Western's *Bristol* and *Birmingham Pullmans*. Full air conditioning, better sound insulation, ergonomically designed seats and wall to wall carpeting were features which combined to provide a totally new concept of train travel. Traditional Pullman service of at-seat meals and refreshments was provided and the trains commanded a supplement.

The Blue Pullmans ran through the 1960s and just into the 1970s. They brought luxury service for a few, but in many ways heralded the HST 125s, though they had nothing like their power. Of course there was no at-seat meal service on the HSTs, but the general standard of comfort was (and still is) remarkable. Today's story is not of the exceptional train of quality and speed but of a vast range of near-standardised super services. That, however, there is always room for the special touch is emphasised by the restoration of Pullman service for first-class passengers on many business trains (albeit using Mk 3 or Mk 4 stock) and the 1980s growth of the luxury-train market (described in *British Rail in the 1980s*, uniform with this work).

By Pullman to the Hampshire coast. One of Nine Elms' Merchant Navy class Pacifics No 35010 Blue Star *runs through the heart of the New Forest at Ashurst on 4 April 1953 at the head of the down Bournemouth Belle. The train loaded seven to ten Pullmans according to season (there are eight in this photograph) and in its final years sometimes up to twelve plus a bogie brake van making it the heaviest express passenger train on the Southern Region's Western Division.*

Western express. The Merchant Venturer was one of the trains named to celebrate the Festival of Britain in 1951. It ran between Paddington and Bristol and vice versa. The up train 17.25 from Bristol is seen here awaiting departure from Temple Meads on a winter's evening in the late 1950s. The name disappeared in 1965 when the Bristol–London service was recast.

A Great Express Train Passes

Almost certainly the world's best known train, The Flying Scotsman has been the East Coast main line's train standard bearer for nigh on a lifespan. Its heyday perhaps was the LNER period when Gresley's A1 and A3 Pacifics carrying names of racehorses ran the summer non-stop services from Kings Cross to Edinburgh with the then new corridor tenders. The crews changed over from and to a reserved compartment in the leading coach en route. With advancement of motive power the glamour dropped a little and now the only sign of a once splendid express is a paper notice attached to the windows of an HST. Soon even that will be history and a slick electric engine will haul the train at ever increasing speeds and silent standardised comfort. Sadly, it is a quicker service but no longer a Great Express Train.

1930. The resumption for the summer season of the non-stop service between London and Edinburgh. A3 Pacific No 2746 Fairway *leaves Kings Cross with the down train on Monday 7 July 1930.*

1953/4. The down train at Newcastle behind the now preserved A4 Pacific No 60009 Union of South Africa. *By this time the train was stopping at Newcastle and there was no need for the corridor tender. The engine is in dark green livery.*

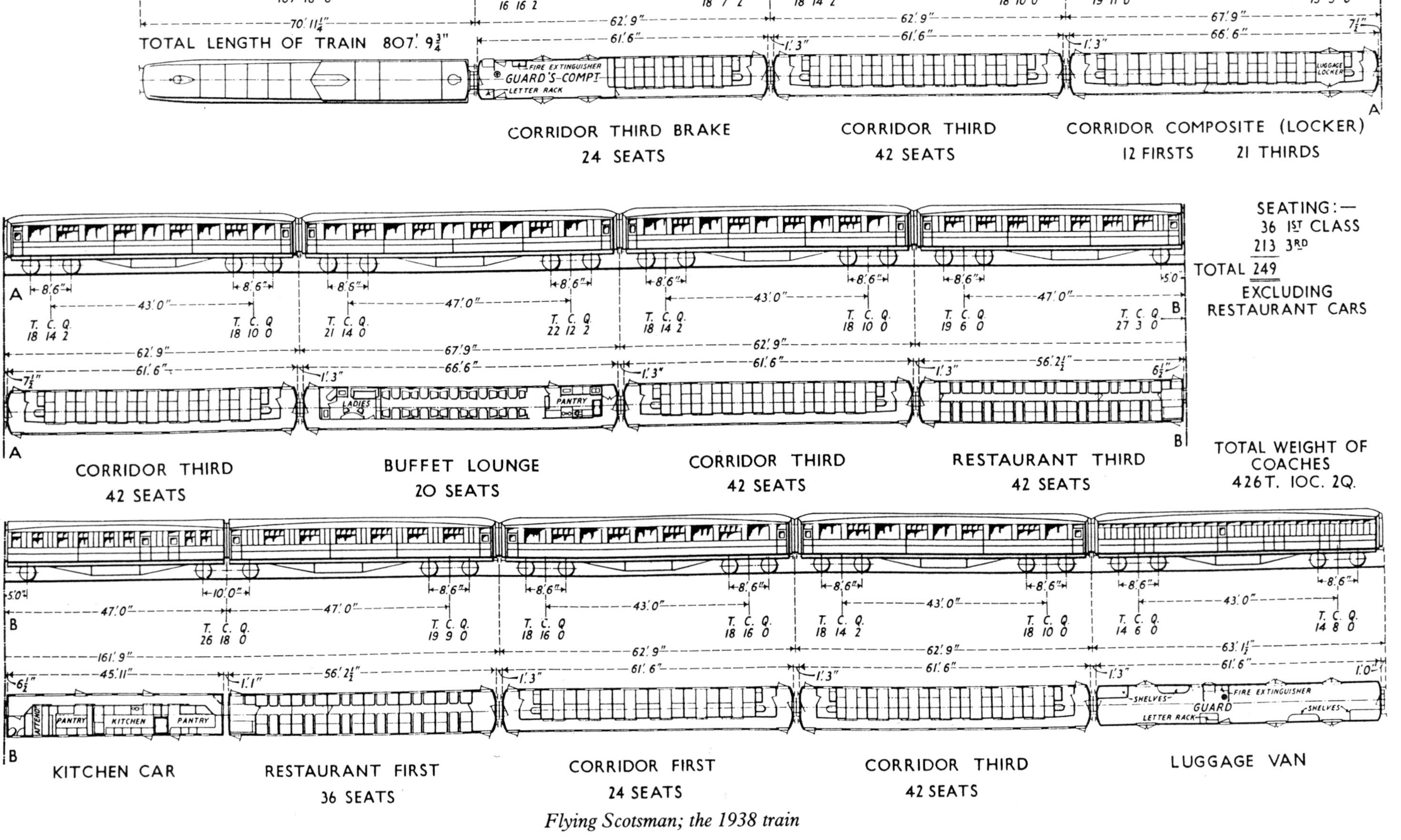

Flying Scotsman; the 1938 train

1965. The age of the Deltics. The Up train now numbered 1A35 and with Flying Scotsman wings above the panel numerals passes through York, a station almost unchanged even today. The Deltic No 9010 The King's Own Scottish Borderer *is in BR two-tone green livery.*

1978. HST 254022/09 (rear) speeds along the cliff tops near Lamberton with the down Flying Scotsman, 10.00 KX to Edinburgh on 6 October 1978. There are two catering vehicles in the train – an eight-coach set.

As Good as Pacifics
I moved to the shed in 1953 when steam was still working to Ramsgate and Hastings and over some Central Section routes. Our mainstay was the Schools class, by now getting elderly, but still capable of brilliant performance and excellent timekeeping. They were worked exceedingly hard. The Hastings line was a gruelling route, with its severe gradients and many slacks, and Bricklayer's Arms took pride that the heaviest steam-hauled train out of Cannon Street, the 5.6pm to Hastings, 359 tons tare, was worked by them on a St Leonards Schools. Little time could be set against the engines; but sometimes delays made punctuality north of Tunbridge Wells very difficult. In the hands of Ted Jakes, an old Brighton man, a Schools would come down through Hildenborough at close on ninety miles an hour sustaining eighty or more over the level track near Headcorn with eleven coaches. They were great engines, ideal for their job; the line without these is the poorer. They were, I think, the only 4-4-0s to work regularly in a link with Pacifics.

One feature that surprised me about Bricklayer's Arms was the use of grade two Welsh coal whereas at Camden we had grade one Barnsley Hards – that is when there were not trucks of firebricks or drums of oil emptied into the hopper by mistake! Much did depend on the fuel and the Welsh seemed more uncertain than the Yorkshire. – Norman Harvey.

Preparation on the shed. A rebuilt Royal Scot, No 46127 Old Contemptibles *still in the last LMS express-engine livery of black with straw lining gets a final polish on Holyhead shed in the summer of 1950. Its trip to London will take 5 hours 24 minutes and the locomotive will return on the 20.50 from Euston – the night mail service.*

7
DAY TRIP TO LONDON

THEY of course know that in a few hours they will be the crew of merely one of a string of expresses chasing each other into the capital, but now they relish the thought that they are about to take out the locomotive for the day's most important service. 'Lovely morning and all should be well with the world,' says the foreman to the driver, knowing that he will welcome today's extra income. This top turn in the top link comes up about eight times a year, and has everything in its favour: the best engine the shed can turn out, the longest mileage (how he enjoys earning a whole hour's pay each fifteen miles at full speed once the first 140 have been clocked up, though you have to work for the 75 minutes' pay for preparation time), a pleasant ride back on the cushions (they couldn't afford to pay you to drive it both ways!), and the feeling of general responsibility with the chance of the local MP, bishop and titled passengers in your care.

The fireman likes it too: civilised hours, no hanging about, and the driver always in a good mood. And they are bound to have sorted out any minor technical problems reported last night. Here we go; ten minutes for signing on and reading notices (no major problems on the road today), five for finding the engine (not that hard here, it positively stands out for all to see), and the mileage to look forward to. He recalls how several hours of overtime were earned when they were caught by a flood on the return run years ago and thinks it would make more sense to pay extra for getting there punctually.

Half an hour before starting time the engine is signalled off shed and backs on to the main down through the tunnel towards the station. They pass two engines also tender first coming back to depot after working an overnight passenger and a parcels. With steam lifting the safety valve, there is no doubt which of them is ready to start its day's work. They have the calling-on signal and hook up twenty minutes to go. First a final check round. The fireman goes to buy his *Daily Herald* and reports that Lady So and So was standing next to him. Since there won't be time once they are under way, they have an extra cup of tea, the driver almost draped over the cab window so he can see what is happening along the platform, especially first class.

Ten minutes to go and the guard (who reported at the station and has a shorter day) comes to report the load. Nine bogies. No surprise there. It is nearly always nine in summer, eight in winter, steam heating equalling one as they all knew. It is Monday, and yes, as expected, the MP boards straight into the restaurant car. They'll have kept his usual seat. 'Guess what,' says the station inspector. 'Mr Whatsit is travelling

6P
6127

Day trip to London. Britannia Pacific No 70032 Tennyson *leaves Manchester London Road (now Piccadilly) with a London-bound express around 1955 – probably the 12.05 to Euston. No 70032 is a Manchester Longsight-based engine.*

Confirmation
'At what time does the 10.10 go tomorrow?' asks the passenger.
'At ten past ten,' replies the booking clerk. 'Next.'
Every booking clerk had them . . . people who knew the answers but somehow needed confirmation before setting out on the journey of the year.

third.' They are outraged that someone so prominent and well-to-do should deprive their employer of its just due.

The doors of the rear van close as the ticket collector passes somewhat late. Trouble at home, perhaps. Meantime the seat reservation officer has sorted out an isolated case of two people being booked for the same seat, though why anyone bothers to reserve at all from here is a mystery since the train is never more than a quarter full on departure. Joining at the next city, that's different.

One minute to go. All doors are closed, and one has to be opened for a late arrival, a young man who looks as though he doesn't mind going to London today or tomorrow. The guard and ticket collector exchange glances. Then the station inspector blows his whistle, the guard waves his flag, the driver sounds the whistle, and off they go . . . just as the chief steward calls the train for first breakfast, though most going to have it have long taken their seats and regulars have started on their tea or coffee. Unlike the rest of the crew who take this crack train only occasionally, the restaurant-car staff are on it permanently, five days a week in winter, six in summer. Good regular work with (as one of the young stewards with an expensive taste in motorcycles puts it) plenty of rest days on which you can earn overtime.

Climbing starts at once. Over the Alps first and then after the stop at the largest city en route over the Rockies, as local parlance has it. Several small stops before the city, though, one of them with a branch connection that on good days might provide a dozen through to London. The city stop is the only one on the whole route where things get temporarily disorganised. Usually more passengers join here than

Shropshire junction, Shrewsbury station looking north in the very early 1960s as the roof is being demolished. In the platform is LMS built Stanier Black Five No 45189 of Crewe North (5A) shed whilst on the right is an unknown Hall with train code number V89 (in full 1V89 indicating that it is an express bound for the Western Region) waiting to take over for the run to Bristol. The train is the 08.35 Liverpool to Penzance (SO).

Sunday Standards. A return 'Television Excursion' to Glasgow waiting to leave Oban station on 24 May 1960. The engines are BR Standard class fives Nos 73108 and 73072.

45189
7
V89
73108
310
73108

THE
MID-DAY SCOT
71000
71000

The Duke of Gloucester *works hard on Camden Bank shortly after leaving Euston with the Midday Scot. This painting by Alan Fearnley was commissioned by the 71000 (Duke of Gloucester) Steam Locomotive Trust, and appears in* The Railway Paintings of Alan Fearnley *published by David & Charles. As Alan Fearnley points out, the run must have been early in the Duke's history, since the locomotive proved unreliable and soon became relegated to less important duties. The locomotive is now preserved after restoration to running order.*

46225
DUCHESS OF GLOUCESTER
46225
45272

Western tea. One of the more civilised aspects of rail travel is the ability to take meals/refreshment whilst en route. Afternoon tea on a Penzance–Paddington express in BR Mk II 'open' stock.

everywhere else together, and there is a general dashing to and fro as the classes sort themselves out and some people try to bring their luggage into the restaurant car and are told to take a seat in the train and wait until second sitting is called. There are several barrowfuls of baggage, too. The driver has time to go round the engine with oil can, the fireman to trim the fire and bring some coal forward for the sharp climb up the Rockies. The safety valve lifts before they have the right away.

Thus far they have really been a local train ferrying people to school, office, shop and hospital and just happening to pick up a few for London. Now the tone is quite different. Only one more stop before the capital, and that is at a country junction where few people will get out. This is now a real London train, and for the first time it becomes a real express, although it has had express headlamps from the start. The hardest work of the day is done on the first half hour out of the city, by the fireman and by the restaurant crew as they get into swing with second breakfast. Only the guard and ticket collector have it easy; the collector went through the train the first time before the city but will wait until the final call has been made before going through again and collecting the London-bound tickets since they will not be needed again. The travelling lavatory attendant who got on at the city joins them after making her first inspection of the lavatories complete with brush and other equipment. She is an innovation and welcome too.

It is, by the way, the mid 1950s, one of the best periods for great express trains, though you would need to be a real expert to tell the

Two typical Indian Summer shed scenes. No 46225 Duchess of Gloucester *on the turntable at Camden shed in February 1959 and Barrow Road shed (ex MR) Bristol in July 1961 showing a number of Stanier Black Fives and one of the Ivatt class 2 2-6-2 tanks in the centre. On the right is an ex Midland class 3F 0-6-0, a Jinty 0-6-0 tank and an 8F 2-8-0. The passing passenger train appears to be headed by a Black Five.*

Driver's eye view. A down express approaching the east portal of Box tunnel taken from the footplate of an unidentified Castle class 4-6-0. The date is probably the late 1950s as the up road is laid with flat bottom rails. The small tunnel on the right originally served underground stone mines but before World War II these were taken over by the War Department and used as an ammunition store. The siding was lifted c1963.

difference from the mid 1930s. The world as a whole is in a turbulent state, but the railway offers solid continuity, though the branch lines are not as busy as they used to be and so much freight is now going by road. This particular express is one of a familiar breed: not in the top ten or even twenty nationally, but the most important for its locality, providing by far the quickest and best quality link with the capital. With no crew change and no stop in suburbia, it carries its district's flavours and values into the heart of the metropolis. Many of the passengers (and crew) know each other; much social business is done in the restaurant car and first-class compartments.

Starting its journey around eight and finishing shortly before eleven, the train is very much in the old tradition of providing the best service for those who have some business to transact but no need for a long day in London. It is also at a decent time for those travelling beyond London, perhaps to the Continent. The return around half past four likewise is acceptable to those coming from further afield and those who have been to see their stockbroker or uncle. And because the train is only in London just over five and a half hours, the accountants have not seen it necessary to pool the locomotive and rolling stock. The local people take pride in it, some regulars choosing the same compartment and enjoying the same photographs of beauty spots each trip.

The mood does, however, vary sharply according to season. The January sales see quite a few women go to London as a regular social occasion. School and university term beginnings and endings bring one- or two-day rushes. Local festivals in May and June attract the musical and literary fraternity including a substantial handful of London reporters. Easter to September see an increase in tourists, who sometimes outnumber the locals on the evening return trip (the morning departure being too early for most), but then many local people are also then setting out on their holidays and everyone knows that this train is the way to start in style. A couple of dozen people including two MPs usually travel up on Mondays and back on Thursdays or Fridays. Mid week is the most popular time for business day trips to the capital, and there have been occasions when cheaper tickets have been available then. The biggest cause of complaint is that BR cannot make up their minds whether to allow day returns to be used on this service or not. Currently they are available third class but not first, enormously increasing the differential. Not that that worries an increasing variety of first-class passengers: those whose fares are paid for by some government or local government agency. And despite complaining, most businessmen still go first! Business travel quietens down in summer, and some of the emptiest runs of all are now on summer Fridays, for the weekend is gaining importance. When things settle down in the autumn the loadings reach their most consistent highest, but the restaurant-car crew wait for their biggest tips of the year to nearly Christmas when farmers and their families going to Smithfield flood the train, all demanding full meals. 'Don't tell me that farmers have it hard.' Then and only then is a third sitting of breakfast needed. And the Christmas period itself is of course also very busy. The chief steward decorates his car and extra tips are cajoled by providing occasional extra touches like a free mince pie. One thing about this train: they don't worry you. The whole Region knows it is well run, and anyway since it does not stop anywhere on the main line it is difficult to inspect.

So we have finished our climb up the Rockies, the exhaust from the locomotive echoing across the valley below with its quaint villages and old mills, and thunder into the summit tunnel just as the guard returns to his van having closed all the windows. A local will have preceded us a few minutes before and have set back into the refuge siding at the junction. Speed builds up on the descent until the driver slows for our rural junction stop – and yes we see short branch trains at the two outer platforms and the local that preceded us. Yet these days most of the fifty or sixty passengers waiting at our platform will have arrived by car, leaving home much later than they would need to have done to catch one of the three connecting trains.

Invariably the stationmaster is on the platform to greet us here; this is the most important moment in his day. He positively urges his porters into action, and doors are all closed with a good half-minute to go. 'London only,' he shouts (as he only can) this once a day lest anyone be

Quicker Get-away

I cherish those days when the 11.15am Nottingham to St Pancras non-stop was due in on platform 3. Standing by on the middle road, a Meadow Lane shed Compound, shining like a mirror, with coal carefully stacked high above the tender sides, awaited its charge. This train was usually worked from Derby by a Lincoln class 2P which came off at Nottingham and went forward on a slow train to its home shed. The reason for this working, I was told, was that the class 2P could make a quicker get-away from Derby than a Compound. This sounded rather queer, but the explanation was always the same. With all pegs 'off' the local lads moved away and the bark of the Compound smashed its exhaust skywards as round London Road Junction she went, the driver winding into his first notch. – Philip Spencer.

in doubt. We note that though the down local has already left the two branch-line trains due to start their return journeys fairly soon have less than ten passengers between them. Only three women are waiting on our platform for the local that we overtake here and will follow us to all stations. But the managers of the bookstall and small refreshment room have obviously had a successful fifteen minutes trading and are busy tidying up before finding time heavy on their hands. Still five seconds early, the stationmaster beams as he give Right Away, the guard waves his flag for the last time, and the engine's whistle responds before the driver makes a cautious but determined start on damp rails in a deep cutting.

Breakfast is not advertised at this point but two who have just joined are fitted into the restaurant car while the rest of those on second sitting are paying their bills and tables are being prepared for morning coffee. This is still before the days of buffet cars and the formal sitting of morning coffee and biscuits (yes, you *can* have tea but are made to feel a real non-conformist) is an important social occasion, especially for the ladies. It is also profitable for the restaurant-car people, a much better margin than with breakfast. The ticket collector is doing his rounds, the travelling lavatory cleaner her less desirable ones, though people from this part of the world don't make a mess. [Her problems will start when higher authority steps in and forces this train to stop at the junction with the main line; a quite different class of passengers then . . . 'You don't know where they're from'. But that is another story, actually the beginning of the end of this train. The modern equivalent runs sans restaurant car two hours earlier up, an hour later down, and gives people who really want to work in London nearly an extra four hours, since the journey itself is quicker. But it is just like any other, pooled rolling stock, of course, never the same railwaymen out and back.]

The moment the driver likes best is when his fireman tells him the distant is off as they approach the main line. He allows his train almost to freewheel round the curve and then, with a long blast on whistle, really opens up as he goes through the large station. That of course has a service of dozens of trains to London, yet those waiting on the platform look enviously at this obvious country quality service. But further along the line most people just see it as another train, and that is what indeed it has become, just one of a succession of such formations racing a few miles apart en route to the capital at the same speed. At least at these traditional timings the suburban rush hour is long over and we keep going at a steady eighty almost all the time. Exhilaration, the challenge of the day ahead, have replaced the relaxed atmosphere of the journey's start. Inevitably one signal check before we roll into the platform, but still on time. A few of the passengers, regulars, wave at the driver as they hurry by to their tube or taxi.

Soon a tank engine is on the back, our loco of course cut off, and the empty stock is taken out to the carriage sidings three miles away. The engine follows to its depot where the driver (but not the fireman) clocks up his final ten minutes booking off and reporting that nothing is wrong. That's more than can be said of many engines being turned in from big

The Distant Story

With the introduction of the high-speed streamlined trains on the LMS and LNER, speeds rose to new levels, over 90mph, sometimes 100mph or even more. Even with direct admission valves on the coaches, this meant increased braking distances. (In passing the railways were remarkably reluctant to use the quicker-acting, more sensitive Westinghouse compressed-air brake, having opted to standardise the vacuum system only a decade before.) So both companies embarked on a programme of moving distant signals further out.

On the LMS (and to a lesser extent on the LNER) the resited distants were in fact colour-lights, easier for the driver to see and avoiding heavy manual pulls for the signalman and just in case the high-speed streamliners could not stop within the braking distance for a signal at danger, double block working was introduced for these trains. A signalman could not accept a streamliner from the box in the rear if the forward section was still occupied. In some locations two sections had to be clear before the streamliner could be accepted. The LMS made sure their signalmen knew that the *Coronation Scot* was approaching for it was signalled by the special Is line clear? bell signal.

The introduction of colour-light distants did not, alas, necessarily mean they would be seen, the most serious accident in the last half century, at Harrow & Wealdstone in 1952, being caused when in fog a Perth express ran past signals into the back of a stationary commuter train and the wreckage was run into by a down express. Only automatic train control, introduced by the GWR years before but only made standard on BR (in a more sophisticated form) following Harrow & Wealdstone, gave the driver an audible indication of whether the

continued opposite

city depots this morning. The footplate crew have a wash and go to the mess room before getting an unofficial lift back light engine for a return journey on the cushions, having to change twice and of course taking much longer . . . unless they do that walk about London they have been promising themselves for years and catch the return fast working.

In the carriage sidings ours is one of a score of trains from many different parts simply idling time away before their late afternoon and early evening returns. There's cleaning to be done, yes, and the chef has to make a start on dinner, and they did not quite finish laying up in the restaurant car. But most of the time the crews of several trains get together playing cards. Occasionally one of them will do an errand for his wife in London, unofficially slipping off duty when he is being paid continuously, the others ready to offer an explanation if needed, though it never is. Hanging around is the bad part of this job. Time for a bit of kip, though, if there has been a run of late evenings.

Four o'clock, and everyone has smartened up. The tank engine sets off for the terminus, the empty train overtaken by several incoming

Roast beef, sir? A first-class dining car on the LMS in the 1930s. These comfortable vehicles were twelve-wheelers and lasted well into the BR period. A scene which would make today's so called 'Pullman' passenger envious.

continued

distant was clear or not, and applied the brakes if need be.

Train travel has always been safe, but used to rely much more on the human element, and only their incredible commitment to their job enabled railwaymen to handle huge volumes of traffic at very different speeds with such a proud record.

expresses. There is a short delay for the departure of the previous express and its tank engine behind it from what is now our platform, and with eighteen minutes to go we come to a stand. The reserved-seat attendant checks his seat labels against the paperwork, the loading of mail and baggage starts, and soon the first passengers are being allowed through by the ticket collector. The chief steward takes his traditional pose by the restaurant car door proffering dinner tickets (normally only one sitting but they will do afternoon tea first) to the knowledgeable, though today there will be plenty of seats even for those who wait for him to come round canvassing the train.

Eight minutes to go and the passengers feel a slight bump as the engine (the same one but with a different crew who have come up on the cushions by a later train) backs on. The restaurant car is almost full for afternoon tea by the time they leave, half a minute late waiting signals. The return through the suburbs is during the rush hour and they are allowed rather longer for the same non-stop run back, an uneventful journey except that they have to cross the up main to join the branch and are almost brought to a halt since an up express is adrift.

The atmosphere becomes more relaxed now that people are being

The quick lunch and snack bar on platform 1 at Paddington. It was opened in 1935 after the station was rebuilt. It provided a quick service of hot and cold meals and snacks and was very good value. The decor was of the period with chromium-plated fittings and the GWR circular emblem much in evidence. The bar finally closed in the sixties with the rationalisation and, some might say, deterioration of railway catering.

returned to their private world and have thrown off the tension and anonymity of London. The speed is the same, dinner proceeds rapidly in the restaurant car, yet this is no longer just any train. Back at the country junction the two branch-line trains are waiting, but note how many cars and taxis there are in the yard. Wives who brought their husbands to the station this morning greet them on their return as though they had been to Africa, and indeed they have spent a few hours in a totally different world. Over the Rockies again in glorious early evening sunshine, the engine doing her stuff, and then into the city where we lose over half of our passengers, a handful transferring to connecting services but most walking straight out of the main exit.

The last drink is downed and the chief steward at last gets his cash to balance (his boss will be pleased with today's takings) as they leave the last intermediate stop, a hillside village bathed in sunshine. But not a single truck in the yard, and we have heard they have been talking about withdrawing freight from all of these small stations. There was nobody on the platform, by the way, since the stationmaster has been withdrawn and the sole booking clerk closed shop hours ago. The ticket collector is drawing on his pipe while listening to the guard tell the story of the night of the flood. They reopened the restaurant car and did forty dinners, and some people wrote in with their thanks, but the office forgot to pass it on to the crew, of course.

It is dusk as we arrive at our destination just under twelve hours before the whole thing will start again, though there will be a lot to do on the engine meantime. The young taxi driver with a broad local accent says he's never yet been to London and obviously lacks curiosity. The capital indeed already seems light years away and in truth it *is* much further by any other means than this fast daily service. Several people who have come to retire here only did so with the reassurance this train gave them. And so it still is over most of pre-motorway Britain, the railway being the great connector, the very character as well as prosperity of countless provincial centres depending on the quality of their best train to the *capital*.

Arrivals board. Euston station at 3.15pm (15.15) on 1 June 1948 showing the train arrival indicator, a precursor to the modern computerised train information now standard practice at the main-line termini. It shows, clearly, the variety of traffic on the Western Division and the availability of connections to be made at such junctions as Carlisle, Penrith, Preston, Wigan, Warrington, Crewe and Bletchley.

Allocations

Each of the Big Four had begun their motive power modernisation by the middle of the 1930s. Stanier was settling into the LMS and exciting new classes were beginning to evolve; not yet the super Pacifics but certainly Jubilees and the first Black 5s. Gresley also was yet to produce his masterpiece the A4, but there were A1s and A3s in plenty though here much greater reliance – for economic reasons – continued to be placed on pre-grouping types. On the Great Western Collett had set their pattern a decade ago with *Caerphilly Castle* out of G. J. Churchward's Star; he followed this with the Kings and Halls. And on the Southern Maunsell produced his King Arthurs and Lord Nelson, in this case supported by a plethora of older classes not worth replacing with the expansion of electrification.

How pleasing it was to see a brand new sparkling red Jubilee, but how sad that the last Jumbo went in 1934 and the last pure Claughton in 1935.

World War II saw little new in the way of express classes though Oliver Bulleid kidded them all with the introduction of his unique Pacifics, supposedly mixed traffic. Come the early 1950s and the kaleidoscope had been well and truly shaken. The LNWR classes had been virtually decimated; all the express classes in fact went by 1949. New batches of specific and well-tried Big Four engines appeared as a stopgap before the Standard classes began to appear.

The following tables made up from the allocations at typical express locomotive depots show just how great that change was over two decades.

CAMDEN

Wheel Arrangement	*Class*		*1933*	*1954*
4-6-2	Coronation	8P	–	15
4-6-0	LNW Prince of Wales	4P	6	–
	LNW Claughton	5P	7	–
	Rebuilt Claughton	5XP	2	–
	Patriot	5XP/6P	8	–
	Rebuilt Patriot	7P	–	5
	Jubilee	5XP/6P	–	8
	Rebuilt Jubilee	7P	–	2
	Royal Scot	6P	15	–
	Rebuilt Royal Scot	7P	–	12
4-4-0	Compound	4P	8	–
	LNW George The Fifth	3P	4	–
0-6-0T	LMS	3F	18	13

EXMOUTH JUNCTION

Wheel Arrangement	*Class*	*1933*	*1954*
4-6-2	Merchant Navy	–	8
	West Country	–	28
4-6-0	King Arthur	9	–
	S15	5	6
4-4-0	K10	1	–
	L11	3	–
	S11	4	–
	T9	9	8
0-4-2	A12	4	–
0-6-0	0395	4	3
	700	4	–
2-6-0	N	30	19
0-4-2T	D1	2	–
0-4-4T	02	9	3
	M7	16	15
4-4-2T	0415	2	3
0-6-0T	G6	4	–
0-6-2T	E1/R	3	4
2-6-2T	LMS class 2	–	3
	BR class 3	–	10
0-8-0T	Z	1	1

HAYMARKET

Wheel Arrangement	*Class*	*1933*	*1954*
4-6-2	A1 Gresley	3	–
	A1 Peppercorn	–	5
	A2	–	6
	A2/1	–	3
	A2/3	–	1
	A3	3	15
	A4	–	7
4-6-0	B1	–	8
4-4-2	C7	3	–
	C11	7	–
4-4-0	D11/2	8	10
	D29	1	–
	D30	7	1
	D31	2	–
	D34	1	–
	D49	4	6
0-6-0	J35	1	–
	J36	5	2
	J37	2	–
2-6-2	V2	–	4
0-6-0T	J83	4	5
	J88	2	2
0-6-2T	N15	4	2
2-6-2T	V1	1	3

LAIRA

Wheel Arrangement	*Class*	*1934*	*1954*
4-6-2	BR class 7 Britannia	–	4
4-6-0	King	6	12
	Castle	10	6
	Hall	10	20
	Grange	–	7
	Manor	–	5
	County	–	5
4-4-0	Bulldog	7	–
2-6-0	Aberdare	1	–
	43XX	9	3
2-8-0	28XX	4	2
	47XX	2	–
0-6-0T	1361	4	4
	Old pannier tanks. Various classes	13	1
	64XX	4	6
	57XX	4	18
	94XX	–	5
2-6-2T	44XX	3	1
	45XX	11	10
	3150	2	2
	51XX	–	2

KINGS CROSS

Wheel Arrangement	*Class*	*1934*	*1954*
4-6-2	A1 Gresley	8	–
	A3	3	3
	A4	–	19
4-6-0	B1	–	7
4-4-2	C1	23	–

Camden shed 1932. Home depot for Western Division London loco men working out of Euston. Camden was rebuilt during the early 1930s with the original pitched roof over all five roads being replaced by a new one. At this time the Royal Scots were in regular use on the Scottish & Liverpool trains plus the Irish Mail but apart from the Compounds which had recently replaced the George the Fifths on the Birmingham two-hour expresses ex-LNWR engines were the norm. This photograph (an official one taken during the rebuilding) shows LMS-built Compound No 1134 (shed 13 Wolverhampton Bushbury), Prince of Wales class 4-6-0 No 5686 Anglia, *three Claughtons, an unknown George the Fifth, two further Compounds, two Jinty 0-6-0 tanks and a red-painted LNWR tender, almost certainly attached to a Claughton.*

Camden shed 1955. Almost a quarter of a century later Camden is a dirty place indeed. At most steam depots the whole servicing process was dependent on the ashpits; the LMS looked towards wheeled ashtubs on rails into which ashes could be raked or paddled and then pushed to a hoist for depositing the contents in wagons. There was a lot of spillage which needed hosing down. The yard layout improvements plus the new twin 150 ton bunker coaling plant and ash handling plant were brought into use in 1936. Modern motive power on shed includes three-cylinder Jubilee and Royal Scot 4-6-0s; the only one identifiable is No 46157 The Royal Artilleryman. *(See also page 130.)*

KINGS CROSS continued

4-4-0	D2	3	–
	D3	3	–
0-6-0	J3	4	–
	J6	7	–
2-6-0	K2	5	–
	K3	13	–
2-6-2	V2	–	11
4-6-2T	A5	1	–
0-6-0ST	J52	26	20
	J53	1	–
	J55	2	–
	J57	1	–
0-6-2T	N1	13	–
	N2	59	57
0-6-0 Diesel electric	350hp	–	7

LEEDS HOLBECK

Wheel Arrangement	*Class*		*1933*	*1954*
4-6-0	LNW Claughton	5P	4	–
	Patriot	5XP/6P	9	–
	Jubilee	5XP/6P	–	18
	Royal Scot (rebuilt)	7P	–	8
	LMS	5	–	23
	BR	5	–	2
4-4-0	MR	2P	9	2
	Compound	4P	11	6
2-6-0	LMS	5	7	3
	LMS	4	–	3
	LMS	2	–	3
0-6-0	MR	2F & 3F	32	–
	MR/LMS	4F	20	5
2-8-0	LMS	8F	–	12
0-8-0	LMS	7F	4	–
0-4-4T	MR	1P	4	–
0-6-0T	MR	1F	7	–
	LMS	3F	–	4
2-6-2T	LMS	2	–	1
	LMS	3	–	3

OLD OAK COMMON

Wheel Arrangement	*Class*	*1933*	*1954*
4-6-2	BR class 7 Britannia	–	5
4-6-0	King	12	12
	Castle	20	31
	Star	9	–
	Hall	22	26
4-4-0	Bulldog	1	–
0-6-0	Dean	3	–
	2251	–	4
2-6-0	Aberdare	3	–
	43XX	31	–
2-8-0	28XX	11	–
	47XX	2	7
0-4-0T	Sentinel	1	–
2-4-0T	Metro	6	–
2-4-2T	36XX	1	–
4-4-2T	2221	6	–
0-6-0T	Old Pannier Tanks. Various classes	14	–
	57XX	49	49
	94XX	–	12
	15XX	–	4
2-6-2T	61XX	20	14
0-6-0 Diesel electric	350hp	–	10
Gas Turbine		–	2

NINE ELMS

Wheel Arrangement	*Class*	*1933*	*1954*
4-6-2	Merchant Navy	–	12
	West Country	–	13
4-6-0	H15	17	14
	S15	6	–
	T14	10	–
	King Arthur	18	12
	Lord Nelson	5	3
4-4-0	K10	5	–
	L11	9	–
	L12	3	–
	S11	3	–
	T9	1	3
	D15	–	2
2-6-0	U	6	3
	U1	–	2
0-6-0	700	2	7
0-4-4T	T1	3	–
	02	5	1
	M7	28	15
0-6-0T	G6	6	–
	756	1	–
0-6-2T	E4	–	6
Co-Co diesel electric	LMS 10000/1	–	2
1Co-Co1 diesel electric	SR 10201/2/3	–	3

8
AN ENGINEER ON THE FOOTPLATE

THE LMS, and in BR steam days the London Midland Region, had four or five mechanical inspectors at the headquarters of the chief mechanical engineer at Derby. They were the eyes and ears of the CME, directed towards the working and mechanical performance of the locomotive fleet out on the line and in the running sheds. Technically qualified men, they were expected not just to report, but to get action to overcome problems. No nine to five job, it involved a lot of travel, irregular hours and hard work, but gave a tremendous degree of satisfaction. Here is the story of a typical week in the life of one of those inspectors in the early 1950s. Let us call him Jack, as a number of others did . . .

Living fifteen miles from Derby means early starts and often late finishes. So the rising sun is still casting long shadows as Jack climbs on to the Midland Red bus in his village at 6.35 for Burton-on-Trent; he is on his way to his first assignment of the week, and he needs to get the 7.56 from Derby to Leeds. A short bus ride from City station, one of Farnley Junction's Class Fives, No 45340, is stopped for special examination because of severe axlebox knock since she came back from intermediate repair in Crewe works. So many drivers have booked her unfit for express passenger work that she is now confined to local freight trips and has been specially proposed for the works at an abysmally low mileage; naturally the shopping bureau wants to know what it is all about.

Her normal stamping ground is the trans-Pennine route from Leeds to Manchester and Liverpool via Diggle, not one on which you can handle a class Five with kid gloves, and Jack has already ridden on her, double-heading on the morning Newcastle–Liverpool express. He could not fail to note the vicious knock in the left hand trailing coupled axlebox, particularly hard with the second valve of the regulator open, and virtually unchanged over the whole cut-off range. He found the coupling rod bushes OK, no tell-tale grey smears of whitemetal dust around them, coupled axleboxes tight, reversing gear true, the beat at the chimney fairly even. So he has arranged for her to be in the shed this morning, cold, front valve chest covers off, allowing him to check the valve setting, the most common cause of these symptoms. By eleven, overalls on, he is getting down to it. The measured leads prove to be not quite accurate in allowing for expansion when hot, but are not far enough out to account for the knock.

Jack is puzzled, but then has an idea, a sort of last fling. The fitter removes the crosshead gudgeon pins and levers the crossheads along

Training a Traffic Apprentice
While stationed in the Doncaster motive power superintendent's office, one month was allocated to footplate. Many classes were sampled. One day the *West Riding* was taken to Kings Cross, the engine being the comparatively new A1, 60118 *Archibald Sturrock*. What beautiful locomotives they were! On the return another A1, 60125 *Scottish Union* had a strong wind and it was pouring with rain. The driver was straining his eyes looking for the oil lamps in the signals. No AWS to help him then. What a job, with smoke beating down in his face.

On 13 November 1953 the morning Doncaster to Kings Cross express was hauled by A3 Pacific No 60109 *Hermit*. The driver, a Doncaster man, really set about the engine on the rising gradient from Grantham to Stoke Tunnel, going over the top at increasing speed and accelerating down the bank to over 90mph at Little Bytham; not excessive by *Mallard*'s standards but the fastest the writer had then travelled on the footplate. That old Pacific really galloped along.

But approaching Finsbury Park all boards were on, and one of the station supervisors was running up the track pointing to the top of the train. A pall of smoke could be seen along the top of the coaches from a fire on the tender, no doubt caused by sparks igniting some waste matter mixed with the coal. A signalman had sent 7 Bells (Stop and Examine).

What might have been a very early arrival at Kings Cross was converted into a late arrival. 'Might have been' for up expresses running early had a habit of being stopped south of Holloway, waiting a platform at Kings Cross, alongside what used to be the Star Brush Co (now Pitt & Scott). In those days Kings Cross district commuters referred to it as 'Star Brush Halt'. – F. Harrison.

LNWR cross-country route. Until the coming of the Stanier 4-6-0s this service between Liverpool and Hull was the preserve of the stalwart Prince of Wales class based on Edge Hill shed. Here in the mid 1950s LMS-built Compound No 41188 (Farnley Junction 25G) double heads Black Five No 45340 over the Pennines near Slaithwaite with a westbound express. Note the tall LNWR signal above the bridge and the ex-LNER leading vehicle – probably a Saturday strengthener making the train over the load for a Five.

with a brake stick until the piston heads strike the cylinder covers at each end, while Jack wields a trammel. Now he gets to the milk in the coconut, for on the left hand side there is a bare ⅛in bump clearance at the back end and nearly ½in at the front. Off comes the cylinder cover and it is evident that the works had fitted a new piston head at the overhaul. In their zeal to get the engine out through the works gate to boost their output figures, the bump clearances were either not checked and evened up – or even ignored. A real Friday afternoon job! 'Send the piston and rod in for rectification, and I'll have a word with the works maintenance assistant about it. Let me know when you get them back and I'll ride with her again to see if it's done the trick.' He picks up a late afternoon express back to Derby, riding the Jubilee for the fun – not that there is much fun until after Sheffield, because the route is littered with permanent way slacks, and those resulting from colliery subsidence are very evident to the eye.

Tuesday is going to be a chance to get some phoning done and to keep the paper moving. There are the monthly casualty statistics from the

Camden Shed 1948

Quite unlike Willesden, Camden was primarily a main-line passenger shed. The only freight workings were Jinty, Class 3F tanks, trips to Victoria Docks and Maiden Lane. There was a front-line stock of Stanier Pacifics reinforced by converted Scots and the remaining Fowler Royal Scots, by this time getting run down and unpopular with the enginemen. A few Jubilees completed the stud, mainly used as cover for the Scots and on the Birmingham/Wolverhampton turn back workings. These did not come on to Camden shed during the day but were serviced between trips at Euston.

During the locomotive exchanges the shed hosted two stars: Nos 46236 *City of Bradford* and 46162 *Queen's Westminster Rifleman* (their continuous blow down disconnected to equalise with other Region's power) working from Kings Cross to Leeds, Paddington to Plymouth, and Waterloo to Exeter as well as over their own road to Carlisle. There was natural disappointment that the King was not allowed over the home system with a feeling that it was time *Launceston Castle* was avenged. One night, when they were waiting for the Merchant Navy to come in from Carlisle, a running foreman was heard to sigh for a Claughton that would steam; round the corner lived a retired engineman who had fired in the Race to the North of 1895 and some of the more recently retired masters would call in to see how things were going. It is on record that a driver from Nine Elms (after bringing his Merchant Navy in) observed that their main line was 'too long'.

Engine crews for the test engines were selected from the top (or Carlisle and Blackpool) link and each driver retained his regular mate. They could scarcely believe their eyes when they were shown the Dainton and Hemer-

continued on page 132

Motive Power Department to be examined, and those which are subject to continuous scrutiny graphed. It is a rather depressing job when you see all the hot boxes up and down the system and visualise all the delay caused; mainly the Midland types but also on G1s and G2s. But he has hardly sat down when the Divisional motive power inspector comes on the phone. A Jubilee working the down St Pancras–Edinburgh sleeper has dropped her middle big end this morning near Appleby, causing serious delay, and after dismantling the inside connecting rod on site the engine is being hauled to Upperby shed. Heavy damage all round. He is going down on the Thames–Clyde; is Jack free? Well, this is a lot more interesting than graphing casualties, though sure enough it will turn up next month in the casualty statistics anyway. Phone the wife that he will not be home tonight, pick up his bag and away.

The new Upperby roundhouse is light and airy as the two inspectors walk over to the casualty. Externally everything looks deceptively normal, but the connecting rod and big-end strap laid out alongside give the game away. No big-end brasses – they have vanished in a haze of dust, along with the steel glut plate. The strap is badly deformed and gouged and blue from running on the journal; the oilwell cork is missing, the oilwell empty. The two long bolts are bowed and shouldered, areas on the shanks worn, and the big-end cotter is mangled but still in place, held by the through bolts and serrated locking plates; that is one modification that works! Going into the pit, things are more or less as they expect. The underside of the boiler clothing, crank webs and frame stretchers are coated in what looks like gold dust, the big-end journal looks like a ploughed field, and the front cylinder cover is missing apart from the flange still on the studs. The cylinder casting appears undamaged, fortunately. The garlic hot bearing detector in the big-end pin is discharged.

They ascertain that the driver, when interviewed, heard nothing untoward until the bang when the cover went. Yes, he had a breath of steam on coming down from Ais Gill (Jack mutters 'liar' under his breath, for not one man in twenty ever did so). No, he had not smelt the stink bomb go off or he would have stopped. Yes, he had prepared the engine himself, and the big-end cork was not new but sound and screwed in firmly. The ganger is still looking for the missing cover and glut, but in the long summer grass at the lineside they may never be found. The motive power inspector phones Leeds for the mileage details; 57,000 miles from works, 22,000 miles from valve and piston examination and coming due for No 4 exam when the big end would have been stripped down and re-metalled if necessary. Cause? Probably the oilwell cork was lost, and for the want of a twopenny cork, loss too of much goodwill from delay to an important express – and the availability of an express engine. Hundreds of pounds worth of damage. The DMPS will have a 'suitable conversation' with the driver to watch it for the future. Now it is a bed for the night in the enginemen's hostel. Pretty sleepless, that.

Next morning the Upperby engine board temptingly shows 46238 marked up for the 8.25 to Euston. This train is really a semi-fast, stopping at all principal stations and even at Shap. It has no less than 52 minutes standing at stations and fifteen minutes recovery time to Crewe, a real temptation for slovenly working! Still, Jack reckons he has earned a little treat, and will be back in Derby quicker that way than waiting for the Leeds train. As he climbs on to *City of Carlisle* and shows his footplate pass, preparation is nearly complete. The fireman has already put on a heavy fire, using at least a couple of tons on that big grate and piling high the back corners where a Duchess demands feeding. He can now close the tender coal doors and sweep and wash the cab floor. He gives the coal pusher three or four strokes to nudge coal forward into the void at the shovelling plate, while the driver goes to ring off the shed. Then it is back to the station to attach to their train in platform 3. 'Twelve on for 383 tons,' says the guard; that's a doddle for a Duchess on Full Load and Limited Load timings.

'Right Away' comes spot on time, and the driver takes her out easily and surefootedly over the pointwork and up the sharp 1 in 110 rise to the goods line bridge. First valve of the regulator is adequate, and by No 13 box the reverser is back to 25 per cent. Jack listens approvingly

Pennine railway. A down express over the Settle & Carlisle line comes off Ribblehead viaduct and approaches the isolated Blea Moor signalbox almost at the summit of the fifteen-mile climb from Settle Junction, over 1,100 feet above sea level. The engine is Jubilee No 45739 Ulster, *by the early 1950s allocated to Leeds Holbeck shed, and the nine-coach train is entirely composed of ex-LMS vehicles. Ingleborough, 2,373 feet, forms the backdrop.*

Assault from the North. Today's electric trains are forced to ease to 75mph for the curves at Bessie Ghyll, between Penrith and Shap, but Duchess No 46238 City of Carlisle, *on a Perth–Euston express about 1960, is not making much more than 40mph on the 1 in 125 as she comes out of them, all staccato sound and fury.*

continued from page 130
don gradient profiles on the Western. The first crew to go into action was Brooker and Short, on a preliminary trip from Kings Cross to Leeds. The atmosphere was tense as those on the shed waited for the news. At last a telephone call came through – Brooker had had a good trip up and had been spotted 'right time' at Potters Bar coming home!

Frank Brooker came from an old railway family, his grandfather had been a driver at Brighton under the martinet John Chester Craven; his father began work at Brighton but came to Camden when still young and took a cleaner's job ultimately rising to the very top. It was not surprising that he performed so well in the exchanges with the ability to seize rapidly on the salient characteristics of the various routes. By his last and final trip over the Southern he had mastered the difficult road west of Salisbury with a run rightly held to be one of the finest achievements of which a British 4-6-0 had proved capable. He always had a fresh white collar and the traditional LNWR black bow tie and could step from his footplate as clean as when he mounted it. Short was an artist in his firing
continued opposite

to the quiet, even purr from the double chimney, the rail joints clearly audible. The fireman does not touch the fire until the engine leans to the Wreay curves, by which time it is hot and bright. On the level past Plumpton the driver brings her back in stages to 15 per cent, and pressure is deliberately allowed to drop back to 210 pounds to avoid blowing off at the Penrith stop. But now come the first signs of trouble, for signals are on at the platform end and the crew are puzzled to see an old LNW Cauliflower, smoking well, put out main line in front of them. Up comes the porter: 'Freight failed at Eden Valley, can't get clear into the loop.' It is going to get a venerable shove at the rear.

By the time they get away the train is 22 down, and the driver starts to make up lost time, putting *City of Carlisle* at the long 1 in 125 up to Harrison's Sidings with the second valve open and cut off at 30 per cent. They pass the Cauliflower in the up loop on the back of a sizeable freight, the woebegone Class Five at the front hiding her face behind Clifton box as the fireman paddles the fire out. Suitable gestures are exchanged! The engine is making beautiful music as she rides smoothly into the Bessie Ghyll curves doing 45 on the grade. Past the limeworks she's accelerating slowly, but now it is time to shut off and brake smartly for Shap station. No passengers, a little parcels traffic, and they are off again, pulling hard up to Shap Summit and accelerating sharply down through the cutting before shutting off by Scout Green distant and coasting to the Tebay stop. There are one or two passengers on the platform, but this is a railway town and it shows.

Eighteen late away, and the engine is put to it hard to make some speed before Dillicar troughs. But Low Gill distant is on, and they are brought to a crawl at the home before it is pulled off to the accompaniment of a flag from the bobby. 'Sheep on the line between here and Grayrigg, proceed at caution.' The driver remarks to all and sundry that it looks like being *one of those days* as he takes the train gently round the curves as Jack and the fireman keep their eyes skinned. But the woollies are congregated up the bank by the fence, and they stop again at Grayrigg box to report. So (despite the recovery time) by Oxenholme they have dropped another five minutes. They have to draw up twice and Jack climbs down behind the box to catch the guard's flag round the curve. The station work is unhurried but even so they can economise on the nine minutes allowed, and they leave twenty minutes down.

Now the driver is intent on making speed, and they go off down the bank on the second valve and 30 per cent, slowly wound back to 18 per cent. Milnthorpe flashes by at eighty, the Yealand pimple is hardly noticeable, and 46238 brakes into Carnforth and stops in just 12½ minutes. The five-minute station stop is cut to three, and they get away barely fifteen late. Another two minutes saved (including one as recovery) to Lancaster by dint of some hard running, but they run into a rain squall coming in off Morecambe Bay, and that bodes ill for the restart.

With the green flag the driver takes the train very gingerly through the crossover and on to the fast line eleven late, his hands never leaving the regulator handle, and faces up to the 1 in 98 climb up to No 1 box. *City of Carlisle* slips on the greasy rails, and skittishly keeps on slipping. The driver keeps the cut off long to keep an even pull, sanders on continuously and the regulator hardly more than cracked. It is touch and go – perhaps the driver wishes he had taken a banker, but that is a bit *infra dig* with a Duchess! They manage to keep going – just – and with two more heavy slips they stagger round the right hand curve which brings No 1 into sight. By now the rails are dry, and she will keep her feet, so second valve and down to 20 per cent is the order of the day on the level to Preston. The fireman quenches 46238's thirst on Brock troughs, as she rolls over them doing 75, but when they come to a stand in the platform even the three minutes' recovery time has been mopped up, despite the effort.

Once again the driver takes her away sharply, eight late after a curtailed station stop, only to be almost stopped by signals approaching Euxton Junction; they are all infuriated to see a Manchester–Blackpool brought across in front of them. 'Signalmen,' says the fireman in disgust, 'they couldn't operate a Hornby Dublo,' and has a go at the coal pusher to vent his spleen on innocent coal. They pull away hard when the board comes off, but there are slacks at Coppull and Boars Head and they drop a minute to Wigan, though the station staff pull that back and they leave still eight down. Another slack at Bamfurlong – this is a miserable stretch for subsidence – but after that they make good time, and with the Warrington platform staff on their toes, despite a lot of parcels and

continued

and a worthy second to Brooker.

Harry Byford had the additional responsibility of the Pacific and it was noteworthy that *City of Bradford* was the only engine to take part in all the tests, in contrast to the failure of *Mallard* whose selection may well have been more for publicity reasons than mechanical ones. No 46162 *Queen's Westminster Rifleman* would have done the same if she had not been run into at Crewe while being paired with the WR tender to work on the Southern Region. No 46236 had in some ways an unfortunate Press as her performance was often notable and she achieved the highest draw-bar horsepower set-up in all the tests whilst climbing the lower part of Seaton Bank – a momentary 2,400 was recorded on 22 June. And as one would expect her crew was particularly pleased that they only used four and a half tons of coal working from Paddington to Plymouth, markedly less than the normal amount issued to the Kings.

There was still that tribal feeling at Camden in 1948. Harry Byford used to refer to the fast Birmingham trains as some of the most demanding trains he had worked on, as schedules became faster the allowance was only 1 hour 55 minutes to London including a Coventry stop. In the early days of these accelerations there was not a minute to spare and he would recall trips with his beloved No 5322 *F. S. P. Wolferstan* and contrast them with those made by the Compounds. It was Laurie Earl who insisted that Camden had taught Midland enginemen how to drive their own engines! Indeed thirty years after the 1923 grouping a driver who returned to the Camden top link after some years at Kentish Town working the Leeds expresses was told by his superior that 'he wasn't on the Midland now' and would have to keep better time!

an enormous crate to manoeuvre into the rear van they are only seven late as they blast out of the station and up the bank to the Ship Canal bridge. The driver goes to the locker and forages in his old gas mask bag for the Working Timetable; after poring over it he announces that they should get the road all right at Weaver Junction, since they will have an eight-minute margin in front of the 11.40 from Liverpool. So it proves.

Now there is just the Hartford stop before Crewe, and they do not need the booked four minutes for that. So they are rolling past Coppenhall Junction just four minutes late when the distants come crowding in on time. They have *eight* minutes' recovery time for the three miles into Crewe, and there is precious little chance of getting into a platform four minutes early; it is not called 'Stop'emall Junction' by enginemen for nothing! Sure enough they are brought to a stand at Coal Yard, to watch the Class 2P pilot draw some parcels vans out of the station for stabling, before getting the road and easing into the platform just two minutes down. The fireman has given the footplate another hosing down, and washed his hands, so that all is Bristol fashion for the relief. The Camden men climb aboard. 'Good trip? You're nearly on time!' 'Yeah, apart from an engine failure in front of us, sheep on the line, and signal checks. It's all this bloke's fault,' grinning at Jack. Is he pulling their legs, they wonder? 'Twelve on. This is a good Lizzie.' The two enginemen make for the North shed and then the Gresty Road lodge, and Jack strolls to the bay for the Derby train. No chance to drive the Tutbury–Burton push-pull on the way home today; the office and those casualty figures call.

Next morning there is an enigmatic message on his desk: 'Crewe North. 46120 12.20 Crewe–Lime St Thursday.' That happens to be today. It is a throwback from the study he did a few years back into the rough riding of rebuilt Royal Scots. With modifications to bogie side control and with stiffer coupled wheel springs they have been tamed and are satisfactory for the fastest express work, but just occasionally a rogue appears, and *Royal Inniskilling Fusilier* is one to emerge recently with a nasty random kick at her back end. Jack has ridden on her as a result of the bad reports, and given her a good going-over; the bogie has been checked, axlebox clearance feeler-gauged, rear coupled springs changed and weight distribution checked on the works weighbridge. No improvement. Finally, he asked Crewe North to part the engine and tender at the next washout and fit packings behind the intermediate buffer springs to increase their pressure on the engine dragbox faces, which can be inadequate on these earlier 4,000 gallon tenders. This has been done and today is the outcome.

The 12.20 is a light stopping train, but can get a gallop on between stations. So it is away on the next Crewe train; what a boring journey when you do it so often, all cows, canals and bottle kilns. But at least he can get some reports and reading done on the way. The station staff seem surprised to see a Scot on this three-coach job, but the sight of the third member of the crew, in boiler suit and cloth cap rather than bib-and-brace and grease top, suggests that there may be reason behind it.

Jammed Regulator

LMSR Pacific No 6234 *Duchess of Abercorn*, figured in a curious mishap at Watford Junction, on Easter Saturday. Shortly before 1pm it was checked by signal on approaching the station with an express on the down fast road. The regulator was reopened, but for some reason it moved to full open and jammed in that position. Finding it impossible to close the regulator or, presumably, put the engine into mid gear, the driver brought the train to rest with the brakes at the platform with the engine slipping so furiously that before the trouble could be cured, the friction generated had ground well down into the heads of the rails under the coupled wheels, the driving wheels in particular. As a result, the down main line had to be closed at a peculiarly inopportune time, until the damaged rails had been replaced. 2-6-4 tank No 2489 was used to remove the Pacific to a siding; and the fourteen-coach train had to be transferred to the down slow road, and taken on from Watford to Bletchley by another 2-6-4 tank No 2444. – Philip Spencer, 1945.

Top of the hill. You can almost hear the fireman's sigh of relief as the final Duchess 4-6-2 to be built (just into BR days in May 1948) No 46257 City of Salford *pounds up the last few yards to Shap Summit with a down express, doing 25–30mph on a day of low cloud and drizzle. The year is not known, but the LNWR home signal with miniature arm for the goods loop has survived all that winter weather on the fells can throw at it. From here it is downhill almost all the way to Carlisle; giving the enginemen a chance for a bite of food and the fireman a wash in the tool bucket.*

Away they go with a hoot, and without pushing the *Fusilier* unduly they make seventy between some stations only then to have to wait time! She (can a Fusilier be female in this context?) still wags a little, especially where there are soft spots in the track to trigger it off, but the greater stabilising force of the tender has made a definite improvement compared with last week. So on his return to Crewe Jack looks over to the North shed and tells the assistant DMPS that she should be OK for express work again. He is not sorry to see his bed that night.

Only one more full day this week, and he decides to devote it to the Jubilees. There are mutterings from the motive power people about poor steaming, and though he does not think there is anything fundamentally wrong – more a case of poor coal or inexperienced firemen – a trip to London and back will not be wasted. So he gets the local from his home to Leicester to pick up the 7.25 Manchester Central to St Pancras, with Trafford Park men on a lodge turn. It runs into platform 3 spot on time, No 45628 *Somaliland* commendably clean. Before climbing into the cab he casts a glance at the front of the firebox clothing and is pleased to see that she retains her straight throatplate boiler. Jack prefers these to the later sloping throatplate type, which always seem to have too much grate for the size of the barrel. The enginemen are out taking water, having got none from Loughborough troughs. The driver is a little dapper white-haired man and his fireman in his mid-twenties, experienced, boots shined and overall trousers bagged out over cycle clips. 'She's a good 'un all right. We've got nine on and we sailed up to Peak Forest.'

Regimental roughrider. Rebuilt Royal Scot 4-6-0 No 46120 Royal Inniskilling Fusilier *was the engine used in the flange force recording tests between Derby and Manchester in 1949/50 to find a cure for the rough riding of the class. About three years later, following a general repair at which bogie modifications were made and smoke deflectors fitted, she accelerates an up train away from the Rugby slack. Above, the Great Central line bridge which saw its last train in 1969; though still in position it now stands in splendid isolation, its approaches gone.*

They have a good clear run to London. On the successive climbs to Kibworth, Desborough, Sharnbrook and Leagrave the regulator handle is up to the stop and the reverser towards 30 per cent. She steams consistently well, the fireman putting on about eight shovels at a time in horseshoe pattern. The last two go more or less under the door, over the flap, letting the draught suck the coal off the shovel. But by Bedford the coal is well back in the bunker and the fireman is having to reach in with the coal doors open, and there is the long drag up to Leagrave in the offing. So without a word, merely the fireman's gesture that says 'Watch your head' Jack is back in the bunker with the coalpick, pulling lumps forward. As they plunge into Ampthill tunnel he is in a splendid position to watch the steady stream of incandescent coal particles bouncing from the tunnel roof and falling either side of the tender. They would have been into St Pancras early but for a severe signal check at Carlton Road; one client is so pleased that as he passes the engine he proffers a ten bob note!

A wash and a bite to eat later, Jack is walking into Camden shed for a discussion with the superintendent, mainly about Royal Scot self-cleaning smokeboxes and how much char remains in them when they come on to the ashpit. They are proving a little tricky to get really right. Duchess ashpans are also talked over, both hopper and plain, and a visit to the ashpits is made to examine one just in; locomotive fortunes are made, or lost irretrievably, at disposal!

Connaught *on Camden bank. The Bushbury (Wolverhampton) based Jubilees did some grand work on the fast trains between there and Euston, and none more so than No 45742* Connaught *which was fitted with double blastpipe and chimney from 1940. She is seen here pounding up the final 1 in 77 out of Euston with ten or eleven coaches on the 17.50 Midlander express in the early 1950s.*

Then it is on a light engine to Euston for the 14.25 Wolverhampton as far as Brum. The engine already hooked on to a ten-coach train is No 45742 *Connaught*, with double chimney. She turns round at the little loco yard by platform 15 and the Bushbury crew have been busy getting coal forward in her 4,000 gallon tender, for she can get none at Euston. They have a big fire on, sufficiently burnt through that the pull up to Camden will get it really hot. The driver is not a man of full regulator persuasion, but on XL Limit timings of ninety-three minutes for the ninety-four miles to the Coventry stop you cannot hang about, so he compromises, opens the regulator handle about half way, getting some benefit from the second valve, and ferrets about for a small piece of coal to hold it there against the quadrant. The engine is a real cracker, steaming beautifully as the fireman feeds his heavy fire regularly, much of it over the flap. *Connaught* is bettering her running time, so in spite of permanent way slacks at Cheddington and Roade the driver can pull her up below 20 per cent, even on the steady banks. They are spot on time through Rugby, and with a final burst of 75 they pull into Coventry a minute to the good.

But the final run into New Street is ruined by a signal stop at Proof House, and arrival is 2½ minutes late. Jack has been keeping tally in his notebook log of the tank water gauge at start, at the three sets of troughs and at Birmingham, and overall she has used just under thirty-three gallons a mile, or about forty-three pounds of coal, excellent for a fast train of this weight. He makes a mental note to go through her repair cards on his next visit to Bushbury shed and get their experience of the state of her smokebox after a trip, and the birdsnesting on tube and stay

Once A Year Express
Once a year they had a great and glorious shindig at Towcester Races. And the vigilant LMS commercial department ran a train on Easter Mondays from St Pancras and Bedford to Towcester via Oakley Junction and Ravenstone Wood Junction, thence over the ST&MJ portion of the SMJ. It was always packed to the doors and made the class 4F 0-6-0 feel it had a real day's work to do for once.

ends at washout, and anything else that may be relevant. A quick run to Burton and he is sitting down to tea by 18.30.

Saturday mornings (remember when they were part of the working week?) are a time for catching up with report writing, reading those of the other mechanical inspectors, and keeping the chief technical assistant, his boss, au fait with what is happening in the big wide world. That double chimney on 45742, for instance. It might be worth trying opening out the blastpipe caps by ⅛in to soften the draught on the fire and check again that steaming has not been impaired. In the meantime, if the motive power people at Euston House continue to complain about the Jubilees, here would be a package to offer them. The CTA says it may be overtaken by work being done at Swindon, and a Jubilee may be programmed for one of the Test Plants. 'But by all means get the caps bored out and keep me posted on the results.'

Precursors to Heathrow

First, second or third class: the choice was yours not only on the great ocean liners but on the boat trains which ran from the long platforms at Waterloo, Victoria or Charing Cross over the Southern's busy tracks to Southampton, Dover or Folkestone. But how many people knew that you could actually get a passage on the *Queen Mary*, or the *Queen Elizabeth* or the *Amsterdam* for the paltry sum of £3 as late as the 1960s? But you *could*, and the knowledgeable enthusiast who also had an interest in things French added a trip to Cherbourg shed to see the SNCF Pacifics into the bargain. True it was only a cross-Channel trip, but it could be overnight including a good dinner and breakfast on board. What a thrill to ride the boat train to that evocative 1950s-style Ocean Terminus at Southampton and be on one of the last of the great ships starting off to New York.

Southampton became the prime terminal for the transatlantic liners in the twenties, taking over from Liverpool which was left with the secondary services to Canada and the USA, plus the Africa trade. Another south coast port had its moments of modest glory: from the turn of the century Plymouth was an important call. Passengers and mail tendered off could be in London many hours earlier and for half a century, not ending until the 1950s, records were made by the special trains.

Dover and Folkestone, dedicated to the cross-Channel packet routes, were not without their railway joys. Folkestone was notable for the return trip from the Harbour station to the Junction when the train was pulled and pushed by up to four R or R1 class ex-SE&CR 0-6-0 tanks (some with cut-down boiler mountings for use over the Canterbury & Whitstable line) or later a slightly less number of ex-Great Western pannier tanks. The sound of those little engines thrashing themselves up the 1 in 30 grade was ear splitting. The exhausts roared sixty or seventy feet up into the air, and echoed off the houses and the cliff. And what a sight it was to see a spotless Bulleid Pacific standing peacefully at the summit waiting to back down to take the train to London.

The other out of the ordinary way to get to the Continent – and very pleasant it could be – was by the famous *Night Ferry*, through sleeping cars London Victoria to Paris or Brussels at 10 every night. The motive power on the English side (until the coming of the Bulleid Pacifics) was usually double-headed 4-4-0s, often a mixture of rebuilt SE&CR locos and a more modern L1. Even after the arrival of the Pacifics, a 4-4-0 could be added if the loading was heavy. But on reflection this might be as much precursor of the Channel Tunnel as of Heathrow and Gatwick.

Many other services ran to the Continent. The LNER always provided a good service from Harwich Parkeston

Luxury on the Southern. The Golden Arrow approaches Dover Marine c1938 hauled by Lord Nelson class 4-6-0 No 862 Lord Collingwood. *The engine is fitted with Kylchap blastpipe and double chimney which it carried from August 1934 to May 1939. The building on the right is an extension of the Lord Warden Hotel which was later converted to offices.*

Noisy departure. The Folkestone Harbour branch was always difficult to work in steam days due to the 1 in 30 gradient up to the main line. For many years James Stirling's 0-6-0Ts of class R and R1 were used in multiple (up to four to a train) but from about 1957 GWR 0-6-0PTs of the 8750 class were imported and these lasted until electrification in 1961. Two of these engines are leaving the Harbour Station in 1959 and are about to tackle the 1 in 30 up to the Junction with the up Golden Arrow. No doubt there were another two banking. All trains had to reverse in the Junction sidings where the main-line locomotive came on to the train.

SOUTHERN
862
3

During the 1950s Trans-Atlantic traffic was still important at Liverpool in spite of Cunard transferring to Southampton. The Mersey Docks & Harbour Board maintained its own station at Liverpool Riverside specially for boat trains. Due to a weight restriction over the swing bridge until March 1950 the main-line locomotive was detached at Edge Hill and the train was worked through the tunnel to Riverside by two small tank engines. For many years two LNW 0-6-0STs fitted with condensers and named Euston *and* Liverpool *were used but after these were scrapped two Webb 0-6-2 coal tanks became the usual power. When in the Dock estate the train was preceded by a man on foot carrying a red flag.*

Harbour train. One of the few passenger railways to run through town streets was the Weymouth Quay Tramway from the Town to the Quay station for the Channel Islands. Only specially authorised stock was allowed on the tramway and due to sharp curves gangways had to be disconnected and couplings slackened off. Small locomotives were always employed, latterly the 1366 class 0-6-0PT shown here.

Quay, from where DFDS also served Denmark. Ships for Scandinavia sailed from Tyne Commission Quay, the LNER running whole boat trains or just through coaches from Kings Cross. Tilbury was an important embarkation point for Australia. The big Strath liners, with their tropical white hulls and one or three buff funnels, were served by boat trains from St Pancras via the Tottenham and Hampstead line to Barking. The locomotive power was likely to be prosaic in the extreme, usually nothing bigger than a Fowler 4F 0-6-0. There were also cruises by other companies, particularly the Orient Line whose yellow-funnelled ships took you on a holiday of a lifetime for thirteen days from twenty guineas if you applied to 5 Fenchurch Avenue, London. However, if your Orient Line cruise was to the Norwegian fjords, it might well sail from Immingham with a boat train from Kings Cross.

Liverpool almost certainly provided the most dramatic exit and entry because its Riverside station lay at the bottom of heavily inclined cavernous tunnels reached via Edge Hill station where the express engine from Euston was detached. For twenty-eight years, two of Francis Webb's 0-6-0 special shunting tanks named *Euston* and *Liverpool* were put on the front. When eventually they were replaced by Webb 0-6-2 coal tanks, the noise, smoke and sparks on the up journey were just the same.

By the 1930s the magnificent twelve-wheel LNWR coaches built specially for the Liverpool American boat trains, considered inappropriate for the secondary services to which the Riverside jetty had been reduced, had given way to standardised rolling stock. On one occasion a train stalled about half a mile short of the tunnel mouth. The driver of the banker (which was not coupled) waited patiently in the stifling atmosphere believing that the train engine driver had run ahead for assistance. But, nothing happening, after three-quarters of an hour he decided to grope his way forward, and found the driver and fireman of the first tank flat on the floor with handkerchiefs tied over their faces. Likewise the driver of the pilot which was still coupled; his fireman had been sent ahead for help. Eventually a Bowen-Cooke 0-8-0, whose driver had signed a note taking full responsibility

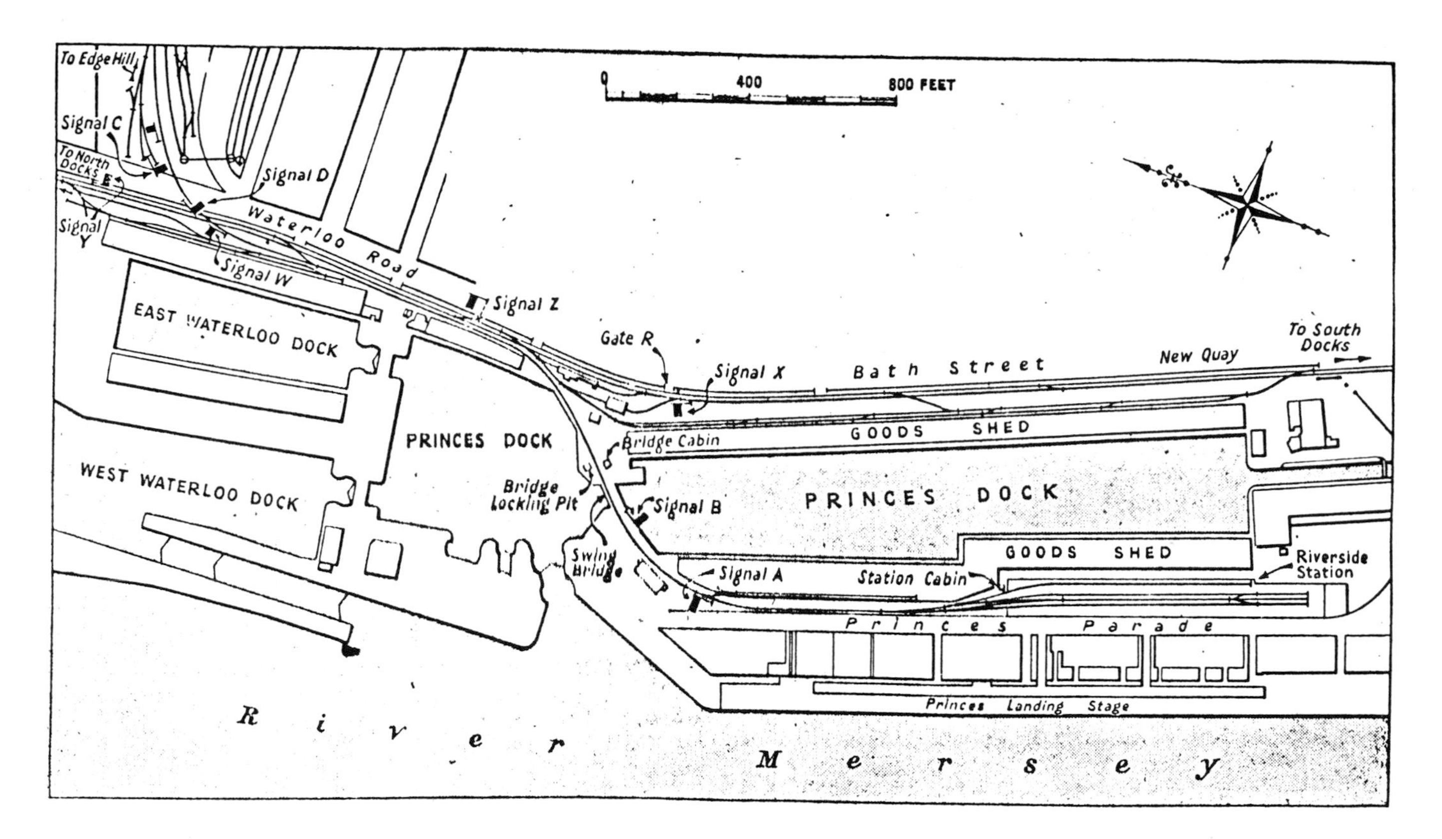

Liverpool Riverside

as there was no wrong line order available, came down to rescue them. It appeared that the fireman – a young passed cleaner – had taken fright and gone home.

World War II brought a whole new panoply of boat trains, though hardly of the comfort and regularity of those for pre-war liner sailings. Some of these involved ships leaving or arriving in the Clyde, the biggest liners (including the two Queens) anchored off Gourock, transfer of passengers being carried out by Clyde paddle steamers now painted in all-over grey. But some of the medium sized ships ventured further up the river, leaving vivid memories of a troop special from King George V dock at Shieldhall, overnight during the bitter weather of January 1947. To say the least the heating was inadequate for thin-blooded Britons coming home from steaming India as the trains wandered around Glasgow in the dark, via Shields Junction and the City Union line to High Street Junction, Bathgate and Edinburgh before setting off behind a V2 for York and demobilisation.

It has to be said that with few exceptions (notably the fast Plymouth Ocean Specials some of whose saloons survive in preservation) the nation has never offered its overseas visitors or returning nationals anything like its best (leave alone quickest) trains. Even today some who might prefer to cross the Channel by ferry must be deterred by the poor train connections through Kent. Air travellers are much better served by the *Gatwick Express*. But there was undoubtedly romance even in the boat trains for Weymouth (for the Channel Islands) which had to thread their way through the resort's streets, and in those for Ireland going as far as the land would take them at Fishguard, Holyhead or Stranraer.

Overnight to the Continent. The Night Ferry service with through sleeping cars between London & Paris (also latterly to Brussels) ran until 1980, when the special Wagon Lits cars built to the smaller British loading gauge became life expired. This was one of the heaviest trains on the Southern and was frequently double headed. Here class L1 4-4-0 No 31789 and a Battle of Britain 4-6-2 await departure from Victoria c1956.

9
CROSS-COUNTRY INSTITUTIONS

The Banbury connection. An ex-GCR class 8C 4-6-0 as LNER No 5196 approaches the Great Western station at Banbury c1936 with the 11.52 local from Woodford. This is one of a pair built in 1904 for comparison with the Robinson Atlantics and became LNER class B1; later class B18. The train arrived at 12.12 giving the engine time to be turned to return on the 12.44 from Swansea to Newcastle.

Nottingham Victoria. A view taken in LNER days showing one of the numerous cross-country expresses which used the GC Main Line via Woodford and Banbury to and from the Great Western, probably a Newcastle–Cardiff. It is ready to leave, with the lower quadrant signal off for its departure, double headed by a GC 4-4-0 (LNE Class D9) and a GC 'Jersey Lily' 4-4-2 (LNE Class C4). In the bays are local trains with old GN rolling stock. Next to the main line is what may have been a Derby train hauled by an ex-GN 0-6-0 No 3551 (LNE Class J6) behind which is a GC engine, probably another 'Jersey Lily' waiting to take a main-line train forward. A Sentinel steam rail car can be seen in the background and then an ex-GN 4-4-0 (LNE Class D2).

No 5261 stands in the north bay at Banbury, a handsome but somehow alien machine wearing a black livery lined out in red. Technically this is an ex-Great Central Railway class 8B (LNER class C4) and an Atlantic as well – a type not seen on the Great Western since the days of the reconstituted French engines used by George Jackson Churchward to act as midwives to the Stars and Saints. It is a Woodford engine which has worked the 11.52 local passenger tender first and has arrived only twenty minutes ago.

Sharp on 12.35 a watcher at the up end of the Great Western's disgraceful station (scruffy, dirty and certainly not the image of a modern forward-looking company) sees a plume of steam on the horizon sweeping majestically past the loco shed. In a trice a Mogul is on him with anchors hard on with the whee-tim, whee-tim, whee-tim sound of the vacuum pump as she sweeps or rather rolls by, followed by a large train of chocolate-and-cream coaches (including a dining car whose crew speaks with a Welsh lilt) and roof boards proclaiming that this is very much a cross-country train: 'Swansea, Cardiff, Banbury, Leicester, Sheffield, York and Newcastle upon Tyne.' No doubt only a few passengers travelled the whole way, but when the link with the LNER was still open one used to see many heavily loaded cross-country trains at Banbury.

By the time the observer has walked down under the degenerate wooden overall roof and reached the front of the train, No 7319 has been unhooked. The calling-on arm under the starting signal just short of the road bridge comes off. And in seconds they are away light engine. The GC Atlantic is soon out of the bay and back on to the train, the cords are pulled to allow the vacuum to be destroyed and recreated (the GWR ran at 25in, anyone else at 21in) and the guards change over (the GWR man resplendent in gold-braided peaked hat being replaced by a cheerful Yorkshireman in more workaday uniform), Even the train's tail lamp is changed and the coaches are checked by a carriage and wagon examiner with their numbers recorded for Railway Clearing House purposes.

The starter drops with a clang, whistles blow down the platform, a green flag shows from the rear van with an answering poop on the locomotive whistle. No 5261 moves off towards Banbury North Junction box and the spur connecting it with home. It will work as far as Leicester, over the great girder bridge crossing the West Coast main line of its LMS rivals at Rugby through the shires and northwards over the last main line ever to be built in England. It is the summer of 1936 and the service has some twenty years to go.

North to South. The 09.20 Birkenhead to Bournemouth has combined with the 12.20 Wolverhampton to Paddington and passes Acocks Green, Birmingham on 6 November 1959, behind No 5025 Chirk Castle. *This is a new working in the winter timetable, the Birkenhead portion being attached at Wolverhampton and taken off at Banbury.*

Originally this train was known as the *Ports to Ports Express* connecting Newcastle upon Tyne with Barry in South Wales but it was extended in later years to Swansea. In LNER days a through coach from Hull and Goole was attached and detached at Sheffield. It was composed on alternate days of LNER and GW stock, leaving Newcastle at 9.30am and, after 1935, it was looped between Northallerton and Thirsk to let the *Silver Jubilee* pass. On the GC main line there was some fast running behind GC Atlantics, Director 4-4-0s or 4-6-0s, the fastest section being on the northbound run between Leicester and Nottingham, 23.4 miles in twenty-six minutes start to stop. Beyond Banbury speeds were much less, because the train crossed the Cotswolds over the single-line branch from King's Sutton to Chipping Norton, Stow-on-the-Wold and Bourton-on-the-Water. The GWR had to use their Moguls because gradients were too steep for the ageing Dukes in normal service and no heavier engines were permitted over the branch. Eighty-two minutes were allowed for the forty-five miles 'over the alps' from Banbury to Cheltenham. This train was an example of how an out of the way section of line could suddenly acquire prominence because it was brought into use as a direct link in a cross-country service.

After World War II these trains ran via Oxford, Reading and the Severn Tunnel, a longer route but one which allowed larger engines to run through. In 1952, it terminated at Banbury (where passengers had to change) because Newcastle had, by then, a far faster service to and from Cardiff by way of the NE/SW line through Derby and Birmingham

New Street. Everything finished with the closure of the GC section in 1966.

Banbury was also host, in pre-war days, to the through coach making the longest journey in Britain – a summer-only operation from Aberdeen to Penzance. It left Aberdeen at 10.20am travelling via Montrose and Dundee to Edinburgh Waverley on an East Coast luncheon-car train. At Edinburgh it was attached to the rear of the 2.5pm express to Kings Cross, and detached at York at 6.14pm. York made up a train for Swindon consisting of the Penzance through carriage, a Glasgow–Swindon through coach, a buffet car and additional coaches and parcels vans. This left via the Swinton & Knottingley Joint for Sheffield Victoria, whence it ran up the GC main line through Nottingham Victoria, Leicester Central and Rugby to Woodford. It was handed over to the Great Western at Banbury at 10.7pm, the through coach having travelled 489 miles over the LNER. The train went on via Oxford and round the west curve at Didcot, reaching Swindon at 11.32pm. The Penzance coach was then attached to the 9.50pm from Paddington to Penzance which ran via Bristol, arriving Penzance at 7.45am after a journey lasting twenty-one hours twenty-five minutes covering 794 miles. The through coach was used by many intermediate passengers, and was frequently quoted in LNER and GW publicity, but few were likely to have ever covered the whole journey in it.

Another regular via Banbury was the 7.30am Newcastle to Bournemouth. Here the rolling stock alternated between LNER and Southern vehicles. At Sheffield Victoria a through coach from Bradford was coupled on giving even more variety for the run up the GC. Banbury, as usual, was the locomotive exchange point and a GWR engine then worked the train through Oxford and Didcot to Reading, where it took the west curve to Basingstoke; the Southern had charge for the rest of the journey to Bournemouth. Southern engines also regularly worked as far north as Oxford.

Before World War II there was a 12.44pm from Newcastle upon Tyne via the S&K Joint Line, GC main line and Banbury to Southampton, to connect with the Channel Islands steamers. At Leicester Central it frequently collected loaded fish wagons which had just arrived from Grimsby. Running was slow, and the restaurant car was detached at Oxford. The train did not arrive at Southampton until 10.44pm, after a

Locomotive Names

When the Footballer 4-6-0s of the LNER were due for withdrawal it was decided to mount the nameplates on a piece of polished wood and present them to the appropriate football teams. Many of them can still be seen at the football grounds. About two months before No 61648 *Arsenal* was withdrawn the nameplates were removed. Until she disappeared for scrap, she bore the painted name 'Real Madrid'. Several years later the Deltic *Argyll and Sutherland Highlander* bore a car window sticker under its nameplate bearing the legend 'God save the Argylls' as the Government had said they were about to disband the Regiment. Someone had endorsed it 'To hell with the Argylls . . . God save the Rangers'.

Banbury North plan
An Historical Survey of Selected GW Stations
Volume 4; C. R. Potts; OPC 1985

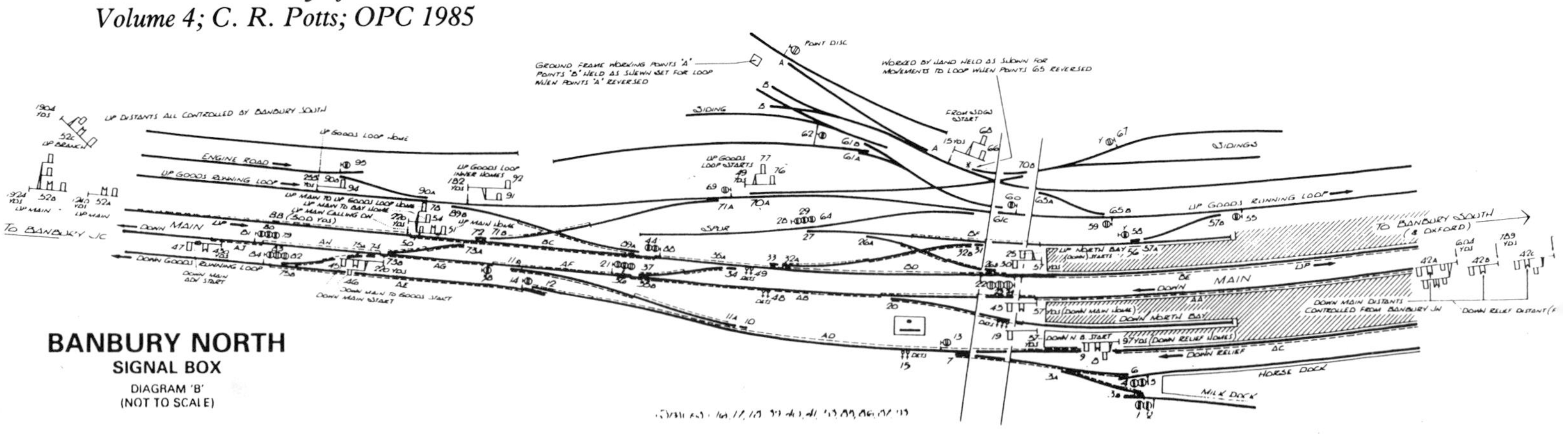

ten-hour journey. The northbound run was even slower, being routed from Winchester over the old Didcot, Newbury & Southampton single line, calling at every station. It did not even pretend to be an express until it left Oxford.

There were three independent routes between the North and Midlands and the South and West of England and many important cross-country trains worked over them, including of course the *Pines Express* and the *Devonian*. They used the LMS West of England main line south westwards from Birmingham, on which all the remaining cross-country expresses are now concentrated so that today Birmingham New Street is *the* station for connecting services from the South and West to the North West, North East and Scotland. But traditionally trains between South Wales/Devon and Cornwall to Manchester/Birkenhead/Liverpool/ Glasgow travelled by a joint GW/LMS route via the Severn Tunnel, Pontypool Road and Shrewsbury. That is only a shadow of its former self with only a basic Crewe–Cardiff service worked by Sprinters, though picturesque route it is. Then, thirdly, the Great Western had its 'own' Bristol–Birmingham route via Cheltenham, Stratford upon Avon and Tyseley. This North Warwick line, with a daily Penzance–Wolverhampton train which in BR days became the *Cornishman*, carried especially heavy summer Saturday traffic. But though it left Bristol via what is now Bristol Parkway (it was the LMS route into the city that BR scrapped), the GW had to use LMS rails from Yate to the outskirts of Gloucester where it did not stop cross-country trains as this would

Southwest–Northeast. Southern Railway class N15 4-6-0 No 30736 Excalibur, *fitted with a Lemaitre multijet blastpipe and chimney, leaves Southampton at the head of the 11.16 Bournemouth West to York through train on 27 January 1951. This will run over Southern metals via Basingstoke, thence by the old GWR route to Oxford (where engines will be changed) to Banbury (another loco change) and the LNER (GC) line to Woodford and Leicester to Sheffield.*

Birmingham New Street Midland side as it was. Class 5 4-6-0 No 44839 is just attaching the Sheffield–Bournemouth through coach to the front of the Pines Express (10.15 Manchester–Bournemouth) and will work the train forward to Bath. The railway geography of the Birmingham area is so complex that trains can arrive at either end from the north and depart for the west. Post-war the Pines ran via Bescot and Aston not calling at Wolverhampton and arrived at the south end departing via Selly Oak and the Birmingham West Suburban line.

have needed a reversal. It still does. A Cardiff–Birmingham service also ran via Stratford. In the 1930s diesel express railcars with a buffet counter took 2hr 22min for the journey of 131 miles. A supplementary fare of 2s 6d per single journey was charged.

The *Pines Express*, originally a joint service worked by the LNWR and Midland Railways, started to run in 1910 between Liverpool/Manchester and Bournemouth. The Liverpool and Manchester portions were combined at Crewe, they then ran over what became, after 1923, exclusively LMS tracks via Birmingham (often behind a Claughton to New Street) to Bath Queen Square, later Green Park, the ex-Midland station now a Sainsburys. After reversal there, the Somerset & Dorset Joint Line (LMS/SR) took the train over the steeply graded line across the Mendips, via Evercreech Junction, Templecombe and Blandford to Broadstone Junction near Poole, and then for the short distance (eight miles) over Southern metals to Bournemouth West. Most of the sixty-four miles from Bath to Broadstone were single track. Before World War II departures from Liverpool Lime Street and Manchester London Road (now Piccadilly) were at 9.40am and 10am respectively and arrival at Bournemouth West was at 4.35pm, the 254 miles from Liverpool taking nearly seven hours. En route the *Pines Express* detached a through coach from Liverpool to Southampton at Cheltenham. This was worked over yet another abandoned cross-country link, the Midland & South Western Junction via Swindon Town and Andover. Imagine the sense of occasion on branch lines long shorn of any pretence of being a trunk

Cross Country to Jericho

During the late 1930s a regular seven-days-a-week restaurant-car express ran between Newcastle on Tyne and Liverpool. The set was always the same – but followed four different routes. On Sundays it ran Newcastle – Leamside – Ferryhill – York – Wakefield – Manchester – Bolton – Wigan – Liverpool outward, and Liverpool – Wigan – Manchester – Todmorden – Leeds (Central) – Harrogate – Darlington – Durham – Newcastle return. On weekdays it was Newcastle – Durham – Darlington – York – Leeds (New) – Huddersfield – Manchester – Earlestown – Liverpool outward, and Liverpool – Earlestown – Manchester – Huddersfield – Leeds (New) – Harrogate – Darlington – Durham – Newcastle return. On weekdays it passed through Victoria station, Manchester and stopped at Exchange; on Sundays the process was reversed. The restaurant-car conductor, a known wag, once declared 'We shall be doing this trip via Jericho next!' little realising that ten minutes before speaking he had been doing just that. On Sundays the train ran within three miles of Jericho, a suburb of Bolton.

route (which many of them and certainly the M&SWJ started out with) when the one daily through train arrived. But almost until the end, and certainly through a particularly colourful Indian Summer beginning in the early 1950s, the Somerset & Dorset had genuine trunk-line status and was worked to the bone.

The Southern West Country Pacifics had just begun to come on stream and regular power included Black Fives, class 2P 4-4-0s and class 4 0-6-0s, one or two being old S&D engines. For freight there were the large- and small-boilered 2-8-0s specially built for the line at Derby; these did passenger duty at peak periods, mostly on high summer Saturdays when the traffic was intense – and often very late causing problems on the single-line sections. The holiday season's peak fortnight straddling the old August Bank Holiday was *the* time to go, and in those days Ossie Nock kept generous open house at Bath for the happy few. They were truly fantastic weekends, led by the doyen of S&D photography, the gentlemanly Ivo Peters, who would guide the select in their elderly cars to all the great photographic spots in his Bentley, his driving an example to all road users. Yet the trains were chased with more than adequate success. Not only did Ivo Peters know the spots, he knew everyone on the S&D as well. 'I have seen Mr Arthur Elliott [the shedmaster at Bath] and he tells me the Leicester should have a 2-8-0 on her today and my friend Mr Arthur Clist will be driving.' And he was right, so whether at Combe Down Tunnel or Chilcompton or Masbury summit there was smoke and a cheery wave of the hand. What days they were and what combinations of loco power, a 2P and a West Country, two class 4 0-6-0s, a 2P and a 2-8-0, a 2P and a Black Five with the occasional three-coach local headed by a solitary 2P 4-4-0 or 4F 0-6-0. Evercreech Junction was another place to be, for here all the northbound trains stopped to take on water and a pilot; by midday the latter were standing four or five in line on the centre road waiting their turn of duty for the climb over the Mendips and on to Bath, where the train reversed to make its way via Mangotsfield Junction to the old Midland main line and points north east. The variety of motive power between Bournemouth and Birmingham, taking in the gradients over the Mendips and up the Lickey was almost unbelievable. The last few years of the Somerset & Dorset provided some additional excitement with the importation of a few BR Standard Class 9F 2-10-0s, which in the hands of the keen Bath and Branksome men made an immortal name for themselves on the heavy summer expresses.

In LMS days the *Devonian* was the fastest train of the day between Leeds, Sheffield, Derby, Birmingham and Bristol. Beginning its journey at Forster Square station at Bradford at 10.25am it made the short run to Leeds Wellington where it had to reverse for the journey via Sheffield Midland, Chesterfield, Birmingham and Gloucester to Bristol Temple Meads. The southbound train was allowed 4hr 40min for the 206 miles from Leeds to Bristol Temple Meads, but there the rot set in. The GWR worked the through Paignton and Kingswear coaches forward via Exeter and Newton Abbot, and arrival at Kingswear was not until 7.19pm, the 330 miles from Bradford having occupied almost nine hours.

One of the joys of lingering on railway stations in the old days was the vast number of colourful posters always on display, some of idyllic destinations others showing scenes on the railway or the services it offered.

A Southern Railway poster extolling the Golden Arrow Pullman service of the late 1920s hauled by No E 853 Sir Richard Grenville *one of the new Lord Nelson 4-6-0s. Ever publicity minded the Southern makes the point that copies of the picture can be purchased either as a picture or a jig saw puzzle.*

The early days of BR saw magnificent posters of railway scenes, Cuneo's Greenwood Box and the Eastern Region's Queen of Scots as examples. An unknown A4 heads the latter against a tartan foreground in the early 1950s as the engine is still in blue – one of the early liveries chosen for principal express locomotives. The locomotive number appears to be its pre war LNER one.

One of the LMS Norman Wilkinson 'Lineside' posters showing Camden shed with three Royal Scots and a Compound. Others in the same series included No 6100 Royal Scot *leaving Euston, Willesden No 7 Box and Passenger Express depicting red Claughton No 5920.*

Bryan de Grineau's lovely 'World Famous Scottish Expresses' painted jointly for the LMS and LNER showing the latest express types passing at speed with what is presumably Edinburgh in the background. A really evocative picture and one very collectable if it was still around today.

Night Train to Scotland by Zec another LMS/LNER joint venture. The small print on the bottom of the poster reads 'Full particulars from LMS or LNER offices and agencies'.

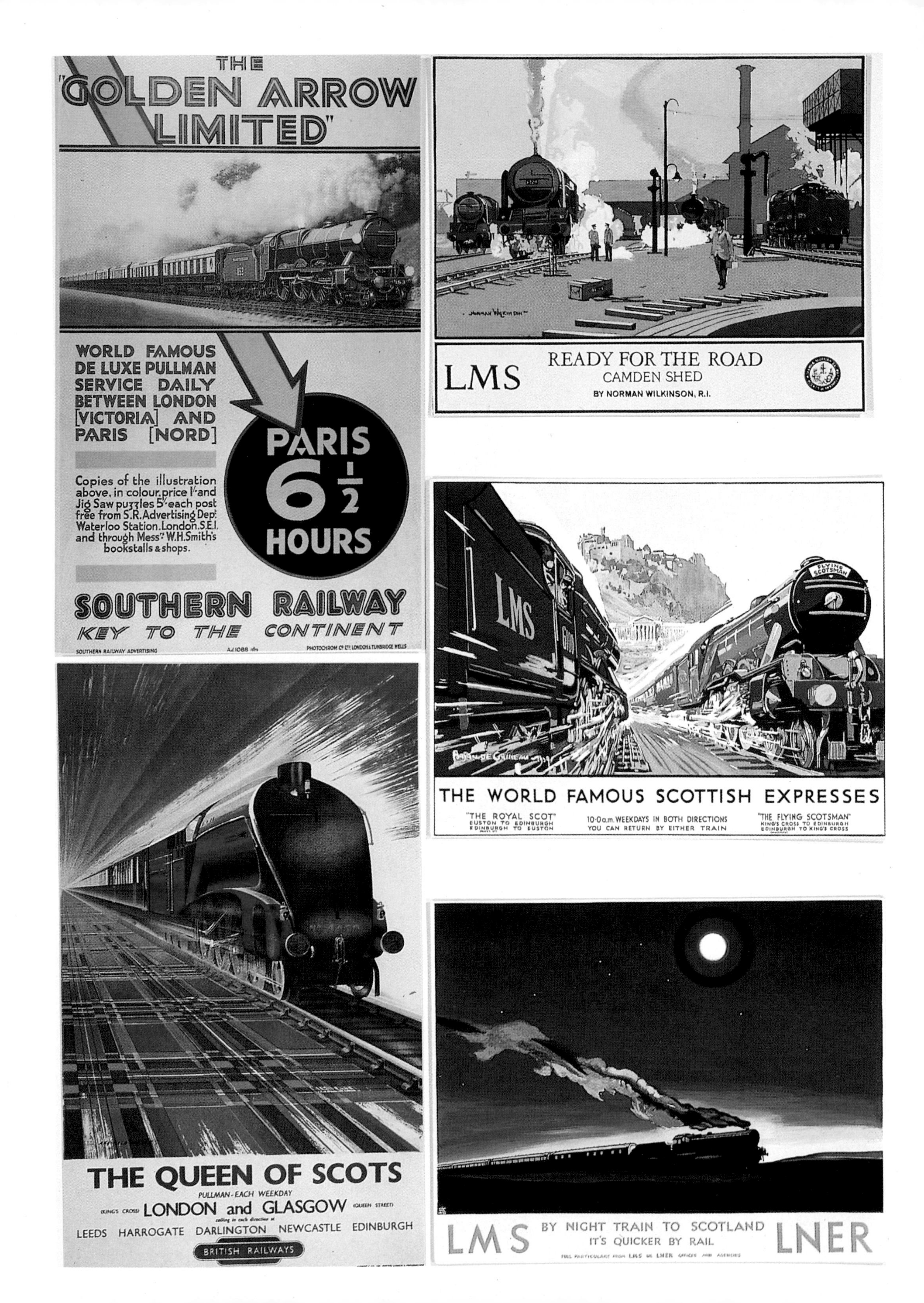
THE "GOLDEN ARROW LIMITED"
WORLD FAMOUS DE LUXE PULLMAN SERVICE DAILY BETWEEN LONDON [VICTORIA] AND PARIS [NORD]
PARIS 6 1/2 HOURS
Copies of the illustration above, in colour, price 1/- and Jig Saw puzzles 5/- each post free from S.R. Advertising Dept. Waterloo Station, London, S.E.1. and through Mess.rs W.H. Smith's bookstalls & shops.
SOUTHERN RAILWAY
KEY TO THE CONTINENT
SOUTHERN RAILWAY ADVERTISING
PHOTOCHROM Co. LTD. LONDON & TUNBRIDGE WELLS
NORMAN WILKINSON
LMS
READY FOR THE ROAD
CAMDEN SHED
BY NORMAN WILKINSON, R.I.
LMS
FLYING SCOTSMAN
THE WORLD FAMOUS SCOTTISH EXPRESSES
"THE ROYAL SCOT"
EUSTON TO EDINBURGH
EDINBURGH TO EUSTON
10·0 a.m. WEEKDAYS IN BOTH DIRECTIONS
YOU CAN RETURN BY EITHER TRAIN
"THE FLYING SCOTSMAN"
KING'S CROSS TO EDINBURGH
EDINBURGH TO KING'S CROSS
THE QUEEN OF SCOTS
PULLMAN - EACH WEEKDAY
(KING'S CROSS) LONDON and GLASGOW (QUEEN STREET)
LEEDS HARROGATE DARLINGTON NEWCASTLE EDINBURGH
BRITISH RAILWAYS
LMS
BY NIGHT TRAIN TO SCOTLAND
IT'S QUICKER BY RAIL
LNER

No 7029 Clun Castle *lifts the 8am Kingswear to Paddington towards Whiteball Tunnel on the Devon/Somerset border on 13 July 1957. Normally part of a Plymouth working, the engine was attached at Newton Abbot, the chocolate-and-cream coaches have been strengthened by standard maroon liveried ones.*

L
505

Z35
DELTIC

The Bankers. With feathers of steam from their safety valves a pair of Jinty 0-6-0 tanks work hard at the rear of a Birmingham-bound train about two-thirds of the way up the Lickey Incline. It is the summer of 1955 and soon, with the Western Region taking over, these LMS stalwarts will be replaced by GWR Hawksworth 0-6-0 pannier tanks, and 'Big Bertha' too will have gone to her long rest. The train is a Bournemouth–Sheffield of mixed LMS, LNER and BR Mk 1 stock.

The LMS trains over this route would usually be headed by a Compound or Jubilee – in later BR years with the deletion of the 4-4-0 and addition of a rebuilt Scot or a Black Five, even a B1. Whatever the motive power the Lickey was never tackled without a banker (except by a three-coach local), the number of helpers depending on the power classification of the train engine(s) and the load. Northbound they would come to a halt at Bromsgrove. Almost before a train stopped one, two or sometimes three bankers would emerge – either Jinty 0-6-0 tanks (in the days following the takeover of the section by the Western Region aided by Swindon-designed 94XX pannier tanks) which were 'equal one', and/or Big Bertha the ex-Midland 0-10-0 specially built for the job which was 'equal two'. When Big Bertha went to her last rest in 1956 she was replaced by a BR standard 2-10-0 usually No 92079 which had the old lady's headlamp fitted for working after dark. Various other classes from an ex-LNWR 0-8-4 tank, a Great Western 2-8-0 tank to the huge LNER 2-8-0 + 0-8-2 Garratt were tried but were sent packing by the Bromsgrove crews.

Every regular traveller regarded the Lickey Incline as a key part of the journey. Fathers taught sons how down trains tested their brakes before the descent from the Midland plain. Every youngster had his head out of the window for the ascent. Two crows on the whistle from the bankers and an answering couple from the train engine and they were off: two miles at 1 in 37.7 with only a small break at Pikes Pool. For the bankers it was a hard slogging job, the engines needing to go for overhaul

One of the Western Region's Britannias (based on Cardiff Canton shed) No 70022 Tornado *climbs out of the Severn Tunnel with 1Z35 an up excursion around 1960. The Western had few BR Standard Pacifics and these were all used on the South Wales main line.*

The prototype Deltic diesel electric at Acton Bridge between Crewe and Weaver Junction on one of the Liverpool–Euston Express trains probably the 14.10 Manxman in the summer of 1957.

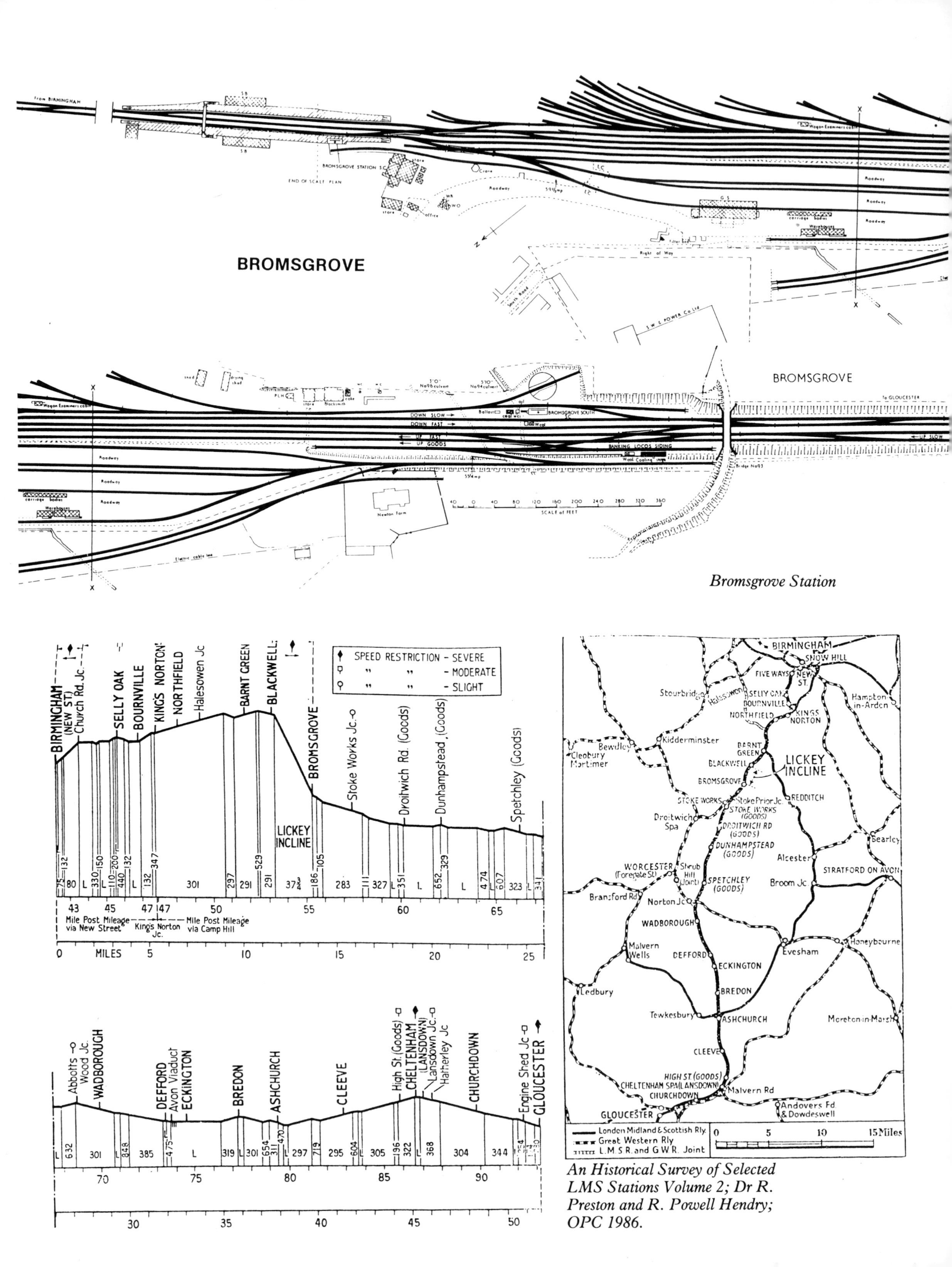

Bromsgrove Station

An Historical Survey of Selected LMS Stations Volume 2; Dr R. Preston and R. Powell Hendry; OPC 1986.

at Derby long before the normal mileage examination was due. For the train engine crew often a welcome break and a chance to repair a poor fire. The few observers who watched from the trackside in the days of steam were never disappointed. Standing at Burcot (about half a mile from the summit) one could see the white (or often black) clouds appearing in the distance as soon as the first train had cleared the intermediate block signal and the track diagram in Blackwell box showed what appeared to the uninitiated to be two trains on line! Up they came with twin- and three-cylinder exhausts reverberating over the Worcestershire countryside followed by the sharp beats from the bankers as they thundered up in full forward gear. Remarkably, there were very few fires, but those were the days of the regular track gang and controlled lineside burning.

To provide a service between northern cities and the Sussex resorts, avoiding London, in 1905 the LNWR and LB&SC companies put on a restaurant-car express between Liverpool/Manchester/Birmingham and Brighton/Eastbourne, known as the *Sunny South Express*. It proved so popular that Kent resorts soon obtained similar facilities by several through coach workings which have long passed into history. In summers before World War II the operation was complicated. Several independent trains were necessary at weekends. The Liverpool and Manchester daily portions combined at Crewe and ran via Willesden Junction, where Southern locomotives took over, working the train over the West London line and Clapham Junction to East Croydon. A portion from Birmingham had been attached at Rugby. On summer Saturdays through restaurant-car trains ran between Birmingham and Hastings and also from Birmingham to the Kent coast resorts, the latter being routed from the West London line through Longhedge Junction on to the SE main line from Victoria. The name *Sunny South Express* was not revived after 1945, but trains continued to run over the West London line to and from the Sussex coast on Saturdays.

The list could go on almost endlessly. There was, for example, a quite separate Margate–Birkenhead SR/GWR service also including a restaurant car. Trains like this not merely made many more journeys possible without changing stations in London but greatly added to the repertoire that could be achieved with only one change. Thus South Devon folk boasted they could get almost anywhere in Britain by through carriage or only one change, the Margate–Birkenhead itself adding many places to the list. It was as much the speeding up of services to London as economies made elsewhere that ended the colourful days of the network of cross-country institutions.

But not all journeys take people anywhere near the capital. Complicated indeed is the story of the Trans-Pennine services, for example. Four pre-grouping companies were involved, the LNWR, L&Y and GC in competition at the west end with the North Eastern holding a monopoly at the east. After the 1923 grouping the all-LNER trains ran via Sheffield Victoria over the steeply graded (some at 1 in 120) route via the three-mile-long Woodhead Tunnel. Down then through Guide Bridge into Manchester, the Liverpool trains being taken over the

Goodbye to the Leicesters

So the once efficient old Midland and Great Northern Joint is to end its career as from midnight on 28 February 1959!

To relieve the gloom of that announcement, were it possible, I made my way through the fog to Spalding Town station on the Tuesday of Christmas week to watch, for one of the last times, the arrival, engine change and departure of a friendly old express. It was a few minutes after 12 noon and a gleaming if somewhat elderly 4-6-0 *Gayton Hall* stood waiting for its right away with the 12.12pm local to Peterborough, but there would be no friendly race today with the up Leicester as the latter was not even signalled.

A violent eruption of surplus steam marked the spot where the relieving engine for the long overdue express was waiting. Although it was masked by a rake of empty coaching stock, I guessed it would be an Ivatt class 4 Mogul from the local shed which had worked the train turn and turn about with its sisters for the last couple of years. It was another of this class – a Yarmouth Beach engine – which brought in the late-running train already some thirteen minutes down but excusable in the foggy conditions and the fact that it was strengthened from the usual seven vehicles to thirteen well filled LMS coaches and an elderly ex-Great Eastern buffet car.

They were quick enough making the locomotive change and eventually the Leicester got away with greater zest and energy than I had ever seen before despite its augmented make-up. No wonder for what I had taken for a class 4

continued from page 155
2-6-0 turned out in reality to be a snappy B1 4-6-0 No 61159 of Immingham shed called upon specially to work the service during the week of heavy Christmas traffic. She was not only the first of her class but the first really modern ten-wheeler to work over M&GN metals so I was lucky enough to see history in the making – the last claim to special note in the long story of the two daily expresses known throughout East Anglia as the Leicesters. – R. S. McNaught.

Cheshire Lines Committee by LNER locomotives. Some Hull–Liverpool trains diverged at Godley Junction, east of Guide Bridge, and worked forward via Stockport to Glazebrook. The Woodhead route was also used by the cross-country trains from Cleethorpes to Manchester as well as the GC/LNER Marylebone–Manchester expresses. The L&Y Trans-Pennine services from Lancashire via the Hebden Bridge route remained on L&Y, later LMS, metals until they reached Normanton or Goole, but the far more important LNW/LMS trains via Diggle were handed over to the NER/LNER at Leeds.

Since nationalisation the Woodhead route has been closed, the Diggle line taking all the expresses, though from May 1989 these were diverted at Stalybridge to run via Guide Bridge, Manchester Piccadilly and the CLC calling at Birchwood and Warrington. For some years the Hull–Liverpool services were worked by special six-car diesel sets known as Trans-Pennines. Little do those whose only train journeys are to or from London know of this other and totally different England served by trains spending all their lives going east and west and climbing the great Pennine divide.

Inaugurated as far back as 1885, and unofficially known as the North Country Continental, or to northern railwaymen as just 'the Boat Train', the cross-country from Harwich to the North has a long and honourable history taking many people on especially important journeys. Until a few years ago, the northbound train from Harwich ran via the north curve

Port to port cross country. The eastern approach to Standedge tunnel with Jubilee class 4-6-0 No 45705 Seahorse *on a Hull–Liverpool express c1955. The train is on the 1894 double line, still in use. On the right are the two original single-bore tunnels of 1849 and 1871. A class 08 diesel and brake van stand on the up slow line.*

at Manningtree, Ipswich, Bury St Edmunds, Ely, and March, where the two coaches for Birmingham were detached to be worked forward via Peterborough and (originally) Rugby. The main train then continued down the GN&GE Joint Line through Spalding to Lincoln, where it was split into separate sections for Liverpool/Manchester and York. The former went via Retford, Sheffield Victoria and the Woodhead route, and the latter the Joint Line to Black Carr Junction and Doncaster. By changing at York passengers could connect into the down *Flying Scotsman*. Before World War II the boat train was headed as far as Lincoln by ex-GE Claud Hamilton 4-4-0s or B12 4-6-0s, but Sandringham 4-6-0s eventually took over working through from Ipswich to Manchester. Many changes have taken place since then. Electrification of the Woodhead route diverted the service into Manchester Piccadilly, so it no longer went through to Liverpool although for a short time, to avoid a loco change, a class 37 diesel was in charge of the train throughout. In 1970 Sheffield Victoria was closed, so the train then took the ex-Midland/LMS route from Sheffield Midland over the Hope Valley to Manchester. Finally, in 1973, came diversion from the GN&GE Joint Line to run from March via Peterborough, Grantham, Nottingham Midland and Sheffield Midland, reversing there for the run over the Hope Valley route. Lincoln thus lost the train which, for nearly ninety years, had been its star visitor. Every day there had been the twice daily ritual of seeing away the two northbound services and joining

From northern murk to southern sunshine. Former LNWR Prince of Wales class 4-6-0 LMS No 5676 Petrel *on a portion of the up Sunny South Express probably between Colwich and Rugeley in 1929. This would appear to be a Saturday-only train of nearly one hundred per cent ex-LNWR coaches either from Manchester or Liverpool which would be split on the Southern for destinations such as Hastings, Dover and Ramsgate. The train ran to Southern Railway metals via the Willesden Junction and Addison Road connections.*

up the two southbound. It was a personal loss to many of the staff.

The principal Scottish cross-country route is that between Glasgow and Aberdeen. The ex-Caledonian Railway route was via Stirling, Perth, Coupar Angus, Forfar and Kinnaber Junction near Montrose. However, in 1967 the entire Caledonian line from Stanley Junction, near Perth, to Kinnaber Junction was closed to passengers, and trains were diverted from Perth via Dundee and Arbroath to Montrose. Over the years several named expresses have used these routes, such as the *Bon Accord*, *Grampian*, *Granite City* and *St Mungo*. The last LNER A4 Pacifics in regular service worked the Glasgow–Aberdeen trains. There is now a fast diesel service, running at two-hour intervals and taking less than three hours for the journey across Scotland.

Not merely were the cross-country trains very special for many of the routes and stations they served (they were often the only full-length train and restaurant car of the day) but there was always a distinctive atmosphere on board them. Any train to or from London naturally is busiest and fastest nearest the capital. Many cross-country services had no one major traffic point and therefore no anti-climax the further they went from it. They were mainly well regarded, well used especially at holiday times, with a combination of people travelling a respectable distance and those hopping on for a few stations. Some, such as those going to the major ports, or those linking ports such as the Plymouth–Southampton–Brighton service, of course had a special maritime flavour. They virtually none of them had the latest rolling stock but nearly all were maintained to a decent standard. As with the examples already quoted, where a train ran partly on two companies' territory, each provided one set, and you did not have to be a railway enthusiast to wonder if today would bring say the chocolate-and-cream *Devonian* into Sheffield. Literally dozens of them had restaurant cars whose crews had carefully developed their 'sittings' to dovetail with the schedules and likely demand. Only the restaurant-car crews worked through onto another company's territory, of course; and since so many of their customers were on board only for an hour or two, the stewards would become specially warm to those with them throughout a long journey and taking three or even four meals.

Because so many of them served ports and resorts, the loadings of the cross-country services tended to vary more sharply than those of London trains. Timings took into account the upper limits. At times of quiet or moderate business, therefore, the cross-countries tended to be exemplary timekeepers and often arrived at major stations several minutes early, enabling the platform work to be done in relaxed style. But when things went wrong they went very wrong indeed. Any major delay anywhere could affect them. Disruption out of King's Cross, St Pancras or Euston, and it could tell on the cross-countries heading to the South West. At peak times, or in bad weather, they were naturally given less priority than the key London expresses. Many of them carried huge quantities of mail which led to progressive delays in the days before Christmas. Put fog and heavy mail together, and you needed to be a mathematician to work out how the hundreds of minutes late translated

Welsh Special

All Wales it seems was served by the 10.37 from Euston, which for good measure also served Buxton by a slip at Nuneaton and running via Burton and Ashbourne. The West and South Wales coaches came off at Stafford and ran via Wellington to Shrewsbury, where the Aberystwyth coach went on to Welshpool and over the Cambrian, while the Swansea coach travelled by the Central Wales line through Llandrindod Wells. The main train, with luncheon car, continued to Chester without calling at Crewe and followed the North Wales coast, shedding the Llandudno coach at Llandudno Junction, the last remnants running via Bangor to Afon Wen and Pwllheli.

Who would have travelled all the way from Euston to Swansea, taking 7hr 38min when there was a perfectly good Great Western express in three hours less? However, it did provide a direct service from Manchester and Liverpool to Swansea, linking with the Euston coaches at Shrewsbury, and that was just as quick as going via Cardiff. And of course the through coach from Euston gave a much quicker service to places like Llandrindod Wells than from Paddington. The LMS service was clearly in demand for even at the outbreak of World War II, when some services had been rationalised, there was still a Euston–Swansea through coach off the 10.40 train from Euston to Liverpool.

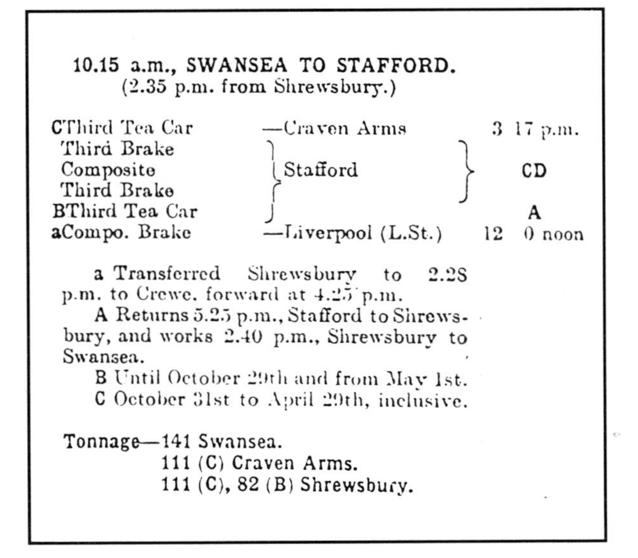

10.15 a.m., SWANSEA TO STAFFORD.
(2.35 p.m. from Shrewsbury.)

Vehicle	Destination	Time / Note
CThird Tea Car	—Craven Arms	3 17 p.m.
Third Brake	Stafford	CD
Composite	Stafford	CD
Third Brake	Stafford	CD
BThird Tea Car	Stafford	A
aCompo. Brake	—Liverpool (L.St.)	12 0 noon

a Transferred Shrewsbury to 2.28 p.m. to Crewe, forward at 4.25 p.m.

A Returns 5.25 p.m., Stafford to Shrewsbury, and works 2.40 p.m., Shrewsbury to Swansea.

B Until October 29th and from May 1st.

C October 31st to April 29th, inclusive.

Tonnage—141 Swansea.
111 (C) Craven Arms.
111 (C), 82 (B) Shrewsbury.

Afternoon luxury. Shrewsbury station south end c1935 – the 10.35 Swansea–Stafford is just leaving with an LNW 'Tea-Car' next to the engine. This was a 57ft cove-roof corridor coach with two compartments converted to a small kitchen/pantry for the service of teas and light refreshments. For some years the tea-car ran through to Stafford in the summer but in the winter was detached at Craven Arms and returned on a down train. A roof board can be seen on the third vehicle which is presumably the Swansea Victoria–Euston through coach.

into hours. 420 minutes late off Birmingham was not unique for the Paignton-bound *Devonian* at such times.

Among its last stations of call was the village of Kingskerswell. Many hours after the solitary porter had turned off the lights and gone home, the train of a dozen coaches would roll to a halt on the rising gradient. The whole village was wakened by the sound of the locomotive struggling to gain adhesion on the slippery rails, and once in BR days (with a Britannia much despised by Newton Abbot men) the hills echoed with the sound of slipping wheels for fifteen minutes, nearly a quarter of a day since a couple of optimistic would-be passengers had arrived expecting the train to be on time.

Somerset & Dorset Interlude

The old Midland and London & South Western joint line (later LMS and Southern) from Bath to Bournemouth handled a prodigious amount of traffic during the summer months with the brunt on Saturdays stretching the locomotives and operating departments to their limits when trains were running block and block first in one direction and then the other. When all was well, that is. Unfortunately trains coming from as far north as Liverpool, Manchester or Sheffield were rarely on time and the congested main line from Birmingham New Street had problems let alone the single line out of Bath. Operating became a nightmare if the south-bound trains failed to run to schedule but they always coped – somehow. During Midland and LMS days the S&D was very much the preserve of Derby 4-4-0s and 0-6-0s. The coming of the Black Fives eased the position tremendously though these were later replaced by the Bulleid West Country Pacifics aided and abetted by some BR Standard class fives and the ubiquitous class 9F 2-10-0s. But on a summer Saturday it was the luck of the draw. What could be certain was that the Mendips would echo the sound of thundering exhausts as the trains wound their way serpent-like over the hills crammed to the doors with outward- or homeward-bound holidaymakers.

Over the Mendips. The Somerset & Dorset, a favourite line for railway photographers if not for the operators due to the long steep gradients and lengthy single-line sections. MR class 2P 4-4-0 No 509 plus an unknown LMS class 5 leave Combe Down tunnel with an express off the Midland at the head of ten well-filled coaches of LMS stock. The date is probably 1948 or 1949.

Masbury summit. A summer Saturday relief train from Bournemouth to the north of England breasts the summit of the Mendips on 23 August 1952; the gradient is 1 in 50. The pilot is LMS-built class 2P No 40696, the train engine Bulleid Pacific No 34042 Dorchester. *The leading pair of coaches is an articulated set built by the LMS for excursion traffic in 1937 as Third opens.*

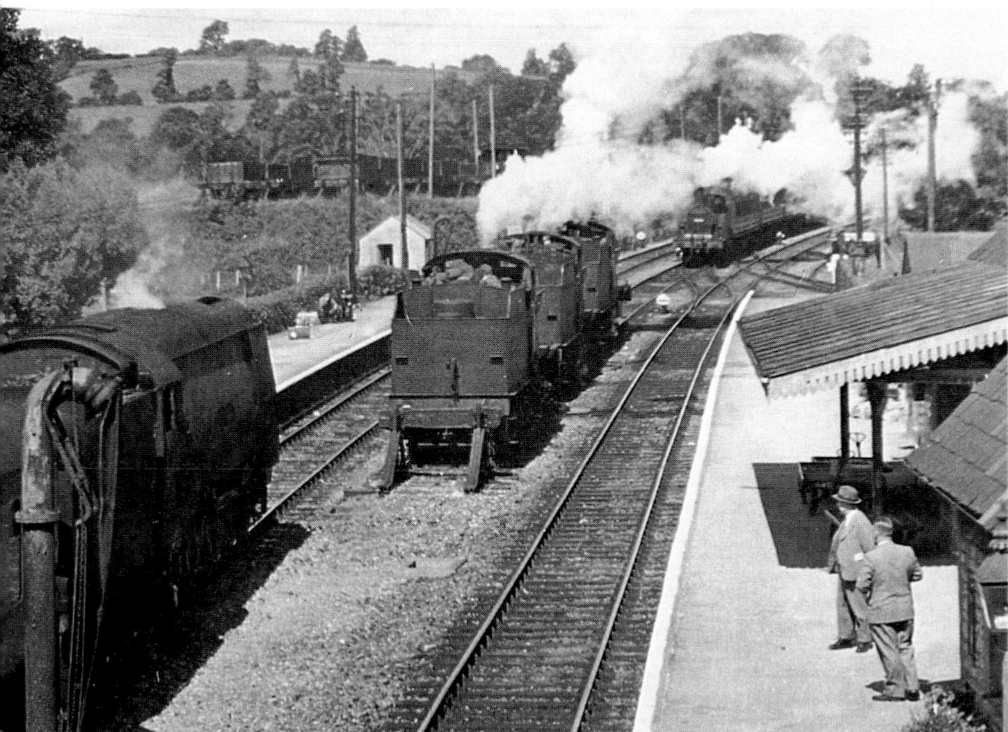

Evercreech Junction. Two views of this mecca for enthusiasts in the 1950s. Evercreech was the watering stop for trains out of Bournemouth en route for the notorious climb up over the Mendips to Bath (Green Park). On a busy summer Saturday engines from Bath shed queued up here for pilot duty on the centre road. Most were class 2P 4-4-0s but occasionally a photographer's luck was in and a Somerset & Dorset 2-8-0 or a class 4F 0-6-0 appeared. These photographs were taken in the early 1950s just after the introduction of the Bulleid Pacifics; they show the scene (a) looking south with five 2P 4-4-0s awaiting their turn and (b) a north-bound express entering behind a filthy West Country, three 2Ps on the centre road and ex-Midland 0-4-4 tank BR No 58086 entering the station off the branch from Highbridge.

Wartime Train Services

3 September 1939, a fateful day which changed the lives of everybody in Britain. The war effectively started two days earlier for the railways. Streamlined trains and other prestige services ran for the last time on Thursday 31 August, and on 1 and 2 September many special trains ran to evacuate children from London, Birmingham and other vulnerable areas. (Unnecessary as it happened as heavy air raids did not commence for another year.)

Industrious Duchess. Probably THE classic Eric Treacy picture taken on a stormy day in March 1942 at Shap Wells, near the summit of the 1 in 75 bank. No 6230 Duchess of Buccleuch, *now fitted with double chimney but not yet with smoke deflectors, has the sixteen-coach 10.00 from Euston – the peacetime Royal Scot – in tow. The white feather from the safety valves and the absence of steam sanding, shows that engine and crew are in full command. The photographer had miscalculated his time and had to run the last two miles. Fortunately the train was held at Shap Wells signal 300 yards away!*

Many regular trains were cancelled to find paths and stock for the evacuation specials.

In the first days of the war the Great Western ran no West of England expresses via Castle Cary, and generally services were much reduced. Everyone expected it 'to be over by Christmas', so a sharp short shock seemed natural.

The first emergency printed timetable dated '25 September 1939 until further notice' was a very paltry affair with what few trains there were averaging not more than 45mph and restricted to a maximum speed of 60mph. This was raised to 75mph in December 1939.

Restaurant cars were withdrawn from all trains for three weeks but were reinstated from 16 October. They were again withdrawn from all but seventy-two trains in May 1942 and completely from 5 April 1944 not being reinstated until late in 1945 after the end of the war with Japan.

Sleeping cars continued to run throughout the war but were reduced towards the end of 1941 when a system of

priority booking was introduced by the Ministry of War Transport for passengers travelling on business of national importance. To increase the number of berths available some first-class cars were fitted with upper berths thus doubling the number.

Travelling Post Offices continued to run but, due to the blackout, all exchange of mail at lineside apparatus was cancelled until 1945. Excursion and most of the other big range of cheap fares were withdrawn as booking offices were given notices: Is Your Journey Necessary? But monthly returns, a third more than single, had became so universally used that they remained standard throughout the war years.

On the LMS, all trains were loaded up to the equivalent, or even above, the 'full load' tonnages. The East Coast main line fared worst as there were no spare paths for reliefs. Many prodigious loads were taken out of Kings Cross with a maximum of twenty-six coaches being recorded on one occasion. It meant loading the train in two platforms and joining the two halves before departure with the engine out of sight in Gasworks Tunnel.

A complete blackout was of course enforced from 1 September and initially carriage lighting was restricted to low wattage blue bulbs. Of course carriage blinds had to be drawn. Gradually restrictions were relaxed and (though blinds still had to be drawn and windows had a 3in black strip painted on) shaded white lights were allowed. The shade cast two rows of light approximately along passengers' knees and it was possible to read with difficulty. Stations with overall roofs usually had the glass removed and replaced with asbestos sheets.

The frequency of trains was gradually increased and the basic winter service dated 28 October 1940 remained in force with minor adjustments throughout the war, except for summer 1944, and it was possible to run some holiday trains in 1941, 1942 and 1943.

Timekeeping was generally speaking poor due to heavy line occupation by the many extra freight trains necessary for the war effort and the build-up to D-Day. The blackout also slowed down operations especially during the long winter nights. 'Summertime' was in force throughout the year with 'Double Summertime' from late April to mid August.

1944 saw the long awaited invasion of Europe and to provide coaches and paths for the many troop trains, train services were again curtailed between April and October with a maximum cut of 290,000 train miles per week in July. This was quite inadequate for the traffic offering and towards the end of the month some extra trains were permitted. One particularly notorious day was Saturday 29 July when it was necessary to close Paddington station as the platforms and concourse were packed with travellers and the queue to enter the station stretched along the approach road and snaked its way into Eastbourne Terrace. It needed intervention at very high level to get agreement for extra trains to be laid on at the last minute. (Reputedly Sir James Milne had threatened to go direct to No 10 Downing Street.) This was of course at the height of the V1 and V2 rocket raids and the loss of life would have been tremendous if one had landed on Paddington. Air raid damage caused its own delays in many areas.

The autumn and winter of 1944–5 saw a partial lifting of the blackout with improved station and yard lighting which no doubt helped punctuality although the system was by this time very run down. It was also possible to run some extra trains at Christmas.

VE and VJ day did not bring any immediate improvements in services but gradually they improved starting with the winter timetable of October 1945 when such trains as the GWR Wolverhampton–Penzance were reinstated. Steam trains never again reached the zenith of the years 1937 to 1939 either in speed or frequency.

Wartime travel was often a grim affair, passengers sleeping as well as standing in the corridor, firemen coaxing ailing locomotives with coal that would have been rejected in normal times. Yet every now and then one came across a locomotive that somehow was in good trim, with coal that wanted to burn, a crew who wished to give their best . . . and a route along which all the freights had been neatly sidetracked. Many a soldier going to or from leave then experienced something of the thrill of a great express train he could not possibly have afforded to travel on in the thirties.

Request Stop

The time I felt important on a railway journey was at the end of a summer holiday at Dunbar. The 1.15pm ex-Waverley was scheduled to call conditionally to take up for the South, and I happened to be the sole consignment. Showing the ticket at the platform gate shook the staff out of their midday siesta and a message to the signalbox sent the points snapping over from the main line to the platform road. In a few minutes Class Z Atlantic No 716 was protesting loudly at the home signal as she was nearly brought to a stand before being allowed to creep into the loop with her heavy train. As usual, the Aberdeen–Penzance portion was full of people who never had been and never intended to go within a hundred miles of either place, but although it only took about three seconds to shove me into a handy corridor it must have been nearer three minutes before the train began to move forward again. If anyone thinks that three-cylinder engines were better at starting their trains than two cylinder, let him observe what happens when the three-cylinder machine is restricted to 65 per cent maximum cut off. I imagine I cost that driver about ten minutes by the time we had laboured up Cockburnspath. – C. B. Harley.

10
SUMMER WEEKENDS

IT is a Saturday in early September, just over a decade into nationalisation and the summer timetable has three weeks or so to run. Britain's railway system has changed little from 1948, steam still reigns almost supreme, the Regions (apart from Scotland) reflect the old big four in their boundaries and the LMR has not yet grabbed the Western Region north of Banbury. So there is yet another decade to go before the shock closure of Birmingham's Snow Hill, a costly error only remedied twenty years on.

The summer timetables still show columns with the magic letters SO, trains which run to the seaside crammed from compartment door to corridor side, for old stock still comes out of carriage sidings to be used on excursions and seasonal traffic needs. Sometimes the engines too are superannuated, Wainwright D and E class 4-4-0s (though in their superb superheated form) along with Ls and L1s regularly head expresses down to the Kent Coast, Compounds run out of Chester to the North Wales resorts and rebuilt Claud Hamiltons to Cromer.

On this Saturday Birmingham's Tyseley shed has charge of the 8.5am SO to Aberystwyth and Barmouth via several stations to Wolverhampton (Low Level) then running fast to Wellington and Shrewsbury, taking the Abbey Foregate loop before the station, thus allowing the train to run direct on to the Aberystwyth road which meets the Cambrian main line at Buttington Junction just short of Welshpool. For this job they need an engine and crew capable of working right through. And it is a long day's work. No real problem here as a number of Tyseley men know the road, and there are two suitable classes available, 43 and 63XX class Moguls and a couple of Manors.

At 7.53 there is a whistle from beneath the city centre tunnel and in a moment No 7819 *Hinton Manor* rushes round the rear of the south end box and into No 1 platform. The family crowd into one of the red-and-cream-painted ex-GWR corridor thirds in the rear Barmouth section, putting the luggage on the racks but carefully leaving the children's impedimenta (buckets and spades, water wings, clockwork boats and string bags full of bathing costumes) on the floor to repel intruders. They make themselves at home; the train is not due at Barmouth until 12.54.

It is very much the same as a trip from any big industrial centre: slow, at least in parts. To start, picking up at Handsworth and Smethwick (with its adjacent Birmingham Railway Carriage & Wagon Company, once the builders of magnificent Pullman cars), West Bromwich, past Swan Village (whose swans have long departed the polluted canal adjacent to the huge gas holders) and then at Wednesbury, Bilston and

Problem on Shap

The diminutive signal box at Scout Green, half way up the 4½ miles of 1 in 75 that is Shap bank, acted as intermediate block post and controlled a very minor level crossing; there were just two signals each way. No points.

A streamlined Duchess is on the ten o'clock from Euston, seventeen packed coaches probably grossing 580 tons. The year 1942. The driver was going nicely when, across the open fell, he picked out Scout Green's home at danger. Hastily taking the speed out of the train, he puts steam on again so to approach at walking pace. He can see the signalman anxiously watching his block shelf. But train out of section and acceptance with the signal pulled off came too late. The driver has run out of track and stopped.

Try as he will, he cannot restart. The rail is dry, he puts down sand, his Duchess does not slip once, it simply cannot lift the train. The bobby knows the drill. After a quarter of an hour (before the guard had got his second detonator on the rail) the steam of a banking engine appears from the Tebay direction. The banker leans on the train while 'crow' whistles are exchanged. Then, slowly and with much noise from either end, the vast caravan begins to move.

Taking the tablet. The Cambrian main line was one of the last strongholds of steam. In the summer of 1965 Manor class 4-6-0 No 7802 Bradley Manor *(with nameplates removed) leaves Llanbrynmair with a down express, possibly the 08.05 Birmingham–Aberystwyth. The stock appears to be one hundred per cent ex-LMS origin. The down signals are still ex-Cambrian (although repainted with vertical stripes on the arms – the Cambrian was one of the few lines to use spots). The fireman has just collected the electric tablet from the manual exchange apparatus.*

Homeward bound. Nos 3209 and 7811 Dunley Manor *drop the three Barmouth coaches on to the main train from Aberystwyth at Dovey Junction on 30 August 1959. The nine-coach formation had come down from Tyseley and Birmingham Snow Hill that morning with No 3209 taking the Barmouth portion from Machynlleth. The 0-6-0 was detached at Dovey Junction and coupled to the front of the Manor coming off at Talerddig summit. The train arrived back at Tyseley a couple of minutes early; only 4½ hours from Towyn where the photographer joined it!*

CAFETERIA CAR EXCURSION

— TO —

WELSHPOOL, NEWTOWN,
MACHYNLLETH, BORTH

AND

ABERYSTWYTH

WITH THROUGH PORTION TO

ABERDOVEY,
TOWYN and BARMOUTH

SUNDAY, 30th AUGUST

FROM TRAIN No. X27	DEPART	Return Fares—Second Class								DUE BACK
		Welshpool	Newtown	Machynlleth	Borth	Aberystwyth	Aberdovey	Towyn	Barmouth	
	a.m.	s. d.	s. d.	s. d.	s. d.	s. d.	s. d.	s. d.	s. d.	p.m.
TYSELEY	9 45	9/-	10/9	14/9	16/3	17/6	16/3	17/-	17/-	11 30
SMALL HEATH & S.	9 48	9/-	10/9	14/9	16/3	17/6	16/3	17/-	17/-	11 25
BORDESLEY	9 50	8/6	10/3	14/3	15/9	17/-	15/9	16/6	16/6	11 20
BIRMINGHAM (Snow Hill)	10 0	8/6	10/3	14/3	15/9	17/-	15/9	16/6	16/6	11 10
WEST BROMWICH	10 10	8/-	9/9	13/9	15/3	16/6	15/3	16/-	16/-	11 0
WEDNESBURY (Central)	10 15	7/6	9/3	13/3	14/9	16/-	14/9	15/6	15/6	10 55
BILSTON (Central)	10 20	7/6	9/3	13/3	14/9	16/-	14/9	15/6	15/6	10 45
WOLVERHAMPTON (Low Level)	10 35	7/-	8/9	12/9	14/3	15/6	14/3	15/-	15/-	10 35
ARRIVAL TIMES		p.m. 12 10	p.m. 12 40	p.m. 1 30	p.m. 1 55	p.m. 2 15	p.m. 2 5	p.m. 2 15	p.m. 2 40	
RETURN TIMES—SAME DAY		p.m. 9 5	p.m. 8 35	p.m. 7 35	p.m. 7 0	p.m. 6 40	p.m. 7 5	p.m. 6 55	p.m. 6 30	H.D.

The Cafeteria Car will Work Through to ABERYSTWYTH

Wolverhampton (Low Level) where they arrive at 8.42 and the train really fills up. There is a further stop at Wellington, then they are right away in summer-Saturday-only style to Welshpool where there is a halt for water. On then through Newtown and Moat Lane (junction for the Brecon line) to Machynlleth where the train splits, No 7819 running through to Aberystwyth with the first five coaches.

After a twenty-minute wait an Oswestry-based 22XX Class 0-6-0 No 3209 eventually backs on the remnant. This is credited as an express but in fact stops at all stations though not the halts. They are into Barmouth Junction at 12.47½, exchange tablets and away over the embankment by 12.49. The family are now leaning out of the windows catching the strong smell of ozone and seaweed which pervades the Mawddach Estuary and gazing up towards Dolgelly and the mountains, a view which George Borrow described as the 'finest in all Wales'. They rumble over the ancient trestle and across the swing bridge, through a small tunnel and out over the Barmouth Harbour trestle. Everyone is now excited and the bags come down from the racks, the children hardly able to contain themselves. Alongside the sand dunes, over the level crossing and into the station. The holiday express has made it to time – well, give two or three minutes – and the adults recall that when things go adrift on this sprawling single-line network the delay can be counted in hours rather than minutes.

The 1950s were not far adrift in their behavioural patterns to those of the 20s and 30s though naturally summer weekends meant different things to different people. To thousands of seaside landladies Saturday mornings involved despatching one lot of holidaymakers and changing the bedclothes in time to get the next lot in during the afternoons. To tens of thousands of children it meant the thrill of a train journey and the prospect of playing on the sands. To many railwaymen it meant a weekend hard at work dealing with the extra Saturdays-only trains. To porters handling mountains of luggage, to taxi drivers extended days and meal times fitted in around the railway's ever-growing demands – for not until 1958 did the number travelling to the coast by train on summer Saturdays finally reach its peak.

Package holidays abroad are now arranged so that the particular airline can get maximum utilisation from the smallest possible fleet of aircraft. No seaside landlady ever volunteered to change over on Wednesdays or Thursdays to ease the load on the railway! The school holiday period in England – it was earlier in Scotland – before the war was mainly condensed into late July and August with a smaller number of lucky people who drew the September straws, but they were usually middle class and better off: some even had cars.

The railway was, therefore, faced with keeping a large fleet of obsolescent vehicles utilised on only a few weekends in summer, on Saturdays-only booked trains and Sunday excursions. Before the start of the summer service special cleaning and maintenance had to be arranged. Some commuter rolling stock, not required for that work at weekends, had to be used on holiday trains. It was unfortunate that many people's only experience of rail travel was the annual holiday trip

Fast Royals

In contrast to what had been expected of the railways during the long reign of Victoria, King Edward VII wanted the royal trains to go faster. On 7 March 1902, when visiting Dartmouth to lay the foundation stone of the Royal Naval College, the royal train ran non-stop from Paddington to Kingswear via Bristol – 228½ miles in 4 hours 22½ minutes – arriving twenty minutes before time. On the return journey from Plymouth Millbay Docks the train covered the 246½ miles non-stop in 4 hours 24 minutes. These were the first non-stop runs over such distances. On 14 July 1903 the royal train, hauled by the 4-4-0 No 3433 *City of Bath*, took the Prince of Wales and his wife, later King George V and Queen Mary, from Paddington to Plymouth via Bristol in 3 hours 53½ minutes, thirty-seven minutes less than the booked time. Times had changed!

in outdated stock. And with hindsight we now know that the season only lengthened when more people went by car and staggered their journeys to avoid spending hours on sections like the Exeter bypass. The railway was still common carrier. It handled the peak traffic with military precision. It never occurred to *refuse* the uneconomic surplus.

All round our coast are seaside resorts which, although they now rely on railways to a lesser extent, and in many cases are not served at all, owe their existence to the arrival of a line in the nineteenth century. Probably the place which received the most passengers by rail was Blackpool, which used to be served by three stations within the town, Talbot Road, Central and South. The 'Wakes Week' in a Lancashire town signalled the departure of a high proportion of its population by train, mostly to Blackpool, and the timing of the trains, diagramming of train crews, and the provision of the locomotives and rolling stock required very careful planning. Oldham was one of the most difficult 'Wakes' with 40–50 special trains over Friday night and Saturday morning. The use of 2-8-0 freight engines carrying express passenger headlamps was not uncommon.

There were a number of pinch points affecting the intensive summer Saturday Blackpool caravan. Leaving aside platform capacity at Talbot Road and Central – and coaching stock, once emptied, had to be quickly removed to sidings or outstabling points – they were the Preston area, the flat junction at Euxton five miles to the south, and the two-track

North Wales excursion. There was no such thing as a typical LMS express! This appears to be a Liverpool–Holyhead train passing Edge Hill c1937. The leading loco is No 2951 one of forty 2-6-0s built soon after Stanier was appointed CME and the train engine ex-LNWR George the Fifth 4-4-0 No 25376 Snipe. *The stock is all LMS, a three-coach 'Inter District Set' leading, which may have been detached at Chester, followed by six or more modern corridors.*

Half way up. A summer Saturday relief from Bournemouth to Sheffield approaches Burcot on the 1 in 37.7 Lickey Incline in June 1961. By now the Royal Scots, displaced from West Coast main-line services, had begun to appear regularly on this route and the train is headed by No 46137 The Prince of Wales's Volunteers (South Lancashire) – *originally* Vesta *and the last of the class to be rebuilt.*

Breasting Dainton. A Newton Abbot Standard class 4 4-6-0 No 75026 pilots an unknown Castle towards the summit tunnel on 18 June 1955. The Bulldogs which acted as pilots have been gone for almost a decade their jobs being taken over by these 4-6-0s and 51XX class 2-6-2 tanks. This is probably a north to west express as it contains LMS stock.

section of the West Coast main line through Wigan from Springs Branch to Standish Junction. The latter stretch had been bypassed from 1886 by the Whelley line, accessed by burrowing junctions at Bamfurlong and Standish and used by heavy coal traffic during the week; it came into its own for Saturday Blackpool traffic after World War I.

Then there was the access to Blackpool itself. There were four tracks (joint LNWR/L&Y) from Preston to Kirkham, from where the principal route to Central also served the coastal resorts of Lytham and St Annes, while the Talbot Road line also took the limited Fleetwood traffic (including that for the Isle of Man steamers) as far as Poulton. But to avoid delays to trains routed straight to Blackpool South and Central was the Marton line opened only on summer Saturdays – arrow-straight and stationless, and saving five miles in the process.

So there was substantial scope for routing Blackpool trains a variety of ways. Obscure junctions, unknown even to many railwaymen, assumed brief importance. All these kept trains clear of the West Coast fast lines and brought them into the west side of Preston station ready to veer off towards the coast. From Yorkshire stations served by LNWR, L&Y or Midland there was a number of routes available – Manchester and Parkside to the main line at Golborne (a flat junction), Manchester and the Bickershaw junctions on to the Whelley, via Manchester and Bolton or Atherton to the Whelley or Euxton Junction, via Sowerby Bridge and over Copy Pit to the East Lancs line, or through Skipton and Colne. There was, too, the standing joke, exercised on summer Saturdays, of trains from Scotland and the North passing Preston *southbound*, turning back via the East Lancs line, Lostock Hall and Farington Curve Junction to appear at Preston again 15–20 minutes later now travelling *northwards* to reach the Fylde coast.

So some of the routing must have baffled the expectant clientele. There was, for instance, a regular early morning Leicester Midland–Blackpool train on Saturday (for a long time it nominally started from Desford) which left heading *south* and ran via Coalville, Burton-on-Trent, Derby, Cheadle Heath (where it remanned and turned on to the CLC), Skelton Junction, Glazebrook, on to the Whelley at Amberswood East, Standish Junction and the West Coast slow lines. Little wonder that special saloons had to be laid on in late spring for train men to refresh their route knowledge. Such paths can no longer be trod, for with the decline in this traffic, many of the alternatives – some only ever used by freight except on summer Saturdays, have been closed and lifted.

Resorts originally received most of their business from industrial areas within a reasonable distance. Skegness and Mablethorpe for example became Nottingham/Leicester-by-the-Sea. Sheffielders moved en bloc to Cleethorpes and Scarborough, and the Lancashire mill workers to Blackpool. After World War I people began extending their sights and were aiming further afield. The railways built up a service of long-distance trains at weekends to move them to their ever more remote choices. People now 'did' North Wales one year, Devon the next. So, while Scarborough was originally developed by the North Eastern

Football Traffic at Marylebone

Special traffic at Marylebone – in connection with the England *v* Scotland football match held on 9 April included seven trains from Scotland and thirteen long-distance specials from the Midlands and the North East coast. The dispatching of these various trains on their return journeys was accomplished between 11.5pm on the Saturday night and 2.50am (or 3.50) on the following morning. Including the regular 11pm departure to Manchester, the time interval between this remarkable procession of 21 expresses averaged 11 min. The variety of destinations served by these trains is indicated by the following list of departures:

11.5 Principal stations on the Edinburgh–Glasgow *via* Bathgate line and Hamilton branch.

11.20 Sheffield and stations to Penistone.

11.35 Edinburgh.

11.45 Ruddington, Nottingham, and principal intermediate stations to Mansfield and Cresswell & Welbeck (Guaranteed excursion).

12.0 Burntisland, Thornton Junction, Buckhaven, Methil, Leven.

12.10 Sheffield and district stations.

12.20 Newport, Middlesbrough, South Bank and Redcar (Guaranteed).

12.30 Derby and Burton.

12.40 Principal GC main line stations to Sheffield.

12.50 Sutton-in-Ashfield, Mansfield (Guaranteed).

1.0 Nottingham and district stations.

1.10 York and Newcastle *via* Sunderland.

1.20 Leicester, Nottingham and district stations.

1.30 Sheffield and stations to Rotherham (Guaranteed).

1.40 Easterhouse, Glasgow, Singer.

1.50 Rugby, Leicester and prin-

continued on page 170

mainly to serve the West Riding, in 1923 the LNER put on the *Scarborough Flyer* from London which, by 1935, was covering the 230 miles in 3hr 55min. On summer Saturdays the train had to be supplemented by a further Scarborough train and another serving Whitby and Bridlington.

Like the 'Wakes Weeks' in the Lancashire mill towns, industrial cities on the east side of the country had their 'Trip Weeks', when factories all closed and most of the population headed for the coast. Special trains were arranged for them, many to long-distance destinations. What a problem it was making sure that someone who saw the inside of a train only once a year actually arrived at the resort he was booked instead of one the opposite end of the country.

And so it was with endless variety throughout Britain, a kind of divine law that said that everyone began and ended holidays on a Saturday when main lines and branches were at their busiest. For example on the Southern Railway route to the West Country the *Atlantic Coast Express* ran in two portions at the height of the summer period even on Mondays to Fridays. On Saturdays no less than eight complete restaurant-car trains left Waterloo for the West between 10.24am and 12.05pm – at 10.24 and 10.35 to Ilfracombe, 10.40 to Padstow, 10.54 to Bude, 11 to Plymouth, 11.45 to Sidmouth and Exmouth, 12 noon to Exeter, and 12.05 to Salisbury and all stations from Axminster onwards.

The Southern, throughout its life, was used to dealing with huge volumes of passengers spread over short periods of time, each morning and evening on the London commuter routes. Fortunately, commuters do not travel in large numbers on summer Saturdays and, even on weekdays their numbers are about 10 per cent less than normal representing the proportion taking their own holidays. Summer Saturdays, however, generated tremendous flows of passengers on the routes to the popular resorts, apart from those in the West Country already mentioned. Packed trains ran from London to Brighton, Eastbourne, Hastings and other Sussex resorts, and also to the Kent Coast. This had to be handled along with the Continental boat trains to Dover and Folkestone. From Waterloo there was the traffic to Southampton and Bournemouth (which was only a seaside village in 1870) and so on, Bournemouth also receiving much business from the Midlands and North via the Somerset & Dorset.

A good friend of the railways was Billy Butlin. He started at Skegness with a big dipper. It was said that the LNER gave him credit to move it in by rail, and he never looked back. His many holiday camps were close to rail, at Skegness, Clacton, Filey, Pwllheli, Minehead and so on, and a high proportion of the passengers arrived by train. At some, like Skegness, buses took them from the station to the camp. At Filey a special Holiday Camp station was constructed after the war (as it was at Pen-y-chain) and the line to Heads of Ayr was reopened.

In spite of all the problems caused by traffic with such a high weekly and seasonal peak, the railways did everything they could to foster the traffic. They produced posters in conjunction with the resorts extolling their virtues and exhorting people to travel to them by rail; indeed they

continued from page 169
cipal GC stations to Chesterfield, Rotherham, Swinton and Conisboro'.
2.0 Leicester, Nottingham and principal stations to Derby.
2.20 & 2.40 Glasgow.
2.50 Edinburgh.

The loads on the majority of these trains varied from 12 to 15 coaches. For probably the first time in the history of Marylebone sleeping cars appeared in service. Eight of these vehicles were observed attached to the 11.5 (3 cars), 11.35 (2 cars), and 2.20 (3 cars).

Locomotives included four 3-cylinder 4-6-0 Sandringham class; two 4-6-0 Sir Sam Fay class; five mixed traffic 4-6-0 B7 class (ex-GC); three 2-6-0 K3 class; one mixed traffic 2-6-2 Green Arrow or V2 class; A1 class Pacifics No 2582 *Sir Hugo*, and No 2575 *Galopin*; two 'C7' class Atlantics of the former NE Z class (both on the same train); and A4 class streamlined Pacific No 4482 *Golden Eagle*.

The usual arrangements for dealing with the large crowds to and from Wembley were supplemented by the use of loudspeakers, and the provision of three additional Bakerloo railway booking offices erected on the concourse. The switching of traffic from the north from one London terminus to another was not confined on this day to the LNER. St Pancras was dealing with traffic from the ex-Caledonian system, Euston was handling special trains from Nottingham and Sheffield.

A down express passes Penmaenpool on the Mawddach estuary hauled by a GW 43XX class 2-6-0 No 6367 which would have come on at Ruabon where the train reversed. The express is probably the 11.05 SO Snow Hill or 09.00 SO Paddington to Pwllheli.

6367

Right Train, Wrong Coach
There was, of course, the important issue of getting passengers in the *right* part of the train. It was no fun if you dashed into St Pancras as the whistles blew for the Manchester train and dived into the last two coaches, only to find after a longer than usual wait at Millers Dale that you were headed up Ashwood Dale into Buxton. You could put details on the station train indicator, put roof boards or labels on the coaches, make loudspeaker announcements, and put sandwich boards on the platform at the split between sections, but always you could guarantee that someone was blithely sitting in the wrong coach and needed to be moved, usually encumbered by luggage, along the corridor. Or in South Devon, where the staff were less assiduous, you expected a regular dribble of Torbay passengers to arrive in Plymouth and vice versa.

effectively subsidised most resorts' publicity campaigns. Again, nobody questioned whether carrying such peaks of traffic made economic sense. It was the railways' job! So huge quantities of rolling stock were maintained and all kinds of extra facilities brought into play. On the Midland & Great Northern, on the North Wales coast line and in South Devon extra signalboxes with only four or eight levers came into use on summer Saturdays, cutting the headway between expresses though often resulting in them reaching important traffic points before they could be handled. Many railway operators throughout the country spent their weekends in the summer sitting on the edge of their seats. Close supervision in the Controls and on the ground was essential. The Press commented on the weekly performance as though it were some great sporting contest.

It was at Bank Holiday periods that special passenger working reached its ultimate peak. So completely altered were the passenger train workings that then practically the whole service could be said to be of a special nature. Carriage and locomotive workings had to be entirely recast. Rolling stock not normally in use had to be pressed into service. Locomotives used mainly on freight, such as 2-8-0s, Moguls and 0-6-0s were allocated to passenger trains. The Special Working booklets issued by headquarters were pored over at local level to ensure that every detail was properly done. 'It can't possibly be done,' said the man in charge of Old Oak Common (Paddington) carriage depot when each August he was instructed to prepare more (and usually longer) trains. But somehow

it always was. And once normal service had been resumed, at all levels discussions were held to see what lessons could be learnt for next year.

Not merely were record numbers of travellers carried, but a great proportion of them on through trains. You could even travel by through service from Cleethorpes to Sidmouth! Literally dozens of branches that were normally self contained had at least a through coach from London on summer Saturdays, and again dozens of inland links normally with no or only an all-stations local passenger-train service suddenly hosted resort-bound expresses. It has to be said that journey times were not always fast; many all-week expresses were allowed an extra 15 minutes or so on summer Saturdays. And delays were sometimes monumental, especially if the overnights to the coast ran so late that the coaches and locomotives were not ready to start their return trips promptly. Delays tended to compound themselves especially on the long single-track routes such as the Midland & Great Northern Joint from Peterborough to Yarmouth, worked absolutely to capacity on busy Saturdays. But while many passengers were delayed and travelled in overcrowded, older trains, generally seeing the railways at their worst, and so took particularly kindly to the thought of car ownership, many others enjoyed fine service . . . exceptionally long non-stop runs overtaking lesser expresses at every possible point at least sometimes working out just as the timetable stated. With reserved window seats, the whole family perhaps enjoying one of those mid-priced two-course summer-Saturday

Through coaches to Lyme Regis. Two 1885-built ex-LSWR Adams 4-4-2 tanks, once the mainstay of the Waterloo suburban services take their coaches, detached from the Southern Region's main train at Axminster, beyond Combepyne one summer Saturday probably in the early 1960s. Nos 30584 and 30583 were two out of the three engines kept at Lyme Regis for working this steep and sharply curved branch. Tractive effort was not really their forte with two vehicles the normal maximum load per loco.

Opposite: Almost there. At about 6 o'clock in the morning SR West Country class 4-6-2 No 34002 Salisbury *coasts down the 1 in 36 gradient into Ilfracombe c1960 on the 01.00 ex-Waterloo. A weary journey for the passengers without the comfort of a sleeping car.*

specials in the restaurant car (a cold plate already at every place before the train was 'called' for the first, second or sometimes even fifth sitting) the scenery, perhaps the first ever view of the sea for the youngsters, the railway interest, the general air of expectancy, the pictures on the compartment wall . . . many of us recall the journey as the highlight of the holiday.

Saturday on the M&GN. LMS-built class 4P No 44231 crosses the Great Ouse at South Lynn with the 08.00 (SO) from Chesterfield to Yarmouth Beach on 30 August 1958. Summer Saturdays on this joint line could be fascinating to the enthusiast but a nightmare to the operators. Long lengths of single track, trains waiting block to block and domino delays all combined to make a long and interesting day for those in the control office. Note the somersault signals. This was the last summer for the M&GN.

Great Central main line. Jubilee 4-6-0 No 45690 Leander *crosses the river Soar bridge south of Leicester Central with a London Marylebone excursion c1962. Although based at Bristol Barrow Road depot (82E) the coming of dieselisation saw* Leander *work a variety of weekend specials over 'foreign' routes.*

Special Occasions

It is rare that a railway general manager writes the blurb for a passenger's handout on an excursion train but Gerard Fiennes was a rare man, a leader, a communicator and very much a human being. So much of a communicator that his writings led him into a head-on buffer-stop meet with his then chairman Sir Stanley Raymond. But that is another story.

In the mid 1960s Gerry Fiennes was in the hot seat at Paddington needing to restore a deal of broken morale but also to implement a much needed modernisation plan in both structure and hardware. He succeeded, and this example shows how well his sense of communication was put to good effect. Steam on the Western Region was due to finish at the end of 1965 and main-line express steam was as good as dead, though the odd Hall occasionally took over from a failed diesel. The Castles bar one, No 7029 *Clun Castle*, had all been withdrawn. It was decided to make the real end an event, and so a special excursion was arranged. Four paragraphs from the published souvenir leaflet handed to passengers read as follows:

> Today, 27 November 1965, is a very special occasion. For when No 7029 *Clun Castle*, the last splendid representative of a splendid breed, takes its train out from Paddington at 9.18am it is beginning its final journey. After this, there will be no more steam-hauled excursion trains from the terminus.
>
> So this is a very special train. It is arranged by the Western Region as a salute to what was probably the most successful class of steam locomotives ever built by any railway. The route it takes is equally famous: to Bristol via Swindon, Brunel's first main line; north to Gloucester, where the gauge war of the 1840s flared up, and Cheltenham – starting point of the *Cheltenham Flyer* – then back to Paddington. At Swindon, birthplace of the Cities, the Stars, the Castles and the Kings, No 7029 – which started life there as part of Lot No 375 – goes to rest, and the link with the great days of steam is severed. At Swindon the new age of diesels comes clearly into its own: two English Electric type 3 (1,750 horsepower) units take charge of the train for the fastest possible run over the remaining 77.3 miles to Paddington – the very stretch of line which the Castles made so famous with the *Cheltenham Flyer*. The transition is complete.
>
> Most of the individual members of this great fleet have made their contribution to the story of the steam locomotive, and by now the railway journals and magazines are studded with phrases like 'brilliant achievement', 'outstanding effort', 'amazing performance'. *Clun Castle*, at the head of today's special train, has also had a share of fame. In May of last year, hauling a 265 ton train, another special, on the Plymouth to Bristol run to commemorate the *City of Truro*'s 1904 exploit, No 7029 reached ninety-six miles an hour down the Wellington bank, maintained ninety

LMS Royal. Most of the larger railway companies maintained either complete trains or a number of saloons for Royalty. In grouping/BR days the LNWR/LMS Royal Train was used for longer journeys. The full LNWR train of ten coaches, still in original colours, is ascending Shap behind Royal Scot class 4-6-0 No 6119 Lancashire Fusilier *c1934. Many of these coaches are preserved, five in the National Collection and one semi-Royal car privately at Birmingham Railway Museum, Tyseley.*

A Southern Royal occasion. By early 1939 the clouds of war were looming darkly on the horizon and it was deemed politic that a Royal visit to the New World should be made to keep lines of communication as strong as possible. Thus HM King George VI and Queen Elizabeth set out on 6 May 1939 for Canada and the United States. Journeys over the Southern by Royalty were short needing no Royal train per se *and good use was made of the Pullman company's stock. Here T9 4-4-0 (the Southern's favourite class for these light train workings) No 718, beautifully finished with the flags of the three countries on a smokebox board plus sparkling white Royal train headcode discs, passes Bedhampton en route to Portsmouth on the first stage of a successful trip.*

An historic occasion. Although the LNER was the poorest of the four inter-war companies it was probably the most enterprising and publicity conscious. In June 1938 to publicise the introduction of new stock on the Flying Scotsman GNR 4-2-2 No 1 of 1870 was brought out of York Museum and put into working order. On 30 June it worked a train of 1888-built six-wheel coaches from Kings Cross to Stevenage where the Press changed into the new train. After this excursion No 1 and its historic vehicles were exhibited at various stations throughout the system and also ran a public trip to Cambridge on 24 August. A fitting climax to all these events was the running by the Railway Correspondence & Travel Society on 11 September of a trip from Kings Cross to Peterborough and back – the first train chartered by an amateur society. No 1 leaves Kings Cross at 13.15 on 11 September 1938.

for some twelve miles, and cut the seventy-two-minute Exeter to Bristol booked timing by a shade under ten minutes.

And now it is the mighty diesel that has taken over this splendid story. Overall speeds are rising dramatically – and the feat of pulling away and topping 80mph in six minutes is commonplace. Two hours to Cardiff and ninety minutes to Bristol are near at hand.

The power is there. The record breaking will go on!

Unfortunately No 7029 was poorly maintained and her last public excursion did not show her up well, though it was still a trip to be remembered. Now the engine rests happily in preservation running from time to time over BR tracks acquitting herself with credit.

While this was a special occasion aimed at the enthusiast public (and obliquely as a good staff relations exercise) there have been and still are many thousands of others, some particularly dramatic, some euphoric, some sad, some glad. Royalty perhaps comes top of the list for since the days of Queen Victoria the Royal Family has travelled extensively by rail mostly in its own train though the short-reigned King Edward VIII preferred either the air for day travel or an ordinary sleeper for an overnight journey. Occasionally he borrowed the official saloon of the LMS president, Sir Josiah Stamp, tacked on to a service train. Since railways began all British monarchs who have died in harness have made their last journeys by train, in recent years from Sandringham to Windsor, usually behind ex-LNER and GWR locomotives; when HM King George VI died in 1952 the then new standard Pacific No 70000 *Britannia* was used from King's Lynn to Kings Cross. Sir Winston Churchill was hauled to his final resting place by train, this time out of Waterloo by a Southern Region Battle of Britain class Pacific, well chosen and carrying his name. Foreign monarchs, presidents of republics and other foreign statesmen in their hundreds have travelled the routes from the Channel ports to London behind Southern engines before the coming of their own special aircraft which have now replaced trains, though some dignitaries still travel by special train from Gatwick to Victoria.

For almost 160 years the railways have been involved in most of the special occasions which have taken place in this country; maybe if a comprehensive list of all the excursions and special trains the railways have organised over the years could be compiled it would provide a unique record of social history over the period. It is difficult today to realise just how different things were only a few years ago before the days of regular air services, motorways, radio, television and FAX.

Then there were the enormous volumes of wartime traffic. For example, between November 1914 and Armistice Day 1918, some 14,000 leave trains ran to and from Victoria carrying 6.5 million officers and men. If the movement of men to and from the training camps on SE&CR territory were included the aggregate number was 14 million. They were perhaps not great expresses but still overtook numerous freights including armament trains. When World War II started in 1939, the railways put their long-planned intensive service of evacuation specials into being and repeated it when the V bombs started falling on London. But everyone knows that the greatest challenge met by the railways was in connection with the evacuation of the BEF from Dunkirk in 1940. In one week 620 specials carrying 320,000 men were moved away from the coast. Later in the war, when the tide had turned, 100,000 men were carried by rail through Southampton in the six days after D-Day. Such were their resources that there was little that the railways could not do. But speed and volume were ever in conflict, one special that had to run at speed and to time taking the capacity of several more mundane trains. Thus it is that Americans who only used wartime troop trains in Britain went home with the mistaken belief that our railways were much slower than theirs.

The power of the box. Between 1959 and 1961 BBC TV screened a regular monthly half-hour programme devoted to railways called Railway Roundabout in which one of the authors was involved. This often presented opportunities for films and photographs normally impossible to obtain. One such programme concerned the running of two ex-North British Railway D34 class 4-4-0s double headed on the through London–Fort William sleeping-car train for two whole days on 8 and 9 May 1959. Both engines, Nos 62471 Glen Falloch *and 62496* Glen Loy *worked the 05.45 ex-Glasgow Queen Street and the 14.56 return from Fort William on each of the two days; they are seen here leaving Ardlui station on 9 May.*

Last steam train to Snow Hill. March 1967 saw the closure of the Great Western's Snow Hill station Birmingham to everything but a few local passenger trains and the discontinuance of the Paddington to the north-west services via Banbury, Birmingham, Wolverhampton (Low Level) and Shrewsbury. To mark this dismal occasion steam specials were run on 4/5 March to Chester and Birkenhead. Reflecting the evening sun No 7029 Clun Castle *climbs Gresford bank on the last journey of all – the return home on 5 March.*

11
KEEPING THEM MOVING: OPERATING AND CONTROL

Time Was
On peaceful dark evenings, with happy heart I very often made my way down platform 5 at Nottingham Midland Station and into the telegraph office on the public side, where all the telegram pads were neatly laid out at the pigeon-hole windows. On the wall a list, around which numerous inspectors and porters were congregated, gave the times at which the London expresses had passed Kettering and Saxby. It was, in fact, really a forecast, because judging from the number of minutes late the 5pm ex-St Pancras was reported, we could safely say 'Compound tonight,' or 'I wonder how they're getting along with that Claughton. They have lost two minutes more at Saxby.' The 5pm St Pancras–Heysham boat train clanked in, both head lamps out, when at a yell from the fireman the brakes went hard on to bring the tender alongside the water column.

It always impressed me that after roaring along through the night for a matter of hours, the driver could bring his train to stand on such close judgement as this. Only on very few occasions have I known them 'set back' or 'open up' to reach the water point. I knew all the enginemen on this turn and as was my practice I handed the leather 'bag' up to the fireman already on top of the tender, and having fixed the cradle support I turned on the water. The driver, with a nod to me, was quickly feeling the wheel centres and motion with the back of his hand, administering oil here and there by the light of a small hand flare. The fireman, pushing coal forward, shouted conversation at me above the increasing roar of steam surging past Ross pop safety valves. The thin scream of a distant whistle sent me frantically turning off the column cock; a green light waved far down the platform, the fire-

continued on page 180

UNUSUALLY, the weak winter sun had managed to break through the seemingly omnipresent clouds for an intermittent hour and by dark there was not only a touch of frost but also a vague hint of fog on the higher ground beyond commuter land. The old Great Western and Great Central Joint Line running north through Buckinghamshire sparkled under the station lights, but passengers waiting on the platforms stamped their feet a little and drew their coat collars up closer round their necks. It was 6 February 1959, the beginning of the evening rush hour and the railways were busy.

In the late 1950s the business traveller went to London by train. Any motorways were either in the planning stage or but small unconnected sections of the now taken for granted network. Electrification had not yet begun on the West Coast route out of Euston and steam, on express train services, was still in the autumn of its years. Dr Richard Beeching had not arrived on the scene and BR was still serving Sir Laurence Olivier his kippers for breakfast on the *Brighton Belle*, and the city-to-city regular-interval services were starting to get their act together.

On the routes out to the West and East Midlands the popular evening trains included the LMR's crack *Midlander* 5.40pm out of Euston, Jubilee hauled on an XL limit loading. Paddington's 5.10pm (still with its Bicester slip coach), and the 6.10pm to Wolverhampton and Birkenhead, regularly King hauled, while the 6.18pm for Leicester, Nottingham, Sheffield and Manchester left Marylebone behind one of Sir Nigel Gresley's A3 Pacifics. The last three used the GW/GC Joint line as far as Ashendon Junction. Traffic was particularly heavy at weekends (though even Mondays to Thursdays you needed to book your seat on the *Midlander*) so on Fridays the Western Region ran the 6.10 Birkenhead in two parts, a fast relief, non-stop to Leamington at 6.08, and the slower Birkenhead train at 6.11.

This evening the regular traveller was later than usual, missing any chance of *The Midlander* which would have been by far the best. As his ticket was valid by either route, he headed for Paddington hoping to get the 6.08; but this was full long before six o'clock. Somewhat reluctantly he made his way to the 6.11 and luckily found a seat in the restaurant car opposite an old colleague. The train left on time. It had been a hard day, and a large gin and tonic went down well – as did the extremely good dinner.

Relaxation had just set in when the train came to an abrupt stop. It was just over an hour out of London, dark outside, but convivial. Unscheduled stops were common enough and at first nobody thought

much of it. But this was a long one; obviously there was a problem. Eventually the regular ticket collector was incautious enough to walk down the train doing his job. He was naturally assailed with questions and the information prised out of him was that the train now reposed on the Great Central main line at Grendon Underwood some eight miles off its proper route! It was going to be a long wait and one which would send ripples of delay back to both Paddington and Marylebone whose controllers now had a fascinating problem on their hands.

It was two hours before a slight bump was felt as an engine was attached to the rear and the train hauled back under the girder bridge at Ashendon Junction to enable Stafford Road's No 6016 to resume its rightful route at Haddenham. No doubt passengers on the 6.18 from Marylebone were held for a similar time and were planning nasty letters to the newspapers which, in the event, they never posted.

Nothing official in the way of a report ever came to the eyes of the traveller, but there is little doubt that the signalman at Ashendon

The Midlander. The down express (the most popular London–Birmingham business train of the 1950s) climbs Camden bank behind a Wolverhampton (Bushbury 3B) based Jubilee No 45733 Novelty, *a name originally carried by one of the Royal Scots (No 6127) before renaming in the Regimental series. Note the earlier type headboard and the small 3,500 gallon tender – there were plenty of water troughs on this route.*

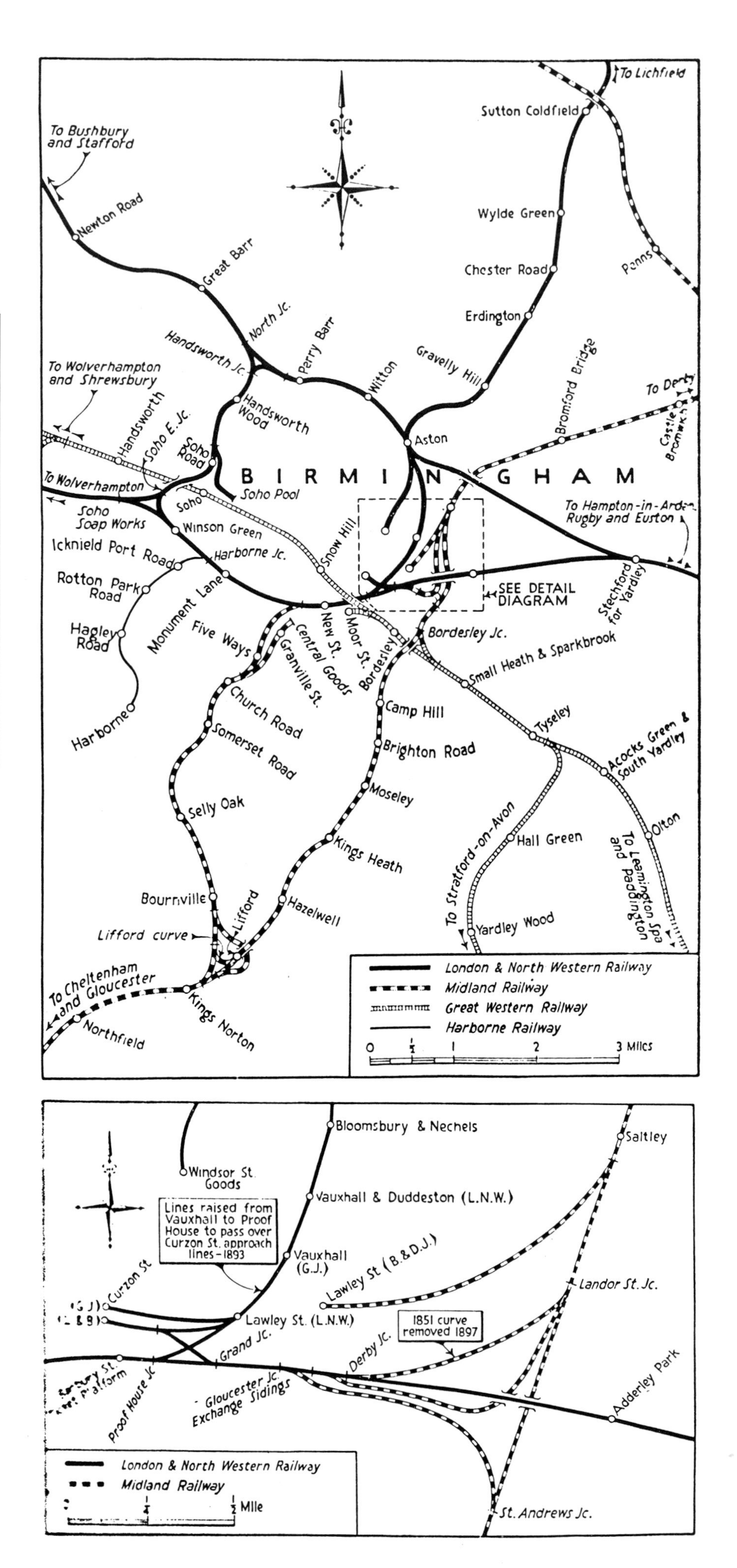

Layout of tracks in the London Midland Region in the Birmingham area.

continued from page 178
man kicked the 'bag' overboard and scrambled down on to the footplate. The ear-shattering roar of escaping steam cut into silence as the driver pulled the regulator open and then eased it closed as the Compound moved, slipped, was held, and finally got under way, her staccato exhaust echoing harshly back from sombre station buildings. The 'clump-clump' of the carriage wheels, the final sizzle of steam from the last vehicle's steam-heating hose connection, and the stolid stare of the tail lamp left me in the silence aching to be on the rocking footplate. – Philip Spencer, 1945.

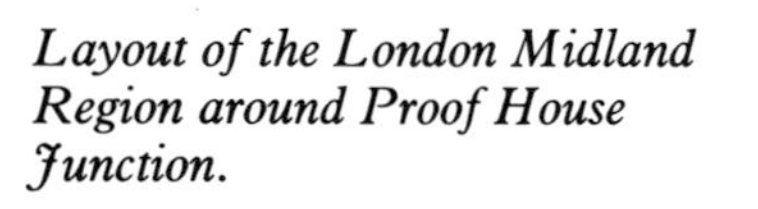

Layout of the London Midland Region around Proof House Junction.

Junction forgot it was Friday and as the 6.11 was running a minute or two down because of the mist, he accepted it as the 6.18 Manchester train, the 6.08 having already swept majestically past on the 6.10's timing. What the engine crew of the 6.11 were thinking about will never be known. Perhaps the driver had an enforced short winter holiday, unpaid, to mull it over and ponder on the fact that while the Great Western Railway had provided ATC to make things safer he still needed to use his eyes and ears.

The Western was not alone with this type of debacle. Around the same time, two early afternoon expresses were booked to leave Birmingham New Street south end within five minutes of one another, one southbound, the 1.55pm Wolverhampton to Euston at 2.30pm and one northbound (via Aston and Bescot) the Bournemouth to Manchester, *Pines Express* at 2.35pm. One day, possibly due to a faulty train describer, the signalman at Proof House Junction accepted the London train headed by Jubilee No 45603 *Solomon Islands* but set the road and pulled off for the Aston line. The driver of 45603 came storming up from the dip after New Street south tunnel and either misread the signals or could not stop in time, and carried on to the viaduct between Proof House Junction and Vauxhall before stopping. The problem then passed to Control. They, though deeming it imprudent to set back to Proof House, were all too conscious of the dreadful problems which further delay would cause – not only to the London *and* the *Pines* but to everything following. Anxious discussion took place. It was discovered that fortunately the driver knew the road, so the train was sent on via Aston, Perry Barr, Soho Road loop and Harborne Junction passing through New Street again some forty minutes later. This time all was well and the train took the correct route. There was of course no feed-back for the passengers who received a free impromptu rail tour of some of Birmingham's less salubrious suburbs!

To those out along the road, Control was often a disembodied voice. Every signalman and station inspector had his own anecdote demonstrating just how out of touch Control could be, sometimes not even understanding the basic geography, it seemed. Yet it was always the voice of authority and sometimes, as in this case, comforting authority. Certainly it was not to be ignored – as the well-fingered telephones at stations or signalboxes (worn of their paint and with their brass earpieces shining) showed only too well.

Controllers were recruited from various grades. Some started their railway life as clerks, some as signalmen or guards or, in the case of those concerned with locomotives or train crew control, as drivers, firemen or running foremen. So the Control offices became places where the many types of railwaymen worked closely together, usually in harmony. But as already hinted, relations between the controllers and signalmen, station supervisors, each end of a phone line, varied considerably. In many places, even though they had never met, controller and signalman were on first-name terms. At others, unfortunately, the signalman would carry out his train-reporting duties with reluctance, sometimes tardily – never the way to ensure the best decision was made. Similarly, the hair

Home and distant. Rugeley No 1 down home signal gantry framing Royal Scot 4-6-0 No 6142 The York & Lancaster Regiment *on the up Welshman. Apart from the removal of the rings from the slow-line signals these splendid skyscrapers remained as installed by the LNWR well into BR days. All other Trent Valley line signals controlled by No 1 box were still pure North Western until electrification. However, signals controlled by Rugeley No 2 box at the north end of the station were replaced pre war by the LMS standard upper quadrant signals on tubular posts. The signals for through running have co-acting arms lower down the post for near sighting. No track circuits were provided at this time, only fireman's call pillars visible in the cess and six foot also indicated by the D sign on the post. The signals were lit by oil lamps of course. Pity the poor lamp man who had to climb about 60ft with two flickering oil lamps especially in a howling gale!*

Signal Gantry. A Bristol express leaving Newcastle Central station hauled by Thompson A2/3 Pacific 60511 Airborne *under a long complicated gantry of electro-pneumatic signals, including a mixture of pre-grouping lower quadrants and LNE upper quadrants, together with small subsidiary signals. All these were swept away by colour-light signalling in 1959.*

of some drivers and guards stood on end when Control was mentioned. One stupid decision made by a controller years ago would continue to be related on footplates and in bothies ad nauseam.

The duty to report trains to Control was laid down in booklets issued to signalboxes by the district operating office, the workload being spread as much as possible. The signalboxes concerned were the more important ones at stations and junctions and those with the ability to make regulating decisions: for example, those controlling turn-ins from Fast to Slow or turn-outs from Slow to Fast. These main signalboxes each reported only certain classes of trains in order to give the full picture to the controllers with the minimum disturbance to the signalmen. Take the Settle–Carlisle line whose two control offices were at Leeds and Carlisle, the boundary at Ais Gill. The reporting boxes were at Blea Moor, Ais Gill, Appleby station, Appleby North and Durran Hill. Blea Moor only reported freight and light engines, Ais Gill the arrival, departure and passing of all types of trains and engines, Appleby North the arrival and departure of all down trains.

The last thirty years have seen tremendous changes on the railways. The one most noticeable to the travelling public has been the disappearance of steam with the emergence of diesel and electric traction, but there have been many just as revolutionary. Chief of these was the replacement of mechanical signalling and block working by power signalling and track circuit block. Operation has been simplified out of all recognition, and there have, of course, been many changes in the traffic flows which have also removed a number of the complications. Examine what has happened on the East Coast main line from Kings Cross to the North.

The first thirty-two miles from Kings Cross to Hitchin (along with several branches) used to be served by steam suburban trains, in parallel with the main-line service, also steam worked. At Kings Cross, many main-line arrivals and departures involved engine movements to and from Top Shed, and the whole of the terminus and its immediate approaches were worked by one electro-pneumatic signalbox with miniature levers. This box was very complicated, so signalmen took a considerable time to learn the frame. Outside the Kings Cross vicinity the line was signalled by a large number of manual boxes working semaphore signals. Until the advent of full power signalling no box south of New Southgate handled trains on both up and down lines. The Finsbury Park area alone was worked by several boxes. This had to be done because points could not be worked manually by rodding at more than 350 yards from a signalbox. There was a further complication until the 1950s of two bottlenecks, the two-mile two-track section over the viaduct at Welwyn through to Woolmer Green, which still exists, and between Potters Bar and Greenwood, through Hadley Wood – the notorious Potters Bar bottleneck. This was immortalised by Terence Cuneo's painting of the signalman in Greenwood box looking through the windows at a northbound A4 entering the bottleneck. Its removal in the 1950s involved the digging of three new tunnels.

Outside the suburban area there have always been a large number of four-tracked sections. The Great Northern paired their tracks by direction, Up Slow, Up Fast, Down Fast, Down Slow. Some other lines, including the Midland section of the LMS and the Great Western paired theirs by usage, Up Relief, Down Relief, Up Main, Down Main. The GN method permitted trains to be switched from Slow to Fast and back again without affecting trains in the opposite direction. There was of course a subtle difference between a line classified as 'Slow' and one as 'Goods'; the former was worked on Absolute Block, as in the suburban area, and could be readily used by passenger trains, the latter was worked on the Permissive Block allowing a freight to enter an already occupied section. Wherever there was a two-track bottleneck, as until after World War II at Huntingdon North and Arlesey, the slow line sections on each side of the bottleneck tended to be worked on Permissive Block. Signalmen could permit trains to accumulate on the approach side and send them forward through the bottleneck in quick succession when a path appeared, knowing that they could quickly clear the main line beyond it.

Before World War II main-line expresses were booked in flights, with fairly lengthy gaps between, giving the slow freights a chance to get moving. After the war, however, with regular-interval passenger services being developed for commercial reasons, the regulation of freight trains

Somersault Signals. A terrible accident in 1876 on the Great Northern main line in which the up Flying Scotsman collided with the rear of a freight train shunting back into a refuge siding caused several alterations to signalling. The main cause of the accident was that the signals, which then dropped into slots in the posts in the clear position, had frozen in 'off', then their normal aspect. The most important alteration was that, in future, the normal position of signals would be 'on'. Moreover the GN designed a new type of semaphore arm which worked clear of the post and was centrally balanced, so could not be affected by frost or the weight of snow. The spectacles for night indications were not attached to the signal arm. This type of signal was copied elsewhere in the country by one or two of the South Wales railways and a few abroad. The signals in this view, Up and Down stop boards for both directions and the distants for the boxes in advance, all on the same posts, were located at Cadoxton Yard on the Barry Railway.

became more difficult. When speeds increased beyond that for which the signalling had been designed, with longer braking distances vital, double block working had to be instituted. This applied before the war to high-speed trains like the *Silver Jubilee* and *Coronation*. Signalmen could not accept them from the box in rear until 'Out of Section' had been received for the preceding train from the box in advance.

One failing of manual signalling by Absolute Block was that the signalboxes had to be placed at junctions, stations or level crossings, not at the intervals which gave the optimum spacing from a line capacity point of view. The number of trains which could pass over a line was governed by the time taken by the slowest train to pass through the longest section.

Between the wars, the more important lines were steadily covered by the district control offices, whose principal function was the overseeing of the movement of freight traffic. The East Coast main line from Kings Cross to Grantham, was controlled by Kings Cross. Although the signalmen were mainly responsible for regulation to ensure punctuality, Control had a duty to oversee the position and step in in an emergency. In the event of an accident or blockage of a line, Control became God, taking immediate steps to ensure that emergency services, breakdown cranes, and so on, were alerted and that train services were altered,

An LMS signalbox. A very large ex-LNWR manual box at Preston. Each pre-grouping company had its own characteristics, their signalmen all sure that theirs was the best system. It can be seen that the levers in the LNW box were released by pressing down on the stirrup on the front of each one. The levers were painted different colours to denote stop signals, distants, points etc. Above the levers is the diagram of the track layout, and beyond that the row of block instruments communicating with adjoining boxes.

cancelled or diverted by any possible alternative route. Train movements were recorded either on separate train cards, train graphs or by cards pegged up on line diagrams. However, in order that the district superintendent and his assistants and staff could see the whole picture and institute any action necessary to improve standards of punctuality, Control kept logs of the running of the principal trains with an explanation of any delays.

A certain amount of power signalling, including automatic signals, was in operation before World War II, but capital was not available for wholesale conversion. In the last thirty years the position has been transformed. While steam locomotives were being replaced by diesel and electric traction power boxes were being built, and semaphore signals and the signalman waving out of his box disappeared from the scene. Then on this East Coast main line the HSTs had a tremendous impact. Multiple unit operation has eased the working of termini such as Kings Cross, already simplified by the opening of the large NX (entrance-exit) power box, in which a whole route can be set up and the appropriate signals cleared by merely pressing two buttons on the panel.

The Kings Cross power box now controls the East Coast main line as far as Sandy, where it links up with the Peterborough box. Now the signals are spaced to give the correct braking distance at the higher

Great Western arms – Newport High Street looking west c1955 with a Pembroke Dock to Paddington train (including a massive twelve-wheeled dining car) entering hauled by No 5040 Stokesay Castle. *Note the fine array of GWR lower quadrant signals (including the 'fixed' distants) on the 'wrong' (or right-hand) side of the line to which they refer. The GWR was always a right-hand-drive line. Those referring to the down platform and main lines have the illuminated indicators P and M below the appropriate arms.*

speeds as well as to give optimum line capacity. From the drivers' point of view they now have very bright colour lights instead of oil lamps, supported by the automatic warning system.

Many new power boxes, with their computerised train describers, include facilities for automatic recording of train movements and operation of platform indicators. The Three Bridges power box on the Southern Region was the first to incorporate automatic route setting worked by the train describer. The new signalling centre recently opened at Liverpool Street has small visual display units in lieu of the large panels used in all modern boxes opened in the last few years. It features the latest solid state interlocking system (SSI) but it is also the first application of automatic route setting (ARS) to such a large terminal, which has eighteen platforms and deals with 1,250 trains in a day. ARS runs the signalling automatically and receives and despatches trains at all times of the day, including the extremely busy morning and evening peak periods when a train comes in or goes out every thirty seconds. The system automatically selects routes and makes regulating decisions to get the optimum performance from the train plan. The signalling centre incorporates the station communications arrangements responsible for the public address system and passenger information displays. In the past there was nothing more frustrating to an operating officer than to realise that trains were leaving late from a station because the station clocks were wrong. Now synchronised digital clocks are available on many busy lines.

Since the movement of trains in such a large area can be seen on the panels of power signalboxes, it is no longer necessary to monitor movements in the district, so along with so many other railway features Control in the traditional sense has also disappeared. Anglia Regional Control is now located in the signalling centre at Liverpool Street.

Overhead electrification is being extended, and soon the whole of the East Coast main line will be covered. Even the High Speed Trains are being left behind. However, for every pro there is always a con. Any railwayman who has had to deal with a derailment which involved demolition of a mast and a long dewirement will agree with this. And it has to be said that the general simplicity of today's railway working has only been made possible by the loss of most freight business. Such have been the increases in passenger volumes that the present system, however sophisticatedly controlled, could not possibly cope with them plus all the coal, perishable and other freights of yesteryear. Ironically, the great days of express trains were those when there were relatively few of them, sandwiched between a mass of much slower traffic. The timetable might have offered a non-stop *Flying Scotsman* from Kings Cross to Edinburgh. Preventing the wheels grinding to a halt used to require teamwork by literally hundreds of people, including of course the drivers of preceding trains who had to work smartly to get their tails out of the way, and the signalmen regulating them whose occasional dash along the frame to pull off the advance starter once Line Clear had been obtained might make all the difference, preventing a heavy train from coming to a dead halt and needing time to restart.

Power Box. View showing the interior of the large power box at Saltley, Birmingham, on the London Midland Region. From the early sixties each Region pressed ahead with this type of signalling, succeeding boxes covering larger and larger areas, eliminating many manual ones. The photograph shows the method of operation. The track layout appears on the large panel and this system, known as 'NX' (Entrance-Exit) merely requires depression of a button at the entrance to a route and a further one at the exit for all points to move to the required position and signals to be cleared. This will only happen if no conflicting movement has already been set up. Once the route is set and locked a row of white lights appears on the track layout. When the train passes along the route the white lights change to red. Since many trains can be on the panel at the same time identification is made by a computer-controlled train describer. Once a train identification is entered by a signalman, or comes into the area from an adjoining box, no further action is necessary. The train number follows the red lights on the panel, and is shown on miniature cathode ray tubes – the small black squares seen on the photograph. In this type of box the staff seated behind the signalmen are regulators and controllers. Signalling has progressed quicker than any other sector of railway working. This type of power box has been superseded in new construction by ones with small visual display units. The first application of this to a complex area was at Liverpool Street, where automatic route setting controls 1,250 trains a day. The system automatically sets routes from the train describer, and also controls the station's public address system and passenger information displays.

On every busy route throughout the country, getting the expresses through called for devotion, expertise . . . and a touch of good luck. Everyone (including the driver of the sidetracked freight which had cleared the Main in good time) took pride in seeing the great expresses flash past carrying the important people who had to travel around the country the railway united. It was perhaps a miracle when it all went well on ordinary days. At busy times, when for example the number of expresses in each flight out of Kings Cross would be increased, it became much harder, and in bad weather often plain impossible. Fog was of course the chief enemy. If it hit just before Christmas, as happened several times in the early years of the century, even though livestock trains bound for the London market were so delayed that some cattle had to be slaughtered en route, express journey times might well be doubled and even then only achieved by railwaymen giving their all.

The Train Now in a Hurry . . .

This book has relied heavily on nostalgia, with the 'great days' largely synonymous with the steam era. It will perhaps be appropriate, therefore, to conclude by bringing the picture right up to date, looking at one particular route, the 186 miles between Kings Cross and Leeds. And rather than looking at operations through the eye of the railway enthusiast, let us occupy for a while the shoes of the businessman from London, having dealings in Yorkshire.

After the unhurried schedules of the 1920s, when competition was minimal, acceleration began in the early 1930s. By 1937 the LNER had introduced the *West Riding Limited* between Bradford, Leeds and Kings Cross. It left Leeds at 11.31 to run non-stop to London in 164 minutes, and northbound from Kings Cross at 19.10 it was a minute faster. The eight-coach train was eye-catching in two shades of blue with stainless steel trim and was hauled by a streamlined A4 Pacific in Garter Blue with red wheels. Inside it seated 48 first- and 168 third-class passengers in pressure-ventilated, sound-insulated luxury, served with meals from two kitchens. It was in marked contrast with the rest of the train service, and commanded a supplementary fare, though its timings were, with the possible exception of the northbound train, not really geared to business travel. With the war it disappeared into limbo.

The 1950s brought a real effort to provide services suited to the business community – an earlyish start, pickup at an outer suburban station, arrival at destination in mid-morning, and return in late afternoon or early evening, leaving time in between for work. In 1952 a new 08.00 service was introduced from Kings Cross, calling at Hitchin and reaching Leeds at 11.21 – hard work with steam. The train was of ex-LNER or BR Mk 1 stock (not noted for its comfortable riding) and the terminal stations were gloomy, unattractive. A major jump in speed came in 1961 with dieselisation; it was now the 07.45, the stock largely unchanged, and it reached Leeds at 11.02. The competition was making itself felt, and with the opening of the M1 motorway through to Leeds a person living in, say, St Albans could, within the law and given no delays, be there by car in little over 2½ hours.

The closure of the scruffy Leeds Central station in 1967 and diversion of the London trains into Leeds New (which it was not!) was an improvement and coincided with further paring of the timing to arrive at 10.30. The superior BR Mk 2 coaches with air conditioning began to appear from 1971. Two years later saw the flowering of Kings Cross's new concourse, at last bringing the station into view from behind the 'African village' which had sprouted between the wars. The new station at Stevenage, on a new site and with extensive car parking took over the outer suburban stop. From 1977 it was backed by electrification of the suburban service. Modernisation was beginning to provide not just speed but a much better overall ambiance.

The next leap forward in both speed and comfort came when High Speed Trains took over the service in 1979. The 07.45 was now booked into Leeds, with Stevenage pickup and Wakefield stop, by 09.59, with the attraction of a quiet, smooth ride in Mk 3 coaches which gave little hint of travelling at 125mph. Perhaps for the first time there was enhanced awareness that the train staff could contribute heavily to the overall satisfaction – the restaurant car and buffet crew in their attitude and style, the appearance of the guard checking tickets, the lucidity of the on-train announcements.

With the October 1989 timetable the electric era began. The 07.50 *Yorkshire Pullman* from Kings Cross features the new Mk 4 coaches, their riding and quietness splendid, decor restful and unobtrusive. No longer do alighting passengers pull down door windows (and leave them open afterwards!) to grope for a door handle; they join and alight through wide conductor-released power doors with local push-button control and via a colourful heated vestibule. Pullman service brings breakfast or trolley snacks to every first-class seat. The timing is a remarkable 2hr 9min; our St Albans man can leave home at 07.45, drive to Stevenage and park, and the Pullman will have him on the platform at Leeds before the clock comes up to ten o'clock, fresh, breakfasted and with an hour's work comfortably under his belt.

Up front the two drivers sit in air-conditioned comfort in the cab of their class 91 locomotive. As they reel off the miles at 125mph, preset on a selector and held automatically by micro-processor, the only sounds over the quiet hum of traction motors and blowers are the tones of the AWS indications approaching each signal and the more penetrating note of the vigilance device every minute. Power and brake controllers are small and at the fingertips. The driver's panel is a model of simplicity, with just two brake gauges and speedometer above warning lights. There is not even an ammeter; the electronics keep currents within bounds. Radio maintains contact with signalling centres and the BR telephone network.

On a recent trip in the company of driver Donald Smith (an Aberdeen man who transferred to Neville Hill over twenty years ago) on No 91001, we were over the Northern Heights at Potters Bar at 112mph where once steam laboured at fifty, and after Hitchin kept up an unvarying 125mph (except for a slight drop when power was shut off for the Little Barford neutral section) until the 110 allowed through the Offord curves. Breasting the Abbots Ripton hump we held 120mph but after touching 125 again had to ease down to 105/115/105 across Holme Fen and through Peterborough. Passing Helpston and seeing the first flashing green signal aspects which govern running at up to 140mph for special purposes, Smith said: 'We shall hold 125 all the way up the bank until we have to slow to 115 through Stoke Tunnel – that's ten to fifteen faster than an HST can do.' Alas, it was not to be, because a fine drizzle and the autumn leaf fall made

East Coast Main Line Modernisation. One of the new BREL/GEC-built electric locomotives No 91008 approaches Doncaster with the 15.50 Kings Cross to Leeds/ Bradford train (The Yorkshire Pullman) on 22 June 1989. A far cry from the wooden-bodied cars of the 1920s/30s and the very individual Pullman service which then pertained. But a faster journey with many more built-in safety features including modern high-speed signalling and all-steel coaching stock.

the rails very greasy, and we had quite a lot of wheelslip as the 91 tried to exert its high power. As a result we came up to Stoke at just 115mph and did not need to ease up.

Thereafter it was an almost boring 125 except for restrictions: 100 through Grantham, 100 over the Newark crossing, 115 on the curves beyond the short Askham tunnel before Retford, and 110 at Bawtry. After the severe slowing through the junction to the Leeds line at Doncaster we were allowed nothing more than 90mph to Wakefield, not omitting a couple of subsidence slacks to 30 and 50, relics of now-closed mines, and 85 thence to Leeds. From the Wakefield stop Smith accelerated the train to go over the top at Ardsley at 73 and coasted down into a drear, drizzly Leeds. Taking an intricate path through the station approach, the train glided to a stop in platform 5 two minutes early.

Over fifty years since the LNER proudly presented their *West Riding Limited*, BR InterCity has brought to fruition something close to the ultimate in rail travel – and without building an entirely new railway, that is – from early morning until late at night. And it is available, without supplement, to all, chief executive and student alike.

12
LIFE AT THE SHED

Rescue In Style
A hot box, a broken oil pipe, a whistle valve stuck open or even melted firebars; all these stopped express trains literally in their tracks, and more frequently, too, than is generally imagined by today's enthusiast. If it happens to one of the bevy of beautifully preserved locomotives plying BR's rails, it makes headlines, especially as there is generally no substitute steam power and passengers are disappointed. In the days of regular steam, it was different. Some failures were disastrous, others were mundane. A few provided great excitement!

It was rare for the LNER's *Silver Jubilee* to be late, even more so for one of the modern A4 streamlined Pacifics to be a failure. But it happened on Friday 4 September 1936. No 2510 *Quicksilver* ran hot approaching York on the up train and had to be taken off. The York station pilot on that day was an ex-North Eastern Atlantic class C7 No 732 and after some consultation driver Samwells and his fireman transferred their bags and bottles of tea – hoping to pick up a Pacific at Doncaster. No luck, the only available engine was 1911-built No 4452, a large-boilered Ivatt Atlantic. They decided to have a go. They covered the 156 miles to Kings Cross in 139 minutes start to stop!

In 1933, on the LMS at Rugby, the driver of No 6131 *Planet* at the head of the up *Mancunian* opened his whistle – and it stuck. They managed to draw up almost opposite the shed, but repeated bangs with a spanner made no impact. They had to remove the shrieking engine and look for another. The first available replacement was the George the Fifth class 4-4-0 No 5392 *Penmaenmawr* which they hooked on to the 295 ton train. They ran the 82½ miles to Euston start to stop in 84 minutes, the 60 miles from Roade in 55 minutes,

continued opposite

'WHEN you've finished there, Bill, turn her and put her up seven road. Then I'll find you another to deal with, just to keep you from nodding off.' This is Bill's fourth disposal of his shift. It is five thirty in the morning, and the outside foreman trudges back along the gritty pathway to his little cabin, picks up the phone and tells the running foreman what he has arranged, so that it can be marked up on the engine arrangements board in the drivers' lobby. 'I've nothing at present for the 8.40. The engine I was going to put on it has the brick arch down and is stopped. But there's a 73 thousand coming on shortly, a rocking grate engine, so we'll do a quick turnround with her.'

Over at the shed proper, the lobby is busy with enginemen booking on duty, and the foreman's assistant is fully occupied keeping track of them. 'Nah, Bert, I'm six forty down side pilot. Has me mate shown up yet?' A driver bawls through the foreman's window: 'What have you given me this b . . . . y thing for ?' 'Go on, Charlie, I saved it specially for you.' Another pokes his head in: 'I'm going to be late off for the six ten. Sanders aren't working. I've got the fitter to 'em.' 'Always find something wrong, Dick.' The nerve centre of the shed is a sound picture of movement, conversation and banter.

Enter the early-turn running foreman, who glances at the engine arrangements board as he removes his cycle clips. Having hung his mac and knife-edged hat in the corner of the dingy office, the handover begins. He studies the log book, noting that the breakdown train has been out most of the night dealing with a couple of derailed coaches in the carriage sidings. He checks the remaining available men in the spare link and their times on duty; there are some blank spaces where men are covering for the inevitable fallout in the other links – sickness, absentees, men on medical examination, practical eyesight tests, route learning, trade union business, you name it. Others are marked up for specials. The coal situation is a little fraught; plenty of grades 2 and 3, but they are hand to mouth for grade 1. Not many cleaners available for cleaning, for this is early summer and many of the passed cleaners are marked up as firemen in the augmented spare link. They are still pretty raw and the foreman is very dependent on their drivers to bring them on; some do, others merely moan about their 'useless' firemen and barely speak to them. The Mechanical Foreman has his full quota of engines for washout and examination save for one, which is lost somewhere within the British Isles. It is a near thing, however and a couple are edging over the maximum examination mileage. He asks the night man about that engine for the 8.40, has a quick word with the outside man, and sinks into the seat of power. He is in charge until the assistant district motive power superintendent arrives at half past eight.

His early-turn assistant has gone through the rosters with his tired opposite number. All the jobs are covered, but the spare men are thin on the ground until lunch time. The foreman leaves his assistant to run that side of the house. Control are waking up with details of various alterations and extras. Engine and men wanted to work urgent empty parcels vans from the yard to the Western. Control are offered the 11.30 spare men, who have route knowledge as far as Birmingham. The up side station pilot is being taken to assist an express in trouble for steam. Can they provide a replacement? Some juggling, and that's arranged with a minimal uncovered period, though it means overtime for a crew just finishing and a move up of several engines on the board. Every good deed deserves another; can Control find out who's using the 'overdue washout' engine and either get it home or get its captors to wash it out and do the X-day examination?

In the shed yard activity is building up to a crescendo. Catering mainly for express passenger work, with some suburban passenger traffic and long-distance freight work, the period from five to eight o'clock sees a major exodus from the shed, with a steady trickle of engines from

continued
actually improving on the *Mancunian*'s tight schedule between Bletchley and Euston. An observer remembers the showers of cinders raining down on the coach roof as they passed under the Great Central girder bridge, and the nonchalant driver Mison at Euston – obviously an old LNWR man reminding himself of *Wild Duck*'s exploits so many years ago.

Why the steam locomotive disappeared from Britain. The filthy work involved in servicing, invariably in the open in all weathers, made it almost impossible to get staff for the job. Here, in the last weeks of steam on BR, a shedman at Carnforth depot shovels char from the smokebox of a disreputable Class Five, maybe for the very last time.

Timetable by Britannia

In 1951 the Eastern Region main line to Norwich could scarcely be called top of the express passenger league but there was a saviour in the offing; in January that year Crewe outshopped the first of twenty-five BR Standard class 7MT Pacifics later called the *Britannias* – their link with the Festival of Britain.

E. S. Cox, responsible for their design, had said they would run 'all day and all night' so two round trips to Norwich and back, 460 miles, would be nothing. They could revolutionise the situation. Twenty-five class 7s would equal fifty-five B1 4-6-0s which needed coal every return journey. The ER indented for their engines and after a minor struggle (the operating member of the Railway Executive was reported as saying 'What! send our first batch of express locomotives to that tramway?') they got them.

The prowess of the *Britannias* meant new engine diagrams and those diagrams meant a new timetable: THAT had not been done on the Great Eastern main line for nigh on forty years. There was a little to-ing and fro-ing with such shibboleths as the *Norfolkman* being retimed from 10am to 9.30 but they won through.

The ironic thing was that three weeks after the engines and the new service were introduced the whole fleet was grounded because water carry over from the boiler

continued on page 195

Armstrong turntable. The Great Western lagged behind the other three companies in modernising their steam depot facilities; mechanical, coal and ash handling plants were almost unknown, and even the turning of locomotives depended on muscle rather than vacuum or electric power. The key Tyseley (Birmingham) roundhouse sees driver and fireman putting their backs into turning 2-6-0 No 9303.

overnight trains arriving for servicing. There is a constant procession of enginemen booking on, collecting tools and preparing their engines. 45 minutes for the smaller ones, an hour for the larger ones, and that means there is plenty for both men to do if it is to be done conscientiously. There is lubricating oil of two types to be collected from the stores, head, tail and gauge lamps to be trimmed and filled, sandboxes to be topped up. While the driver is filling lubricators and oiling round, the fireman is busy spreading and building up the fire and, if he has enough steam, testing the injectors. Engines ease up to the preparation pits across the front of the shed for the underneath oiling and to get the last few hundred gallons of water in the tank. It is a time when the outside foreman keeps a weather eye on the skyline, for when the shed is surrounded by houses excessive smoke can cause wrath, both official *and* domestic! There is steady movement, much hissing of steam from cylinder cocks, as engines saunter down the shed yard to the exit signal and stop for the fireman to ring the bobby with details of the train they are to work. The outside foreman keeps careful tally of it all, for late starts off the shed are serious and will have to be accounted for in detail.

The arrival of the office staff and the boss brings new pressures. Foreman and log book go on parade in the sanctum, and the events of the last 24 hours are gone through in some detail; the boss is not going to be caught napping when the divisional office demand his explanation of untoward events. There is a quick review of the prospects for availability of engines and men for today, with particular emphasis on engines for the top-rank express workings and the tough fitted-freight jobs. There are special items to be dealt with; the need for the outside foreman to carefully monitor the use of grade 1 coal, the late-on-duty cases and any resulting delays, the state of the ashpits and the spillage under the coaling plant, and a number of others. They are interrupted by the mechanical foreman with *his* proforma summarising the stopped engines at the depot. The washouts, those undergoing standard examinations and unforeseen repairs, those waiting material from the works, and those in or waiting to go into works are all accounted for. A summary will be passed to the divisional office soon after nine o'clock and be argued over where necessary.

Now the running foreman can go back to his noisy office and finalise the roster alterations for tomorrow. The rosters displayed in the lobby have to be marked up with all alterations in red by mid-morning so that they can be seen by enginemen when booking off duty. There are other things to be seen to also. There is the odd discipline form to be handed to the offender – always when booking off so that he does not brood over the consequences while on duty. There is the perpetual problem of engine tools in short supply – even such basic items as firing shovels. But by two o'clock all is shipshape to hand over to the two back-shift foremen.

The afternoon man gets a breathing space before being called in to the ADMPS. There will be an LDC meeting in two days' time with the footplate trade union representatives, and the agenda needs to be discussed and facts marshalled. It is in two parts, items for negotiation

9303

Coal hole 1. The financially straitened LNER did some splendid modernisation of its locomotive servicing facilities although many places escaped the process and Copley Hill shed (Leeds) was one of them. So Class A1 4-6-2 No 60133 Pommern *built in 1948, finds herself queuing up at an old coal stage built decades before, where men shovelled coal from wagons into wheeled tubs which were pushed and tipped over the tender by hand. Great Western practice was similar even in their later-built sheds.*

and those for consultation, and it is the first section that can be the most tricky. Several items involve rostering alterations in the past for which claimants feel they are entitled to extra pay; at the bottom of it all is seniority, which governs the depot link in which an engineman is placed. Pity the poor foreman who, under the pressures of the hour, allocates special work to the wrong man! Then there are union proposals for changes in the allocation of certain jobs within the link structure; the implications for route knowledge, general experience of the type of work involved and for earnings are carefully examined. By the time the agenda has been mulled over and the line of approach agreed, the foreman is happy to escape back to his office and a big mug of strong, sweet tea. If breakfast time saw a stream of engines leaving the shed, the back shift sees a reversal of the process.

There are still engines going off, reaching a modest peak in the early evening as power is provided for the overnight fitted freights and others, and then tails off again. But now the coaling plant rumbles near-continuously and the ashpits take on a dull clinkery glow as the light begins to fade. The afternoon coalman is busy with towrope and capstan bringing wagons to the tippler to meet the quality needs of the coaling plant bunkers and clearing the empties. The ashpits become an abrasive inferno of dirty fire falling from ashpans and the scrape of shovels loading the ash and clinker into the wheeled tubs which carry it to the ash hoist. The whole operation has to be kept on the move to make way for the new arrivals; there are no prizes for blocking the main line because engines from traffic cannot be accepted on to the disposal roads.

Meanwhile the repair staff are releasing engines after washout and examination. These need to be drawn out of the maintenance area in readiness for lighting up, and a shed set of enginemen – the driver a restricted duty man whose eyesight is no longer up to main-line standard – is involved with moving these dead engines and inserting them on the shed roads as the outside foreman requires. There is much huffing and puffing and hissing of air from open cylinder cocks as they perform this slow motion dance.

Now the steamraisers can get started on these cold engines as well as keeping those in steam safe and ready. Washout plugs and doors are checked, boilers filled, and in go the blazing firelighters to a nest of small coal under the firedoor. The lung-corroding yellow smoke begins to crawl greasily from chimneys and seeps inexorably from closed firedoors into the cabs. Soon there is a creeping yellow fog through the shed, muffling sounds and well-nigh impenetrable by the lights. It will be three hours or more before there is enough pressure to operate the blower, spread and build up the fire somewhat, clear the smoke and leave the engines to simmer gently, awaiting the ministrations of their new firemen.

The shed yard fades into darkness, broken only by pools of luminosity from the indifferent lighting. A glint on boiler clothing and tender flanks is interrupted by a fairground gallery of moving human silhouettes,

continued from page 192
caused broken piston heads and wheels shifted on the axles. For about a month they had to do what they would have done if B1s had been used instead – namely use a lay-over engine for each round trip.

But the *Britannias* came back and ran a magnificent service which showed just what the engine could do. The Eastern even had a malignant triumph – it still meant something in those days. Their 1951 Christmas card was a picture of the *Broadsman* at speed and headed: 'The fastest train in Britain.' It was short lived. Within weeks the North Eastern Region took five minutes out of a service between Darlington and York. But they had their hour of glory. – Based on Gerry Fiennes's *Fiennes on Rails*.

Coal hole 2. Coaling facilities at locomotive depots ranged from the most modern mechanical plants to prehistoric erections or none at all. At Edge Hill (Liverpool) the LNWR erected a unique coaling plant in 1914 which served until the end of steam; it took advantage of differences in ground level to run wagons directly over the bunker from which it was discharged on either side into tenders. Jubilee No 45558 Manitoba *is getting her ration in the early 1950s.*

Thirst quencher. The steam locomotive's need for water was on a large scale. Here the 5,000 gallon corridor tender of an ex-LNER Pacific is filled up from a water column at Haymarket shed, Edinburgh. As tenders increased in size it became necessary to raise the hinged arm; in this case a 'swan neck' has been fitted to suit.

mufflers round necks against the all-pervading ash, clogs crunching on the clinker lying on the pit sides. It is a scene that few have attempted to capture on film or canvas; no such attempt can be complete in two dimensions, lacking as it must the hiss of steam, the sound of a long rake scraping an ashpan bottom, the musical singing of an injector, the muffled curses of tortured men. And above all it needs the smells, the drift of coal smoke, the acrid ash, wet coal in bunkers, warm oil and soot. For this is something primitive and awesome, the unattractive side of the coal-fired steam locomotive.

A few of the arriving engines will be siphoned off for the mechanical foreman's daily programme. Coal and water, yes, unless bunker repairs or attention to internal tank sieves dictate otherwise. But no residue of fire in the box; just enough steam to get them wheezily on to the washout roads to be cooled down. There is a hollow sound of steam being blown down from injector overflows, laying a veneer of condensation on steel surfaces. Men in waterproof trousers and clogs dance attendance, dragging heavy armoured hoses, unscrewing washout plugs. Water splashes across aisles and cascades into the pits in miniature waterfalls for hours as the boilers are slowly cooled down to minimise stresses. A select pair of engines will be retrieved when cold and pushed down into the little repair shop to await the day-shift fitters for their mileage examinations.

By the time that the running foreman is beginning to relish his usual pint on the way home, the engine arrangements board in the lobby is filling up well and so it goes on.

Preparation made easy. The modern locomotive with two outside cylinders and valve gear could be fully prepared without need for a pit. This driver oiling a post-war Stanier class Five 4-6-0 has an easy task compared with his colleagues of a generation back.

THE FASTEST TRAINS

Our first table lists scheduled start-to-stop runs in August 1939.

Railway	Division	Train	From	To	Distance	Time	Speed
					miles	min	mph
LMSR	Western	6.58 pm	Rugby	Watford	65.1	60	65.1
,,	,,	6.12 pm	Crewe	Euston	158.1	148	64.1
,,	,,	1.30 pm	Euston	Carlisle	299.1	283	63.4
,,	,,	3.17 pm	Carlisle	Euston	299.1	283	63.4
,,	,,	6.15 pm	Nuneaton	Euston	97.1	92	63.3
,,	,,	8.34 am	Watford	Coventry	76.5	73	62.4
,,	,,	6.52 pm	Stafford	Euston	133.6	128	62.6
,,	,,	2.58 pm	Crewe	Euston	158.1	152	62.4
,,	,,	9.26 am	Willesden	Birmingham	107.5	104	62.0
,,	Midland	11.37 am 5.14 pm	Luton	Bedford	19.6	19	61.9
,,	Western	11.41 am	Blisworth	Euston	62.8	61	61.8
,,	,,	5.13 pm	Coventry	Willesden	88.6	86	61.8
,,	Midland	2.22 pm 6.10 pm	Kettering	St Pancras	72.0	70	61.7
,,	Western	10.08 am	Wilmslow	Euston	176.9	172	61.7
,,	Midland	12.10 pm	Appleby	Carlisle	30.8	30	61.6
,,	Western	10.16 am	Crewe	Euston	158.1	154	61.6
,,	Midland	9.01 am	Luton	Wellingborough	34.8	34	61.4
,, ,, ,,	Western	11.30 am 2.25 pm 5.50 pm	Euston	Coventry	94.0	92	61.3
,, ,, ,,	,,	12.08 pm 1.23 pm 2.58 pm	Coventry	Euston	94.0	92	61.3
,,	,,	10.35 am	Crewe	Euston	158.1	155	61.2
,,	,,	10.34 am	Bletchley	Euston	46.7	46	60.9
,,	Midland	10.00 am 12.00 noon	St Pancras	Kettering	72.0	71	60.8
,,	Western	4.35 pm	Euston	Blisworth	62.8	62	60.8
,,	,,	2.00 pm	Euston	Crewe	158.1	156	60.8
,,	,,	9.16 am	Willesden	Northampton	60.5	60	60.5
,,	Midland	5 trains	Luton	St Pancras	30.2	30	60.4
,,	Western	4.53 pm	Crewe	Euston	158.1	157	60.4
,,	,,	9.28 pm 4.28 pm	Rugby	Euston	82.6	82	60.4
,,	,,	1.35 pm	Euston	Rugby	82.6	82	60.4
,,	,,	1.15 pm	Stoke	Euston	145.9	145	60.4
,,	,,	6.00 pm	Euston	Wilmslow	176.9	176	60.3
,,	Midland	8.43 am	Birmingham	Derby	41.2	41	60.3
,,	,,	9.05 am 2.10 pm 6.20 pm	St Pancras	Nottingham	123.5	123	60.2
,,	,,	11.18 am	Nottingham	St Pancras	123.5	123	60.2
,,	Western	10.21 am	Mossley Hill	Euston	189.7	189	60.2
,,	Midland	4 trains	Cheltenham	Bromsgrove (a)	31.1	31	60.2
,,	,,	9.05 am	Manton	St Pancras	90.1	90	60.1
,,	,,	4 trains	St Pancras	Leicester	99.1	99	60.1
,,	,,	7 trains	Leicester	St Pancras	99.1	99	60.1
,,	Western	10.00 a.m.	Euston	Carlisle	299.1	299	60.0
,,	,,	12.16 pm	Carlisle	Euston	299.1	299	60.0
,,	Midland	5.18 pm	Kettering	St Pancras	72.0	72	60.0
,,	,,	8.43 am	Willesden	Rugby	77.0	70	60.1
LMSR	NCC	8.52 am	Ballymena	Belfast	31.0	31	60.0
GWR	—	3.55 pm	Swindon	Paddington	77.3	65	71.4
,,	—	10.00 am	Paddington	Bristol (c)	118.3	105	67.6
,,	—	4.30 pm	Bristol (d)	Paddington	117.6	105	67.2
,,	—	10.10 am 5.35 pm	Oxford	Paddington	63.5	60	63.5

THE FASTEST TRAINS

Railway	Division	Train	From	To	Distance	Time	Speed
					miles	min	mph
GWR	—	5.40 pm	Swindon	Reading	41.3	39	63.5
"	—	8.28 am	Chippenham	Paddington	94.0	83	63.4
"	—	9.03½ am	Kemble	Paddington	91.0	86½	63.1
"	—	11.15 am 1.15 pm	Paddington	Bath	106.9	192	62.9
"	—	5.05 pm	Paddington	Bath	106.9	193	62.3
"	—	10.18 am	Westbury	Paddington	95.6	92	62.3
"	—	12.00 noon	Paddington	Exeter	173.5	169	61.6
"	—	1.14 pm 4.19 pm	Swindon	Paddington	77.3	76	61.0
"	—	9.44 am	High Wycombe	Leamington	60.8	60	60.8
"	—	5.00 pm	Paddington	Kemble	91.0	90	60.7
"	—	9.35 am	Moreton-in-Marsh	Oxford	28.3	28	60.6
"	—	3.17 pm	Oxford	Paddington	63.5	63	60.5
"	—	3.30 pm	Paddington	Westbury	95.6	95	60.4
"	—	1.35 am	Paddington	Taunton	142.7	142	60.3
"	—	10.30 am	Paddington	Newton Abbot (a)	193.7	193	60.2
"	—	9.24 am	Didcot	Paddington	53.1	53	60.1
"	—	5.09 pm	Westbury	Taunton	47.1	47	60.1
LNER	GN&NE	4.00 pm	Kings Cross	York	188.2	157	71.9
"	"	5.30 pm	Kings Cross	Darlington	232.3	198	70.4
"	"	10.42 am	Darlington	Kings Cross	232.3	198	70.4
"	GN	7.10 pm	Kings Cross	Leeds	185.7	103	68.4
"	"	11.31 am	Leeds	Kings Cross	185.7	164	68.0
"	GN&NE	6.33 pm	Newcastle	Kings Cross	268.3	237	67.9
"	GN	9.40 am	Grantham	Kings Cross	105.5	100	63.3
"	"	11.00 am	Kings Cross	York	188.2	180	62.7
"	NE	6.40 pm	York	Newcastle	80.1	77	62.4
"	NE&NB	8.00 pm	Newcastle	Edinburgh	124.4	120	62.2
"	"	4.30 pm	Edinburgh	Newcastle	124.4	120	62.2
"	GN	11.35 am	York	Kings Cross	188.2	182	62.0
"	GC	4.30 am	Leicester	Arkwright Street (b)	22.6	22	61.6
"	NE	9.08 am 9.50 am 8.39 pm	Darlington	York	44.1	43	61.5
"	GN	9.30 am	Huntingdon	Kings Cross	58.9	58	60.9
"	"	7.41 pm	Grantham	Doncaster	50.5	50	60.6
"	"	12.25 pm	Doncaster	Kings Cross	156.0	155	60.4
"	"	3.04 pm	Peterborough	Kings Cross	76.4	76	60.3
"	"	4.45 pm	Kings Cross	Doncaster	156.0	156	60.0
"	"	3.49½ pm	Grantham	Kings Cross	105.5	105½	60.0
"	GC	7.45 pm	Woodford	Leicester	34.0	34	60.0

Notes: (a) Stop for banker, (b) Nottingham, (c) via Bath, (d) via Badminton.

The second table summarises the aggregate daily mileage of trains booked at 58mph or more in August 1939.

Railway	70 mph and over	67 mph and over	64 mph and over	62 mph and over	60 mph and over	58 mph and over
	miles	miles	miles	miles	miles	miles
LMSR	—	—	223 (2)	1,394 (9)	6,902 (68)	8,928 (99)
GWR	77 (1)	313 (3)	313 (3)	1,083 (12)	2,187 (24)	4,725 (52)
LNER	653 (3)	1,293 (6)	1,293 (6)	2,103 (12)	2,896 (23)	4,679 (46)
SR	—	—	—	—	—	354 (5)
NCC	—	—	—	—	31 (1)	31 (1)
Total, 1939	730 (4)	1,606 (9)	1,829 (11)	4,580 (33)	12,016 (116)	18,717 (203)
Total, 1938	730 (4)	1,606 (9)	1,829 (11)	4,714 (34)	11,665 (113)	17,924 (187)
Total, 1937	730 (4)	1,606 (9)	1,844 (12)	4,152 (29)	11,228 (107)	16,019 (179)
Total, 1936	542 (3)	778 (5)	996 (7)	2,245 (18)	6,206 (65)	9,116 (105)

Note: The figures in brackets indicate the number of individual runs making up each total mileage figure.

The third table shows book mile-a-minute runs in the summer of 1956.

Region	Section	Train	From	To	Distance	Time	Speed
					miles	min	mph
Eastern & North Eastern	GN	8.29 am	Hitchin	Retford	106.7	97	66.0
"	"	7.39 pm	Retford	Hitchin	106.7	99	64.7
"	NE	7.57 pm	York	Darlington	44.1	41	64.5
"	"	10.43 am	Doncaster	Darlington	76.1	72	63.4
"	GE	4.46 pm	Ipswich	Norwich	46.3	44	63.1
"	NE	3 trains	Darlington	York	44.1	42	63.0
"	"	*5 trains	York	Darlington	44.1	43	61.5
"	"	2 trains	Darlington	York	44.1	43	61.5
"	GN&NE	9.30 am	Kings Cross	Edinburgh	392.9	390	60.4
"	"	9.45 am	Edinburgh	Kings Cross	392.9	390	60.4
"	"	10.08 am	Darlington	Kings Cross	232.3	231	60.3
"	NE	4 trains	Darlington	York	44.1	44	60.2
Western	—	8.45 am	Paddington	Bristol	†118.3	105	67.6
"	—	4.30 pm	Bristol	Paddington	‡117.6	105	67.2
"	—	1.15 pm	Paddington	Bath	106.9	99	64.8
"	—	5.35 pm	Oxford	Paddington	63.5	60	63.5
"	—	12.35 pm	Newbury	Taunton	89.8	87	61.9
"	—	9.45 am	Paddington	Reading	36.0	35	61.7
"	—	10.40 am	Swindon	Bath	29.6	29	61.2
"	—	10.55 am	Paddington	Newport	133.4	131	61.1
"	—	4.00 pm	Birmingham	Leamington	23.3	23	60.8
"	—	2.27 pm	Chippenham	Paddington	94.0	93	60.6
"	—	12.00 noon	Paddington	Exeter	173.5	172	60.5
"	—	11.15 am	Paddington	Bath	106.9	106	60.5
"	—	10.11 am	Reading	Taunton	106.7	106	60.4
"	—	7.30 pm§	Paddington	Taunton	142.7	142	60.3
"	—	1.08 pm	Swindon	Paddington	77.3	77	60.2
"	—	6.30 pm	Paddington	Chippenham	94.0	94	60.0
"	—	7.15 pm	Paddington	Chippenham	94.0	94	60.0
"	—	9.04 am	Kemble	Paddington	91.0	91	60.0
London Midland	Western	3.15 pm	Rugby	Euston	82.6	79	62.7
"	"	8.20 am	Watford Junction	Crewe	140.7	136	62.1
"	"	1.30 pm	Euston	Rugby	82.6	80	62.0
"	Midland	9.41 am	Luton	Kettering	41.8	41	61.7
"	Western	6.39 pm	Crewe	Watford Junction	140.7	137	61.6
"	"	8.50 am 6.15 pm 6.25 pm	Crewe	Euston	158.1	155	61.2
"	"	8.58 am	Crewe	Euston	158.1	157	60.4
"	"	9.15 am	Watford Junction	Birmingham	95.5	95	60.3
"	"	12.50 pm 2.20 pm 5.50 pm 6.55 pm	Euston	Coventry	94.0	94	60.0
"	"	8.56 am 11.56 am 12.56 pm 4.56 pm	Coventry	Euston	94.0	94	60.0
"	Midland	9.33 am	Kettering	St Pancras	72.0	72	60.0
Southern	Western	11.00 am	Waterloo	Salisbury	83.7	83	60.5

*6 trains on Fridays. †Via Bath. ‡Via Badminton. §Fridays only.

Traffic Inspector's Report

Fancy six or seven weekly trips on the *Flying Scotsman*? A select group of traffic apprentices, including H. H. Webster in 1959 and 1960, enjoyed (or suffered) just that as part of their systematic coverage of East Coast main-line services. We produce several pages from his notes . . . more informative than the normal performance logs.

But, writes Mr Webster, there remain so many other impressions . . . the early platforming of the train with time for leisurely boarding, the maroon-uniformed reservations chap helping passengers find their seats, the roofboards on the coaches and headboard on the locomotive, the attendance of the stationmaster prior to departure, the restaurant-car conductor issuing his first and second sittings tickets, the ability to walk to the diner without being thrown about as in today's HSTs, the progression of telegraph poles, signalbox, wayside stations, freight activity that seem incredible in 1990, the passage of water troughs – would there be a deluge? – the exhaust darkening as steam was shut off at, say, Skelton Bridge for York, the stately run through the centre road, drawing many glances (check the watch and the clock by the footbridge, booked time is 1.44), the haunting chime of the A4s whistle, the exhaust taking up the rhythm again as the driver tugged open the regulator at the platform end.

The boxed figures to the left indicate recovery time allowed. Time lost by signal and pw is referred to as (i) and (ii) in the general remarks column. Booked seating is shown first: second eg 84:282. The *Scotsman* conveyed a SK and BCK to/from Aberdeen. A vehicle with a ladies' retiring room was booked but either it (or the attendant) was often missing. A male 'day train attendant' also looked after the toilets, litter, and so on; guards were not greatly disposed to stir from their vans in those days! We were having a purge on TMs (towelmasters) and LPs (lavatory pans). The first few class 40s had just entered service. One was rostered for the down *Scotsman*, but on 29 October 1959 failed before departure. A1 60130 deputised, needing much work on the fire. Once they had that right, they were away and 14 late out of King's Cross became 2 early at Newcastle.

B.R. 29106

10.0 Am. TRAIN FROM LONDON TO NEWCASTLE ON THURS DAY THE 29TH OF OCT 1959

Name of Driver	Stationed at	Engine No.	From	To
TURNER	KINGS X	60130	KINGS X	NEWCASTLE

Heat lbs.	Stations, Junctions, or District Boundaries	Timekeeping: Booked	Timekeeping: Actual	Mins. Late Dep.	Minutes lost: At Stations	Minutes lost: By Engine	Minutes lost: By Signals	Minutes lost: By P.W. checks	Minutes lost: By other causes	Minutes gained: At Stations	Minutes gained: By Engine	Load: Vehicles	Load: Tons
	Kings X [1]	10.00	10.14	14 L								11	379
	Potters Bar	10.19	10.34			1							
	Hatfield	10.24	10.38½								½		
	Hitchin	10.38	10.54					1½ (i)					
	Sandy	10.47	11.03½			½							
	Huntingdon [2]	10.59	11.15½										
	Peterborough	11.17	11.33½					0 (ii)					
	Werrington Jn.	11.22	11.38								½		
	Essendine	11.31	11.47½			½							
	Stoke [2]	11.42	12.02	20 L				3½ (iii)					
	Grantham	11.49	12.07½								1½*		
	Barkston	11.53	12.11½										
	Newark [4]	12.01	12.19½										
	Retford [4]	12.22	12.36								4½*		
	Doncaster [2]	12.43	12.51½					0 (iv)			5½*		
	Shaftholme Jn.	12.50	12.56								2½*		
	Selby	1.03	1.08								1		
	York	1.18½	1.22½	4 L							1		
	Skelton Jn.	1.21½	1.25								½		
	Alne	1.30½	1.34½			½							
	Thirsk	1.40	1.43½								½	11	379
	Northall'ton [4]	1.46½	1.50										
	Eryholme	1.57½	1.57½								3½*		
	Darlington	2.02½	2.02	½ E							½		
	Ferryhill	2.15	2.16			1½							
	Durham [4]	2.24½	2.25½										
	Newcastle	2.45	2.43	2E							3*		

General remarks as to cause of delay and location. Formation of train, including alteration to load during journey

BSK	34334	34
SK	24221	33
SK	25003	33
FK	13034	33
FK	13239	35
FO	1967	31¾
RF	1667	42½
RMB	1809	34½
SK	24161	33½
SK	24603	34
BCK	21218	35

11 379

(i) Langley 20
(ii) Abbots Ripton
(iii) Corby Glen – Stoke 20
(iv) Bawtry Viaduct 40

Late start due to failure of D206 with fractured steam pipe.

No L.R.R. attendant
∴ Rostered seating 84:282
Actual provided 96:282
ex London 54:201

Exceptional occurrences, deficiencies in lighting, heating accommodation and cleanliness of stock.

BCK: V. hy mails, flowers, papers for north of Edin
Rear BSK: Mod hy. luggage, papers.

Apology broadcast K.X.

Weather

13
SERVING KENT WITH STEAM

It is seven o'clock on a bright warm Saturday morning at the end of July 1954 beneath the arches and behind the great Hamptons depository, the landmark of Stewarts Lane Shed, three parts 'Chatham', one part 'Brighton', for the old loyalties die hard. And the shed yard, stretching to a point at the outlet near the Junction signal box is full of engines being made ready to tackle whatever duties have been planned for them. The exodus started in the early hours and, so far, has gone well.

But will our luck hold? It better had, otherwise a couple of late starts from the shed can paralyse Victoria (E) and that would never do for, in 1954, the Southern could afford to chase every minute lost, the shedmaster would be held accountable – and Stewarts Lane was always conscious of its position in the punctuality league table published each month.

We have twenty Bulleid Pacifics and two Britannias of which fifteen are in service, better than usual. Just as well as 'Engine Workings, Waterloo' have given us thirty-three Pacific jobs this Saturday! So the trusty old Arthurs and our one School will bridge the gap. But, as we have twenty-one KA duties against an allocation of seventeen, the Ns, U1s and of course, the wonderful little Maunsell rebuilds of class E1 and D1 will have to do their stuff for us.

Nor must we forget that the Brighton side has got to be covered. Apart from the booked services, there are bound to be extra boat trains for Newhaven from Victoria (C) and three or four Willesden or Kenny jobs to the South Coast to be covered by our men. And on Friday evening, when all was prepared for battle, Waterloo must phone over three more duties for which we had neither men nor engines. But no shed worth its salt would turn work away, and the London men whether in Battersea or the Old Kent Road will rise to the occasion, however impossible the odds.

A remarkable scene: engines, smoke and steam everywhere. Men going calmly about their business, no absentees, no leave granted – least of all to the shedmaster who has been around since six o'clock – and no late comers despite the early hour. Every five minutes yet another engine moves up to the foreman's office to be rung out for Victoria or Bellingham or Maze Hill or Stewarts Lane Yard.

It used to be the practice to have the engines for the long-distance jobs prepared by shed staff or by crews dragged unwillingly from the peace of Tunbridge Wells or Norwood. They hated our place on a busy Saturday and so we 'modified' the workings to enable our men to prepare their own engine keeping them happy with a suitable adjustment to their

As Safe as on the Sofa

There were many occasions when signalmen felt adrenalin as they were offered the four-beat 'Is line clear for express passenger train' and there was still a freight, perhaps with a badly steaming loco, ahead.

Two bells, the express enters the section, the freight has still not cleared. Smoke and steam are seen down the valley; the express is only a mile away. Then that welcome two-pause-one, train out of section. One beat, answered instantly, four beats, likewise, a quick dash to pull off the signals – home, starter, advance started and finally the distant. Now, has the express driver seen that go clear? Yes, smoke and steam at the chimney, no real delay or 'please explain' this time.

But signalmen who had to decide whether to loop or allow a slower train into the next section could not always get it right, especially on hilly sections where the time taken by freights varied enormously depending on the load (which the signalman would not always know), the state of the engine and even if it rained in the next few minutes. Nor could the right choice always be made at busy junctions between passenger lines . . . the up expresses had priority, but the down one *should* be across well in time.

There were of course many railway accidents, caused by a host of circumstances, human and technical. The signalman or bobby carried a specially tough responsibility in the days before electrical locking – when, for example, the starter was not locked to the block mechanism and it was perfectly possible to pull it off before the previous train had left the section.

Only more serious than forgetting to send two bells, train entering section, when appropriate was to send back two-pause-one when it was not. Imagine: you're tired

continued on page 203

Bound for the Kent coast. A London (Victoria) to Ramsgate, probably the 14.35 (SO), train approaching Dumpton Park in the summer of 1957. The engine is an ex-SE&CR L class 4-4-0 No 31781 – the last of the series (July 1914) – built by Borsig of Berlin, giving the class the nickname of 'Germans'. The shed plate carries the number 74B (Ramsgate). This class was also used on the Hastings line trains.

By King Arthur to Ramsgate. N15 class No 782 Sir Brian *heads a late morning train from Victoria in the Herne Bay area probably in 1939. There are twelve coaches including a Pullman buffet car. The train, likely to be a Saturday one as it has a reporting number as well as its duty number, has been strengthened by a three-coach ex-SE&CR 'Birdcage' non-corridor set with a nice first-class saloon in the middle.*

pay packet. Gone too are the days of tool shortages for each Battersea engine down to the humble P class shunter has a locked tool box with key to be collected and returned 'on pain of death'. The tools are there, the oil too and a driver can get on with his work at once. Minutes saved, more time, less hassle, fewer frayed tempers, preparation well done and Grosvenor Road bank to be faced with every confidence.

Our bland and smiling list clerk (who needs a bullet proof vest) has prepared the enginemen's rosters for the weekend on Friday and while this work of art, breaking many cherished National agreements is being finalised, the engine list for Saturday is worked out. A knowledge of the temperament of each driver is essential for some men are not at their best in the early hours, and with a five-minute headway the last thing a foreman wants is a wordy argument and a last-minute switch of engines.

Not much is needed by way of running repairs for the fitters have done their work well but one can see driver Bailey looking in our direction hoping to provoke an argument. We know Bill, we know he doesn't want 774, a rough King Arthur and we let him alone so that (against his better judgement) he leaves us on time with a final baleful stare. On the other hand, driver Wing has already let drive firmly but civilly at the shedmaster wanting to know what he is supposed to do with 'this thing' on a fast Ramsgate. All the week he has had 34066 but today he gets 1019, a Maunsell rebuild weighing all of 52 tons. He is reminded of what he used to do with No 19A as a fireman, back in the

continued from page 201
at the end of a busy night shift, the box is too hot but because of the horizontal rain you cannot open a window. An up train has just passed, but did the down one which should have been here a few minutes ago ever go by? The temptation to believe it did is real.

Once, immediately after the last war, a soldier stopped an express in mid section so he could get home on short leave earlier. Though it was a selfish act, he was incorrectly blamed by the Press for causing the accident that followed when the signalman *assumed* the train must have passed and allowed a following one into the section. The soldier retires in the year of this book's publication . . . from being a signalman. After the horror of that night he decided to devote his life to ensuring that passengers on express trains would be just as safe as on their sofa at home.

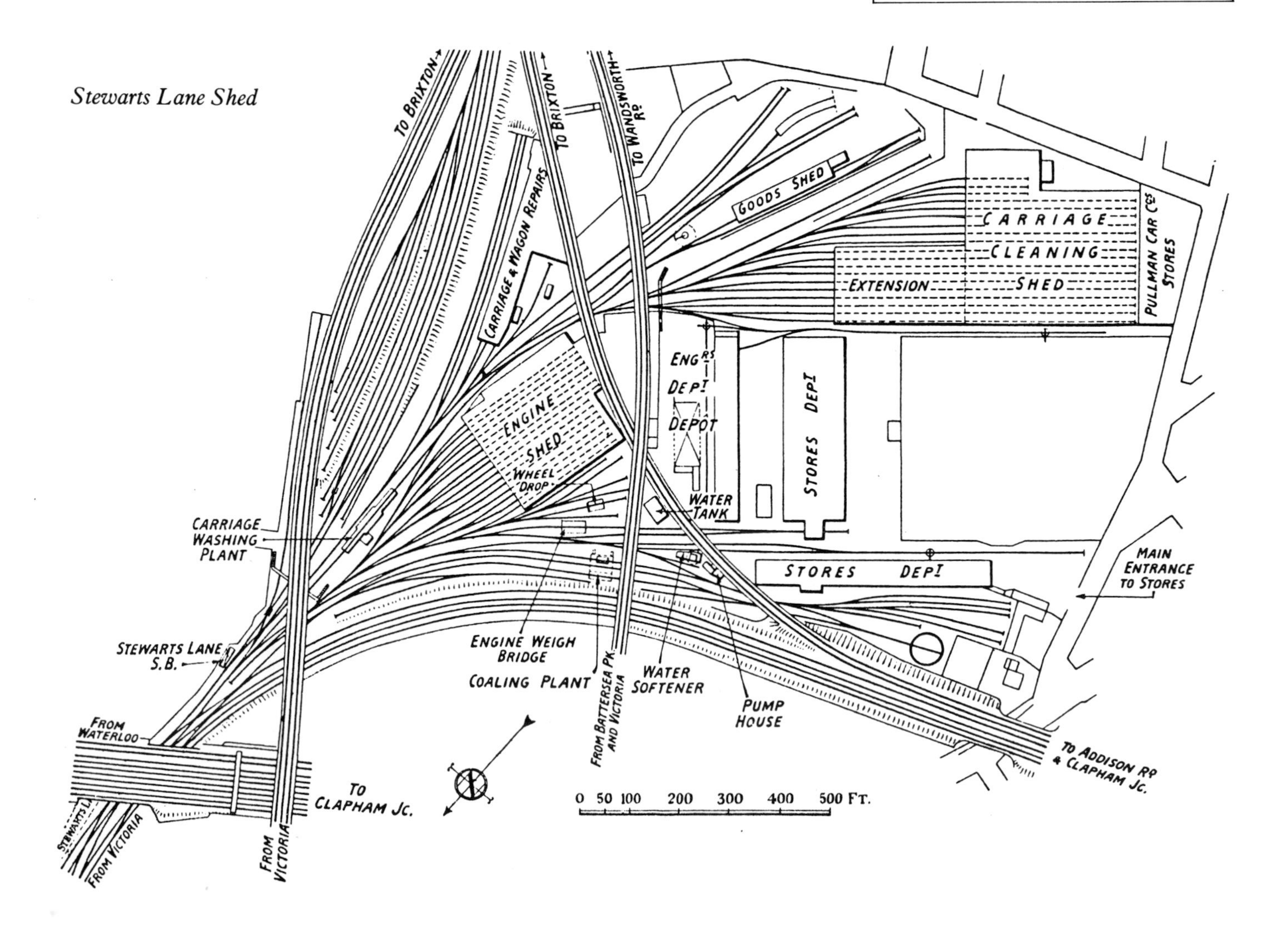

Stewarts Lane Shed

Up Ramsgate. Rebuilt by Maunsell as class D1 No 31487 (ex SECR No 487) climbs Sole Street bank on 30 July 1949 resplendent in the new 'LNWR' livery for secondary passenger locomotives. It has not yet received any lettering on the tender but carries the new LMS type cast smokebox door plate.

The Last Snippet

Memories of enjoying veritable Turkish baths of steam heating (oozing into all one's pores) on cold mornings when the combination of condensation, steam and smoke make it impossible to see out clearly; of hurrying through the newspaper so as to use it as window wiper; of claiming the facing seat to take charge of the window; of foolishly opening it an inch on the sea wall at Dawlish and having to call for a replacement porridge after drops of salt spray mixed with the milk; of long night journeys in stuffy sleepers years before air conditioning and waking to see different landscapes, especially Scottish mountainous ones with solid-built stone single-storey houses set well back from the village street; of being lulled by the pattern of passing telegraph poles and wires and (at familiar places such as Patney & Chirton) catching the point they changed sides; of relishing one's own company as nowhere else beside Bala Lake or Morecambe Bay, especially feet up in the front compartment in harmony with the locomotive's beat; of the exhilaration of getting to Peterborough from Kings Cross in well below the hour, and eagerly waiting for the call to second lunch. They truly were great days.

1920s. Having made his point he goes off to Victoria determined to prove that the old engine can still do it.

About 11 o'clock, the country engines begin to arrive, a Dover Schools, a Faversham German class L and certainly, a Faversham River. And then in the early afternoon, the first of the Rounders worked by a B.Arms engine and men. They have been all round Kent from Charing Cross to Victoria anti clockwise. Our men go clockwise via Chatham, Deal, Dover and Ashford to finish at Charing Cross. A good day's work but not enough for some on the Southern and our foreman will get some B.Arms men to recondition their engine and maybe prepare another before they go home with a final exchange of profanities.

The Faversham River leaves Victoria in the early afternoon and it is likely that the young Stew Lane fireman will have difficulty with that class so the shedmaster decides to go with him to ensure that no time is lost. All is well at Chatham and the first train on the up passes through at speed, Engine 1549 class D with both safety valves blowing off hard. Where else in this country in 1954 would you find a saturated Edwardian engine at the head of a heavy express and in fine fighting form?

The shedmaster returns from Chatham with an E1, No 1504 with nine coaches. They were going well up Sole Street bank of 1 in 100 only to be stopped to assist a boat train with a Bulleid Pacific which had stuck on the bank. With an exhaust like a gun, the old E1 did the lion's share of getting twenty-one coaches on the move and about the same time, away to the west a 24 year old driver and a fireman of 21 on 795 *Sir Dinadan* were successfully fighting Hildenborough bank with a Merchant Navy load and gaining the sort of experience that would set them up for years to come. The whole of Kent was full of trains that day, a miracle of operation. Quite unforgettable. Look at the map, note how each train will have to leave or reach London through not only the suburban network but a myriad of main lines. Then you will begin to appreciate the depth of route knowledge required of so many drivers.

Back at Stewarts Lane, the pressure has never relaxed. Those specials for which, in theory, we had neither men nor engines, left Victoria to time, adequately powered and manned by crews who had already done more than half a day's work. Locomotives have come and gone constantly, reconditioned for service by light work drivers and the youngest passed cleaners, working 12 hours or more. Battersea men got rich in the summer and it was as well for the railway that they were prepared to play their part in the 'Southern Miracle' not only on the Saturday but right through the weekend and well into Monday.

The shedmaster will get home well after the children had gone to bed. He will be back on the job early next morning for Sunday (with fewer men available) is sometimes even tougher. With luck he will see his family on Sunday afternoon. He usually works seven days a week – throughout the year, every Bank Holiday, even Christmas Day. But he has twelve days' annual leave. The pay to lead from the front? £670 pa. He has the best job on the railway, a joy and a real challenge to come to work.

London bound. An up Charing Cross or Cannon Street express has the green light prior to leaving Chatham around 1958. The driver is looking back awaiting the guard's green flag. The engine is Schools class 4-4-0 No 30912 Downside.

Serving Kent with steam and electricity. Cannon Street station, London between April 1958 and January 1959 (the dates of removal of the overall roof damaged during the War) with a Ramsgate (via Chatham) express hauled by a Schools class 4-4-0 (shedded at Ramsgate, 74B) and a Gillingham emu. The Schools is No 30920 Rugby. *The emu will run via Greenwich.*

ACKNOWLEDGEMENTS

This has been another team job. It began a long time ago with railwaymen going about their daily tasks working in disciplined organisations with scope for using initiative – the great days of railways and their express trains did not come about easily or without dedication. This book is a celebration of that dedication; it could not have been written or completed without the constant help and advice given by an almost resident team of ex railway officers. This is the fifth time for John Powell and John Edgington and the second for Frank Harrison. Each of these professionals has risen high in his sector – engineering, operating, public relations. We know they have enjoyed their time on the advisory panels and can assure them that their help has been thoroughly appreciated as has that of another fine railwayman Richard Hardy.

Human memories are fallible and many friends have searched their files to check facts or help dig out snippets; this archival work has been highlighted by the constant help of John Smart of Millbrook House Limited. We would like to thank Richard Hope, the editor of *Railway Gazette International* for permission to reuse line drawings and information from that publication along with John Slater and Peter Kelly editors of the *Railway Magazine* for similar permissions. Drawings are also acknowledged from *An Historical Survey of Selected LMS Stations Volume 2* by Dr R. Preston Henry and R. Powell Hendry, OPC 1986 (page 46 Llandudno Station plan and page 154 Bromsgrove Station) and from *An Historical Survey of Selected GW Stations Volume 4* by C. R. Potts, OPC 1985 (page 145 Banbury North plan). The *Meccano Magazine* has also been a source of useful information as have the various published works of the Railway Correspondence & Travel Society and the Stephenson Locomotive Society. We have consulted and used material based on items appearing in *Trains and Railways* edited by Patrick Whitehouse.

We would also like to thank the photographers, known and unknown, whose sojourns on the lineside have enabled us to select an extremely fine range of pictures to make *The Great Days of The Express Trains* really live: the principal contributors include P. M. Alexander, the late D. S. M. Barrie, C. R. L. Coles, George Heiron (who also painted the picture appearing on the jacket and within the book contents), the National Railway Museum, the late Bishop Eric Treacy as well as others mentioned in the photographic acknowledgements.

The main chapters are based on material supplied as follows: David St John Thomas (Introduction, The Anatomy of the Express Train, Day Trip to London); Patrick Whitehouse (By Train and Platform, Change Here for Journey's End); A. J. Powell (Sleepers and Night Trains, An Engineer on the Footplate, Life at the Shed); Basil Cooper (Sauntering at London Termini); Frank Harrison and Patrick Whitehouse (Cross Country Institutions, Summer Weekends, Keeping Them Moving – Operating and Control).

Fillers between the chapters are based on material supplied by: Patrick Whitehouse (Passing Through, Llandudno Excursion, Precursors to Heathrow, Special Occasions); Richard Hardy (Serving Kent with Steam); Frank Harrison (Excursions Even Further); A. J. Powell (Search for Improvement – Tests and Trials, The Train Now in a Hurry); G. M. Kichenside (Luxury Trains, Wartime Services); John Edgington (Allocations).

The authors would like to make acknowledgement to the following for the use of their illustration.

Black and white photographs are by: P. M. Alexander/Millbrook House Collection (26, 29 *lower*, 34, 36, 63, 106 *upper*, 146, 160 *both*, 204 *upper*); *W. J. V. Anderson (23); H. Ballantyne (174 upper*, 189); D. S. M. Barrie/Millbrook House Collection (83 *upper*, 84 *upper*, 87 *both*); BR/Millbrook House Collection (54, 70 *upper*, 122, 187); W. A. Camwell (64); J. R. Click/NRM (62, 136); C. R. L. Coles (33, 57, 70 *lower*, 73 *both*, 74, 88 *both*, 175 *lower*, 126); Basil Cooper/Millbrook House Collection (139 *upper*); Derek Cross/Millbrook House Collection (139 *lower*); M. W. Earley/NRM (60 *lower*, 32 *upper*); John Edgington (89, 99); L. Ellson (32 *lower*); J. C. Flemons/Millbrook House Collection (Frontispiece); W. Leslie Good/Millbrook House Collection (157); G. F. Heiron (15, 16, 25, 48, 50–51, 66–67, 68, 75 *lower*, 98, 106 *lower*, 117, 172, 185, 196 *lower*); C. C. B. Herbert/NRM (61 *lower*); J. R. Hollick (143 *lower*); John Hunt (177 *lower*); R. G. Jarvis/Millbrook House Collection (59), G. D. King (168 *upper*, 174 *lower*); K. H. Leech (118); LMS/Millbrook House Collection (6, 37, 38, 52, 53, 101 *top*, 121, 123); A. E. Loosley (191); M. Mensing (27, 83 *lower*, 100, 144, 147, 165 *upper*); Millbrook House Collection (21 *both*, 45, 84 *lower*, 107 *upper*, 125, 175 *upper*); National Railway Museum (101 *lower*, 141); O. S. Nock (9); Ivo Peters (161 *upper*, 173); Railway Gazette (61 *upper*); Railway Magazine/Millbrook House Collection (8, 12 *lower*, 47, 140 *both*, 159); P. Ransome-Wallis/NRM (14, 58, 69, 90, 102 *lower*, 202 *lower*, 204 *lower*, 205); R. C. Riley (183); Peter J. Robinson (109 *lower*); E. S. Russell (181); G. H. Soole/NRM (11); H. Gordon Tidey (60 *upper*); Eric Treacy/Millbrook House Collection (4, 12 *upper*, 75 *upper*, 94, 96, 97, 103, 107 *lower*, 109 *upper*, 111, 112, 129, 131, 132, 134, 137, 154, 162, 167, 179, 182, 194, 195, 196 *upper*); C. E. Weston (24); E. R. Wethersett (19, 102 *top*); C. M. Whitehouse (95); P. B. Whitehouse (20, 29 *upper*, 40, 92, 143 *upper*, 153, 161 *lower*, 165 *lower*, 168 *lower*, 171, 177 *upper*, 193, 202 *upper*); T. E. Williams/Millbrook House Collection (105); T. E. Williams/NRM (82).

Colour photographs are credited to the following sources: P. M. Alexander (113 *upper*, 152 *both*); Don Breckon (78–9); Colour Rail/J. G. Dewing (116 *upper*); Colour Rail/Trevor Owen (116 *lower*); Alan Fearnley (114–5); Peter Gray (150–1); George Heiron (77); M. Mensing (113 *lower*).

INDEX

INDEX